China and East Asia's Post-Crises Community

China and East Asia's Post-Crises Community

A Region in Flux

Wei Liang and Faizullah Khilji

LEXINGTON BOOKS
Lanham • Boulder • New York • Toronto • Plymouth, UK

Published by Lexington Books
A wholly owned subsidiary of The Rowman & Littlefield Publishing Group, Inc.
4501 Forbes Boulevard, Suite 200, Lanham, Maryland 20706
www.rowman.com

10 Thornbury Road, Plymouth PL6 7PP, United Kingdom

British Library Cataloguing in Publication Information Available

Library of Congress Cataloging-in-Publication Data

Liang, Wei.
China and East Asia's post-crises community : a region in flux / Wei Liang and Faizullah Khilji.
p. cm.
Includes bibliographical references and index.
ISBN 978-0-7391-7082-3 (cloth : alk. paper) -- ISBN 978-0-7391-7083-0 (electronic)
1. East Asia--Economic conditions--21st century. 2. East Asia--Economic policy--21st century. 3. East Asia--Foreign economic relations. 4. Financial crises--East Asia. 5. Global Financial Crisis, 2008-2009. I. Khilji, Faizullah. II. Title.
HC460.5.L559 2012
330.95--dc23
2012026538

The paper used in this publication meets the minimum requirements of American National Standard for Information Sciences Permanence of Paper for Printed Library Materials, ANSI/NISO Z39.48-1992.

Printed in the United States of America

Contents

Acknowledgements

The work benefited from comments on draft versions of various chapters by Meekal Aziz Ahmed, Ma Changlin, Khalil Hamdani, M. Ali Khan, S. Iftikhar Murshed, S. M. Naseem, and Eric Rahim.

ONE

Introduction: East Asia, old and new

EAST ASIA'S PAST AND PRESENT

Shortly after the end of the Second World War, as British India became independent, to mention Asia was to refer to the South Asian sub-continent. Beyond that lay, with the exception of Siam, the colonies of the European imperial powers such as the British Malay States, French Indochina, and Dutch East Indies, all ravaged by war, and, beyond that, an utterly devastated and defeated Japan. In between was a war-torn China, distraught with human suffering and tragedy, where Communists were in ascendance but were fighting against odds to gain control of Peiping and Shanghai—a bleak landscape as far as the eye could see. The Western representations of this Far East survive in iconic films such as *Hiroshima, mon amour,* and *Indochine*. The region of East Asia had not yet surfaced, or perhaps resurfaced.

Lee Kwan Yew recounts that as a student finishing up his studies at Cambridge and ready for the journey back to Singapore, he had met up with his tutor who advised that the small island of Singapore had little future; it had little future because it did not have any infrastructure, or a hinterland, or a trained civil service, and it did not even have a history. Perhaps the young man should consider not returning, the tutor had mused. Lee Kwan Yew has of course lived to see and say that Singapore "turned that conventional wisdom on its head," as would some of the other nations of East Asia.[1] Beginning with Japan and then Korea, and most recently China and then Vietnam, one by one, a number of East Asian states adjusted to the realities of a new world order, influencing that very order in the process, by rapidly climbing up the ladder of economic and social progress to present possibly the only case in our time of what increasingly seems to be a shift in the making from developing to developed economies. In the long arc of history, such a shift would be unprecedented and is perhaps also unexpected. The wounded lands and the disoriented and submissive peoples from the ignominious days at the end of the Second World War seem to have given way to the prosperous and bustling East Asian metropolises of today with a youth that looks with increasing confidence to a future it seeks to shape.

This continuing shift in the region's fortunes variously fascinates and puzzles scholars of development. For some it is also a case of East Asia's resurgence and a return to prosperity and stability, for it is often claimed that East Asia has been a stable and prosperous region in its past as well. From the fourteenth century right down to the nineteenth, East Asia was structured in a loosely hierarchic order around Confucian China, a phenomenon frequently described in Western scholarship as *the tribute system.*[2] China, the *primus inter pares* state in this *tribute system,* constituted the core together with Japan, Korea, and Vietnam, with the system extending to Southeast Asian states in varying degrees. Kang recounts that for most of this period, the region was politically stable and peaceful, pragmatism was the norm in interstate relations, there was no alliance formation, wars were a rare occurrence, and none of the wars were for a religious cause. On the whole conflict reportedly tended to occur not to check China's influence but rather as order within China itself was decaying. This *tribute system* did not make many demands on the participating states but by most accounts seems to have offered much opportunity for the peaceful pursuit of commercial and economic gains. Maritime trade flourished in the region, with the volume of intraregional trade reportedly outstripping by a large margin the trade with the West. Seen in this perspective, East Asia may thus lay a claim to a past as a self-organized China centric region, working pragmatically for mutual economic gain.[3]

This polity came apart with the advent of European colonial empires in the nineteenth century, but in hindsight the period of European imperial hegemony seems only a brief interlude in the timescale of China's history, and China historically has been the most influential state in the region. The colonial empires began to be dismantled in the aftermath of the Second World War, but this dismantling was not a smooth or a peaceful process in a region already ravaged by war. The Cold War was to follow on the heels of the Second World War and, with the erstwhile colonial powers in retreat, the emerging shape of the region, including its economic development, was determined by the exigencies of the newly perceived threats. The security interests of the two Cold War protagonists constituted the chief influences in the immediate postwar shaping of the region. The defining institutions of this Cold War era in East Asia were the overarching "Communist threat" and the ensuing bilateral treaties between some of the countries in the region and the United States. These treaties covered economic and social development besides the predominant security aspects.

The post Second World War East Asia or East Asia of the Cold War developed as a "hub and spokes" structure: United States was "the hub," and the major spokes were a defeated Japan, a Republic of Korea facing a division of its nation, and a "Republic of China" established by Chiang Kai-shek in retreat in the face of the onslaught by Mao Zedong's forces. Minor spokes were the original SEATO pact nations of Southeast Asia. Substantial crossties among the East Asian countries were discouraged though by the United States. Peoples Republic of China stood excluded because it was a part of the collective "enemy," as then defined. This postwar East Asia, the outcome of a "top down" approach conceived and enforced by the United States with the authority of a Second World War victor and with a defined "enemy" in its sights, was arguably the Asian extension of American security interests. And American security interests also required that its East Asian allies be visibly more developed than other economies in the region. Japan, Korea and Taiwan developed rapidly, albeit with some American assistance, and by the 1980s Japan had become the world's second largest economy.

With the end of the Cold War the focus of American security preoccupations shifted to the Middle East, and American interest in East Asia, including the economic development of the region, seemed to have waned, in hindsight perhaps momentarily. For East Asia though the end of the Cold War meant that the goal of economic development could clearly take precedence over security issues, and with the fading out of American security interests in the region, the global economic forces rather than security considerations provided the immediate milieu for East Asia's development efforts. As East Asian economies rose to prominence, growing at record rates, United States, with its Iraq and Afghanistan efforts stymied, appeared to reassess its role in what appeared to be an area of increasing economic opportunity. Prominent in the economic dynamics at work in the region in the post Cold War phase have been the phenomenon of economic globalization, the Asian financial crisis of 1997, the ongoing global financial crisis of 2008, and the rapid growth being experienced by the Chinese economy.

SCOPE OF THE BOOK

What we attempt to study here is aspects of the coming together of East Asia as an economic space in the post Cold War period, propelled as we see it by its response to the challenges posed by the two financial crises and the opportunities offered by the emergence of China in a globalized world economy. The discussion begins chronologically with the disappointment felt in the region with the multilateral financial system on the eve of the Asian financial crisis of 1997, and the first efforts aimed at ASEAN+3 regional economic cooperation that were set in motion, and takes us to the aftermath of the global financial crisis of 2008, which helped to identify East Asia as an economic region by the dint of the region's performance during the latter crisis, and brought to surface once again the region's dissatisfaction with the international currency system. Between the two crises we see a fast emerging China, its growth facilitating the economic integration of the economies of the region through growing production and trade networks, made feasible by the free flow of goods and investment characteristic of a globalized world economy. The rapidly increasing economic weight of the region seemed to raise questions about the legitimacy and efficacy of the postwar multilateral economic institutions.

The Asian financial crisis of 1997 had caught the East Asian economies in an uncertain situation of adjusting to the liberal market economy model and a globalizing financial system; ideas that were being advanced then by the multilateral economic institutions though with strong support from the US Treasury. The crisis of 1997 was perceived by the affected economies in the region as an instance of the adverse effects of globalized finance working through currency speculators. The transatlantic economies, the multilateral economic institutions and the large foreign commercial banks, that had advanced credit in East Asia, saw the crisis as an instance of lack of financial sophistication among the affected East Asian economies, and also as a result of the prevalence of "crony capitalism" in the region that interfered with the efficient functioning of the markets.

A beleaguered East Asia galvanized almost instinctively to devise regional measures in finance and thus set the scene for regional economic cooperation. The ASEAN+3 conference, called in 1997 to deal with the financial crisis, eventually evolved into an institutional mechanism for economic and financial cooperation, though more by default than by design. Currency swap arrangements were instituted between the countries in the region. Separately and individually, these countries accumulated foreign reserves. The net result of the Asian financial crisis was a more regional orientation in economic matters, the emergence and development of institutional mechanisms for regional economic cooperation in situations where the multilateral alternative seemed not to respond to East Asian concerns, and the beginnings of a build up of a bulwark of foreign exchange reserves, so as to deter a future run on the regional currencies and also to lessen any future dependence on the multilateral economic institutions.

The globalized world economy, while engendering the Asian financial crisis, was also impacting on the region in more positive ways. The initial phase of economic globalization had jived with the historic opening up of China in the Deng Xiaoping era. In hindsight it would seem as if China's policies had been calibrated to maximize the opportunities that this new economic milieu offered. Over some thirty years China emerged as the hub of processed manufacturing networks in the region, growing at rates that present an unparalleled phenomenon of the late twentieth and early twenty-first centuries. These developments had a critical impact on intra-regional trade and investment; the business interests increasingly pulling together the neighboring economies with the process being facilitated by the rules of a globalized world economy. Though the demand for China's exports stemmed chiefly from the transatlantic economies, corporate interests evidently turned to the regional economies to a growing degree for the imports required to produce the exports.[4] China's rapid growth and the growing range of its production and exports put it at the center of the region's development. Regional networks of investment and trade evolved and developed with linkages to China, and these networks continue to flourish. Even though private corporate interests drove the trade and investment flows, these developments combined with the ASEAN+3 forum to arguably nudge the governments in the region towards a number of multilateral and bilateral economic cooperation and trade agreements, some of which were concluded, whilst discussions on other such agreements were initiated and are a work in progress. These economic cooperation and trade agreements and related discussions were greatly facilitated by the regional institutions that had emerged and developed in the aftermath of the Asian financial crisis, chiefly the ASEAN+3 forum. The commonality of economic interests and advantage among the region's economies broadly seemed to trump their political differences in the context of these accords and discussions. Separately, the economic rise of the East Asia region and the rapid growth in its trade surpluses and intra-regional trade gave rise to concerns about the nature of the multilateral trade regime.

But we may note, *en passant,* that it is also the case that China's economic rise was only the most recent chapter in East Asia's development, which had begun with Japan after the Second World War. Japan had visualized its postwar development as heralding the economic rise of East Asia. Japan perceived the region's development as a flight of geese with Japan's economy in the lead and with the other regional economies following in formation, albeit in a global situation of protection and economic controls, and with substantial state direction of economic policy.[5] On the eve of the Asian financial crisis Japan had already become the world's second largest economy, Korea and Taiwan had transformed following Japan, and economies of Southeast Asia appeared to be undergoing a similar industrialization, with China very much on the way to becoming a part of the regional and global economic networks. But by the late 1990s the Japanese economy had also run into problems. The Japanese initiative seems to have petered out; the weakness of Japanese economy was perhaps making it difficult to organize the region around Japan. The Chinese economy was in the ascendance; the regional division of labor had increased in intricacy and complexity and the unambiguous hierarchy with Japan as the leader was coming into question.

Returning to the substantive theme, we note that in a twist that seemed to reflect the multifaceted nature of globalization, the Asian financial crisis linked up with the global financial crisis of 2008: one view importantly proposed that the surfeit of credit in the United States (arguably a proximate cause of the global financial crisis of 2008), was possible only because of the large trade surpluses earned by East Asia and the consequent build up of the large foreign reserves by these economies. Yet others saw the 2008 crisis as an outcome of growing economic inequalities within the United States. But in East Asian perception the basic reason for accumulating foreign reserves was the inability of the international financial system to respond in an adequate and timely manner to the region's needs at the time of the 1997 crisis. In this manner a systemic link was argued to exist between the two financial crises, the global financial crisis of 2008 and the Asian financial crisis of 1997. The fact that economic performance in East Asia fared distinctly different and better than what obtained in the transatlantic economies in course of the global financial crisis of 2008 contributed to East Asia's emerging identity as a distinct economic space, with perhaps its own economic policies and distinctive approach.

It seems to us that the foregoing developments including the end of the security imperatives of the Cold War, the emergence of China, economic globalization, and the financial crises, the economic and financial cooperation that has taken place, the East Asian perception of dysfunctionality of the multilateral economic institutions, all have worked to change the very concept of East Asia from a US-centric formal treaty-based security structure constructed in the aftermath of the Second World War with an ascendant Soviet Union as the chief adversary in view, and point to the making of a regional economic space, an informal China-centric economic cooperative, with the United States emerging both as a partner and a competitor, and this perceptible shift in East Asia's character continues for now, even though the treaties remain in place, and even as the United States reasserts new security imperatives in the Asia-Pacific spaces.

It seems to us that economic and financial cooperation in today's East Asia is driven by a desire to further economic gain and to evolve mechanisms to facilitate economic growth; and it is not driven by a grand vision or by an ideology, and the process seems to have evolved without a "leader nation." Neither for the moment do we realistically see a ready "leader," notwithstanding America's claim to be one, even as the region looks to the future. The rapidly growing production and trade networks have been followed up by free trade agreements that have been negotiated, or are being negotiated, and yet others which are contemplated. The business interests have been active in this effort. The manner in which trade and financial cooperation has built up may perhaps be described as need based cooperation, reflecting both the shortcomings of the multilateral economic system and the opportunties it offers. The cooperation in trade, a brick by brick piecemeal approach that seems to evolve in a pragmatic fashion, and notably, in absence of an overarching plan, would likely grow as China's economy and other economies in the region continue to expand. The new emerging institutions in the region, primarily economic in nature, appear to be inclusive with regard to the East Asian countries, and the countries are free to foster crossties among themselves. The successful development experiences of Northeast and Southeast Asian economies spanning the past six decades offer a choice of development "models," or rather the lesson that a country develops its own model.

The nature of East Asia's economic success raises issues regarding "appropriate" policies. In East Asian perception the state was fundamental to the success of any effort at economic development. The market economy model that saw no positive role for the state in the economy, popularly known also as the Washington Consensus, posited as *the* approach to economic organization and management by the international financial institutions has always appeared as something of a puzzle in East Asia in light of the region's own development experience. Thus in East Asian perception, the Washington Consensus model stood discredited after the two financial crises of 1997 and 2008, and its economic foundations were also more widely questioned. The model was not only seen to be crisis prone, but also lacking in the claimed self-corrective mechanisms. Thus the two financial crises helped to bring to surface and to strengthen an implicit consensus among the East Asians on the role of the state in economic growth and development.

Besides the contested market economy model, the experience with the global financial crisis brought some perennial issues to the fore, and the debate about the role of surplus and deficit countries in any adjustment process in the international monetary system resurfaced, as did doubts about the efficacy of an international currency system based on a national currency. To the extent that China may adjust, it would surely mean a shift away from an export-oriented model of growth to a situation of growth supported through domestic consumption. But any such adjustment by China, though also desired by China itself, could not be instantaneous and would necessarily impact on other countries in the region via the processed manufacturing networks. Such an adjustment would also impact on situations further afield where the consumer-debt financed model of prosperity had taken hold.

The global financial crisis as well as China's rapidly growing role in the world economy arguably served to highlight a continuing but somewhat dormant problem with the international currency system. In the absence of an international currency the American dollar, to a considerably lesser extent the euro and to an even lesser extent the yen, all three being paper currencies not tied to an "anchor" such as a physical commodity, improvise in the current international monetary system, and whilst the dollar's international acceptance and use may be helpful to the United States, it may also cause United States (and consequently the world economy) problems as America's dollar debt mounts. With mounting debt, the United States invariably links this currency issue with other issues in its bilateral as well as multilateral dealings. This dollar issue as a strategic matter has been repeatedly discussed since the 1960s, and in course of the 2008 crisis the debate again opened up. Separately for China, one of the largest traders in the world economy and presently the largest provider of economic assistance overseas, the currency issue cannot feasibly be left on autopilot, that is to say, left to a certain renminbi/dollar parity. China therefore instituted in a step-wise manner a range of measures to create a modest but growing space for the renminbi in the international currency system.

The East Asia that we now see had perhaps started to take shape in the early 1990s, and is something of an indigenous development. It is chiefly a community of interdependent economic interests akin in this respect to perhaps NAFTA or the EU, but unlike the latter two, it is an unplanned one. Also unlike the EU, it is devoid of a security or political agenda, and one that is developing in an environment of a non-protectionist and globalized world economy. Its economic policies are largely determined in the region. Its increasingly China-centric trade and investment links continue to deepen and grow as China-oriented networks develop. United States serves as a large export market albeit of diminishing importance, whilst the region stands out as America's chief creditor. Arguably, the manner in which this community evolves is partially also a reflection of the political reality in Asia, where a legacy of political mistrust perhaps leaves only trade and investment as issues that may be comfortably discussed and implemented.

Though economic forces have on the whole been a beneficial factor in furthering cohesion in the region in post Cold War East Asia, yet other phenomena, some of it rooted in history, point to fissiparous tendencies. Japan's efforts to set up an empire in Asia in the earlier part of twentieth century have left a legacy of considerable mistrust in their wake, and these misgivings persist, radiating their effects in a sort of a "half-life" in the region. A separate aspect is that the smaller countries tend to be wary of the larger ones. China's rapid growth and accompanying rhetoric in particular appears to have created a desire and search for leverage on the part of some of the smaller countries in their dealings with China. In their efforts to acquire leverage vis-à-vis China, a number of these smaller countries tend to look outside East Asia, chiefly to the United States, which admittedly does not discourage such thoughts and approaches. Ethnicity tensions are another factor that pervade a number of the countries in the region. More specifically, in some of the ASEAN economies, a divide may exist between economic power, which may vest with an ethnic minority, and political power that vests largely in the majority ethnic group, thus creating a source of potentially continuing political difficulties. Though such factors are perhaps divisive in terms of any regional economic identity and arguably raise hurdles in the efforts aimed at economic and financial cooperation in the region, possibly impeding the pace of development in some instances and adding an element of fragility, the region's economy as a whole has continued to develop in tandem thus far.

Thus the book explores by way of essays aspects of what we see as an emerging theme: the transformation of the East Asia region, a metamorphosis discernible in its graduated occurrence, from a security-oriented US-centric top down structure, to an informal, China-centric, and increasingly confident economic community with its unique form of need driven cooperation, raising questions in the process about the efficacy of the postwar economic order. The aspects examined in the book include firstly the impact of the Asian financial crisis of 1997 in giving rise to economic and financial cooperation in the region, and that of the global financial crisis of 2008 in furthering these efforts besides raising the identity of the region as an economic space. Secondly, the book examines the integrating impact of the emergence of China in its interaction with East Asia. Third, we consider China's response to the global financial crisis. Fourth, the consensus on issues of economic policy emerging in East Asia is explored, and, fifth, we discern the shift in the region from a US-centric security oriented one to a China-centric economic one. Questions that come to mind, and some of these questions address counterfactual situations, include how important and critical a role have the two financial crises played in the emergence of what we refer to as the East Asian community, would the process of coming together of East Asia have been significantly different in the absence of these crises, or would the rapid development of China have been sufficient for the evolution of the community; in other words, did the two crises (bearing in mind that the second crisis is of course of very recent origin and came when the process may have been well established) no more than expedite the process? The essays in this book attempt to consider these themes. We had intended to write a monograph but the closeness in time to the developments discussed simply did not make a monograph feasible; hence the essays.

It needs saying here that in contradistinction to the ideas advanced in this book, there is a school of thought that holds that the relevant geographical region is Asia-Pacific, that cooperation requires leadership, that America has in the post Second World War period provided this leadership and remains the best placed to do so. In this "top down" approach one of the first government backed regional cooperation initiatives, encompassing the vast and diverse spaces that go by the rubric of Asia-

Pacific, was the APEC, and the most recent initiative is the Trans-Pacific Partnership (TPP). One problem with this explanation is that APEC seems to have lost its way notwithstanding some of the strongest support extended by the United States government, and governments of Japan and Australia, among others, and the TPP initiative too seems to move slowly even though it is strongly supported by United States, Australia and Singapore, among others. There may perhaps be some indifference in the region to what may be seen as "messianic" efforts at cooperation with little in way of near-term tractable economic gain, and this may help explain why initiatives such as APEC and TPP, among others, have failed to capture the enthusiasm of the policy makers and the imagination of the intelligentsia in the region. Such projects perhaps do not answer the region's immediate concerns. Two aspects of these two efforts at building regional cooperation are particularly instructive. Firstly, the approach adopted in these initiatives, a "top down" one, is parallel to that adopted in the postwar reconstruction of East Asia (albeit in the latter case it was through bilateral security treaties). Second, some of these "top down" efforts at cooperation are possibly inspired by motivations that have no immediate relevance for East Asia. The APEC, for example, had as its purpose to alarm and prod the EU to speed up the Uruguay Round deliberations. Whilst the purpose was laudable, there was perhaps not enough in it for East Asia's future as the regional economies perceived it. And at a more prosaic level, when we look across the Pacific we see the transpacific commerce losing out to intra-East Asia trade. Nonetheless, perfectly reasonable arguments have been made and can be made to support the case for APEC and TPP.

The essays in the rest of the book are organized as follows. Chapter 2 explores how the Asian financial crisis helped to create and then galvanize the ASEAN+3 framework and how financial cooperation ensued in the region. It took the Asian financial crisis for the region to realize that the American priorities had shifted, and that the multilateral financial system did not address the region's concerns. Chapter 3 considers how the combination of a globalizing world economy and a shift in China's economic policies led to a networked region, changing the nature of the trade in the process, and with the ASEAN+3 process at the center of these efforts. Between the two crises the intraregional trade grew and economic integration began to shape the region. Chapter 4 explores aspects of China's policy response to the global financial crisis of 2008, seeking in the process a role for the renminbi and an alternative to export-oriented growth that for now may largely be dependent on the needs of the debt-financed transatlantic consumer. Chapter 5 considers the evident differences on economic policies between East Asian economies and the transatlantic economies and the multilateral institutions. Chapter 6 reflects on the changing geopolitics of the region.

We take East Asia to comprise the ten ASEAN economies plus the five in Northeast Asia, that is China, Japan and Korea, as well as Taiwan and Hong Kong, that is ASEAN+3 plus Taiwan and Hong Kong.[6] A large number of configurations that group together various countries of Asia and the Pacific in different combinations exist, but this particular configuration, apart from being a reasonable analogue of an earlier East Asia, seems to be coming together the best in actual fact. Perhaps the same cannot be said of APEC, ASEAN+6, the Trans-Pacific Partnership, the East Asian Summit, and some others.

NOTES

1. Lee Kwan Yew speaking in 1994 in Islamabad.

2. The *tribute system* we learn is a Western invention devised no later than the 19th century and then translated back into Chinese. The Chinese had no conception of it as such, and the tribute system model has been questioned; but the fact that there was a *system* over long periods with a prosperous China at the center of a relatively prosperous East Asia is perhaps not in dispute. See discussion in Zhang Feng, Rethinking the 'Tribute System': Broadening the conceptual horizon of historical East Asian politics, Chinese Journal of International Politics, vol. 2, 2009, pp. 545-574, especially p. 547 and p. 574. One early exponent of the *tribute system* would appear to be the late John K. Fairbank. See discussion in John K. Fairbank, ed., The Chinese World Order: Traditional China's Foreign Relations (Cambridge, Harvard University Press, 1968). Also see John K. Fairbank and Merle Goldman, China, A new history, 2nd edition, (Cambridge, Harvard University Press, 2006).

3. See David Kang, East Asia before the West, Five centuries of trade and tribute, (New York, Columbia University Press, 2010), pp. 7-10, 25-27, 29, 43, 50-51, 53-56, 70-71, 83-86, 90, 93, 107-109, 114 and 133-134, Henry A. Kissinger, On China (London, Penguin, 2011), pp. 5-32; Jonathan D. Spence, The search for modern China (New York, WW Norton, 1999), p. 119; Andrew Gordon, Japan, A modern history (Oxford, Oxford University Press, 2003), pp. 18-19; Anthony Reid, Economic and social change, c. 1400-1800, in Nicholas Tarling, The Cambridge history of Southeast Asia, vol 1, part 2 (Cambridge, Cambridge University Press, 1999), pp. 119-124; Zhang Feng, Rethinking the 'Tribute System': Broadening the conceptual horizon of historical East Asian politics, Chinese Journal of International Politics, vol. 2, 2009, pp. 545-574; and John K. Fairbank and Merle Goldman, China, A new history, 2nd edition, (Cambridge, Harvard University Press, 2006), pp. 112-113.

4. References to "transatlantic economies" refer to the group of countries classified under the rubric "advanced economies" by the IMF, excepting East Asian economies. East Asian economies of Hong Kong SAR, Japan, Korea, Singapore and Taiwan are excluded from the advanced economies category because these economies are treated as East Asian economies for purposes of our discussion. The substantial remaining entities in advanced economies grouping are the transatlantic economies of the United States and Canada, and the European Union, besides Australia and New Zealand. The rubrics "multilateral financial institutions" and "international financial institutions" is used to refer to the two Bretton Woods institutions, namely, the International Monetary Fund and the World Bank. We consider the two institutions to be making common cause in the propagation and enforcement of the same set of economic and social policies.

5. See Kaname Akamatsu, A historical pattern of economic growth in developing countries, in Journal of Developing Economies, 1962, March-August, pp. 3-25.

6. References are to South Korea, that is, the Republic of Korea, unless the context suggests otherwise.

TWO

Asian financial crisis and the resort to regional cooperation

I: INTRODUCTION

The two financial crises that are the Asian financial crisis of 1997 and the global financial crisis of 2008 have been formative in East Asia's understanding of the globalized world economy and in particular the postwar financial system. These two crises have impacted on East Asia's policy choices, and continue to exert influence in the region's interaction with the world economy. This chapter discusses the differences between East Asia and the multilateral financial and economic institutions on the causes of the Asian financial crisis and the differences on policies to best cope with the crisis, as well as East Asia's collective response to the Asian financial crisis. As is discussed in this chapter the Asian financial crisis caused the region to hit upon the ASEAN+3 process almost as a reflex action and the region thus drifted into financial cooperation by the force of circumstance.

The plan of this chapter is as follows. The different perceptions of the Asian financial crisis are considered in the second section. The third section takes up East Asia's response to the Asian financial crisis, including the lessons drawn in the region with regard to its interaction with the globalized world economy, and the efforts to develop a solution within the region.

II: THE DIFFERING PERCEPTIONS OF THE ASIAN FINANCIAL CRISIS

In this section we first set out the events leading to the unfolding of the crisis, and then consider the different perceptions of the causes of the Asian financial crisis and the equally different perceptions regarding policies considered as appropriate in dealing with the crisis. Thus we consider how the causes and remedies were perceived by the afflicted economies in the region on the one hand, and differently by the International Monetary Fund on the other, and with the differences unresolved, how East Asia eventually responded by resorting to regional mechanisms in its search for a solution when looking to the future.

Events building up to the crisis

The Asian financial crisis is an oft-told tale. The crisis caught the region's economies in a period of sustained upswing and for that reason it was seen as particularly capricious. In the economic milieu of the 1990s, these economies had liberalized the external capital account and there was freedom of capital movements, with sums in foreign currencies moving in and out of the domestic banking system. This measure to liberalize external capital flows combined with fixed exchange rate regimes in East Asia, the East Asian currencies were pegged against the dollar, and with substantial interest rate differentials—which is to say that interest rates were higher in East Asia than, say, the United States, Western Europe and Japan. Such a configuration of developments presented a profitable investment opportunity for the foreign investors. Foreign capital flowed in, chiefly as short-term loans, and received a higher rate of interest. The banks then lent out this money that they had received, and the stock markets as well as the real estate sector benefited in particular from the loans resulting from these flows of foreign capital.[1] A substantial risk existed on account of the fact that while a loan had been contracted in a foreign currency, say in dollars, the actual investment by the borrower had been made, after conversion, in the national currency, say in Thai baht. With the loans having been advanced in dollars, as in this example, and repayments of these loans to be made from earnings in the Thai baht, a mismatch of currencies existed. The possibility of an adverse movement in the exchange rates, say a depreciation of the Thai baht vis-à-vis the dollar, created a risk for the borrowers: the risk was that any such adverse shift in exchange rates would make it that much more difficult to service and repay the loan as the amount to be repaid in the Thai baht would increase, thus changing the entire economics of the loan. This risk naturally increased with expansion in the quantum of foreign capital that was flowing in.

As short-term external debt built up, the ratio of foreign exchange reserves to short-term debt, indicating liquidity, being a measure of the ability to service the loans, started deteriorating for the East Asian economies. The foreign exchange reserves as a ratio of total debt for these economies, taken as one indicator of solvency, also exhibited a downward trend. Export growth too slowed down in 1996.[2] It is easy to see how these indicators, which showed a decline in foreign exchange resources relative to external liabilities, may have suggested an opportunity to speculators to bet on the national currency and, for example, try and profit by taking local currency loans, converting them into dollars and keeping the process going until the exchange rate finally came down. Similarly, selling the East Asian currencies "short," which is to say for delivery at a future date, a commonplace transaction in the absence of capital controls, presented an opportunity for quick and easy gains for a holder of say dollars.[3]

A spate of rumors, buttressed in due course by a May 1997 report from Goldman Sachs, suggested that the Thai baht would be devalued. While speculation on baht was building up rapidly, another Goldman Sachs report titled *Malaysia and Philippines: Thailand in the making?* appeared; the very title suggested problems with the Malaysian ringgit and the Philippines peso, and ringgit and peso came under increasing pressure from speculation as well.[4] Other Asian currencies too began to experience similar pressures from speculative forces, even as International Monetary Fund packages to help the afflicted economies were being arranged. The IMF country quotas "were far too small" to enable the afflicted economies "to draw adequate funds, forcing large-scale negotiations to create packages to obtain dollar reserves from other international financial institutions and a variety of other countries."[5]

Table 2.1. Asian financial crisis: Afflicted economies, end of period exchange rates. Local currency units per US dollar.

	Pre crisis			Crisis and post crisis		
	1994	1995	1996	1997	1998	1999
Indonesia rupiah	2161	2249	2383	4650	8025	7085
Korea won	789	775	844	1695	1204	1138
Malaysia ringgit	2.56	2.54	2.53	3.89	3.80	3.80
Thailand baht	25.1	25.2	25.6	47.2	36.7	37.5
Memo: Chinese yuan	8.4	8.3	8.3	8.3	8.3	8.3

Source: International Monetary Fund, International Financial Statistics database.

In this rapidly evolving situation foreign banks refused to roll over debts of Korean corporations, with an eye to their traditionally high debt/equity ratios.[6] As speculative transactions grew, the rumors were realized and the exchange rates plummeted. Table 2.1 indicates the movement in period averages for exchange rates; immediate falls were more severe.

As national currencies depreciated, foreign loans in terms of domestic currencies multiplied correspondingly. Thus the businesses that had borrowed found that their outstanding loans had suddenly increased, and that they simply did not have the earnings streams to repay at the new exchange rates, and were in fact unable to do so: in Indonesia 75 percent of all businesses were put in distress, and in Thailand close to 50 percent of the bank loans became non-performing.[7] Once the difficulties facing the businesses translated into a reduced cash flow to the lending local banks, these banks too were looking at bankruptcy. The table below shows how the foreign loans to afflicted economies spiked up as the crisis set in.

Table 2.2. Asian financial crisis: Severely afflicted economies. External debt outstanding as a percentage of the GDP.

	Pre crisis	Crisis and post crisis		
	1996	1997	1998	1999
Indonesia	51	57	144	98
Korea	28	33	47	34
Malaysia	38	44	62	54
Thailand	60	72	94	78
Memo: China	15	15	14	14

Source: Asian Development Bank.

For the afflicted East Asian economies, it was an instance of speculators in search of profits taking advantage of freedom of capital flows in a globalized financial system. By selling these East Asian currencies "short," the speculators worked to cause the national currencies to depreciate sharply against the dollar, and this led to the sudden and unforeseen increase in national indebtedness summarized at an aggregate level in the table above. The gains by the speculators were thus being made at the East Asian public's expense. In an emotional speech, the political leadership captured the mood then pervading the region; Dr Mahatir spoke:

> We have always welcomed foreign investment, including speculation. . . . But when the big funds use their massive weight to move shares up and down and make huge profits by speculation, it is too much to expect us to welcome them. . . . I know I am taking a big risk to

> suggest it but I am saying that currency trading is unnecessary, unproductive and immoral. It should be stopped. It should be made illegal. We don't need currency trading. We need to buy money only when we want to finance real trade. Otherwise we should not buy or sell currencies as we sell commodities.[8]

To forestall "currency trading" required that the speculators be deterred by national governments. And this could be done through having credible sums of foreign exchange reserves or, failing that, through putting in place controls on external capital flows.

The East Asian perspective on the crisis

Dr Mahatir's assessment very much resonates in Joseph Stiglitz's academic writings on the crisis. Joseph Stiglitz, in his capacity of World Bank's Chief Economist at the time of the crisis, seems to have had the benefit of extensive interaction with the East Asian officials, including during the crisis, perhaps comes closest to articulating the Asian point of view on the academic plane. In context of the Asian financial crisis, Stiglitz makes two points. First, capital account liberalization was not only unnecessary, but "excessively rapid financial and capital market liberalization was probably the single most important cause of the crisis." It was also "partially responsible for the onset" of the crisis. In his view, capital account liberalization was done at the behest of IMF and US Treasury, because Wall Street institutions wished it. Stiglitz asserts that in the early 1990s the IMF and the US Treasury pushed the East Asian economies to undertake capital account liberalization, a counterintuitive position because a high saving region such as East Asia did not need to import additional foreign capital. The argument advanced at the time though to support capital account liberalization was that it would help diversify sources of funding and hence enhance economic stability, even though the data showed the flows to be procyclical, and hence furthering instability. The IMF and US Treasury were in Stiglitz's view pursuing the matter under the influence of Wall Street institutions, the latter seeking to profit from East Asia's booming economies.[9]

The East Asians according to Stiglitz realized that the hot money flows generated by the liberalization of the capital account were the source of their problems, and some of the finance ministers said as much to him at the September 1997 IMF-World Bank annual meetings. However they feared an international withdrawal of capital if they did not follow IMF advice. (In the end only Malaysia was able to overcome such fears; it ignored the IMF advice, took the risk and imposed capital controls.)

The second point made by Stiglitz is that pursuit of IMF advice made matters worse. IMF misdiagnosed the crisis in East Asia, and the policies imposed by the IMF only deepened the crisis. Stiglitz writes that IMF saw the East Asian difficulties as just another instance of Latin American style profligate government spending and high inflation rates. Such a diagnosis overlooked the fact that East Asia had good macroeconomic indicators going into the crisis, including budget surpluses, low inflation levels and high GDP growth rates. It was the best performing region in the world, and its problem was not so much excess demand as insufficient demand. The downturns, as developments in Korea and Malaysia showed, were no different from the ones that historically plague the "major advanced economies." The only area where East Asian indictors did not look good was high corporate debt.[10]

The standard recipe for an economic downturn was to stimulate demand by easing fiscal and monetary policies, reducing taxes, and increasing expenditure. In a sharp contrast to this commonsense standard response, the IMF conditioned its offer of funds on implementation of policies that were quite the opposite: contraction in aggregate demand including cuts in government spending, a significant hike in already high interest rates, and increases in taxes. Such conditionality could only worsen East Asia's plight. Political and economic changes of an institutional kind were also sought.[11] The high interest rates were arguably directed at attracting capital inflows; but instead they only caused widespread default amongst businesses: as noted earlier, in Indonesia 75 percent of all businesses were put in distress, and in Thailand close to 50 percent of the bank loans became non-performing.[12] Subsequent lowering of the interest rates could not and did not "unbankrupt" the firms that were wiped out, argues Stiglitz. Already weakened financial sectors were made worse.

To better understand Stiglitz's perspective, it needs bearing in mind that he had previously served as the Chair of Council of Economic Advisers in Clinton's cabinet, and thus brings the awareness of a US government's cabinet rank person of the IMF's work and working to his writing. Stiglitz's views are also informed by his work on the World Bank study on the Asian Miracle in which he had a leading role. This study found that the East Asian economies had been so successful "not only in spite of the fact that they had not followed most of the dictates of the Washington Consensus, but *because* they had not." These findings, according to Stiglitz, had been toned down in the published report; nonetheless, the "study laid out the important roles that the government had played."[13]

The markets seemed to ignore the IMF rescue packages, and the fall in exchange rates continued unabated. An embarrassed IMF, unable to restore the confidence of the markets in economic policies being pursued under its conditionalities, blamed the governments, and this only furthered the panic in the markets. An important complicating factor was that the IMF packages did not include a stand still clause for the foreigner creditor banks. This was a departure from the practice seen in earlier IMF assistance packages for Latin American countries experiencing economic and financial crises, and meant that loans from foreign banks had to be repaid as per schedule, regardless of the severity of the crisis, and this factor only compounded an adverse situation.[14] East Asia (and also some outside the region) developed a perception that the loans extended by the IMF for an important part amounted to the use of public funds supplied on conditions that aimed to secure a bailout of the foreign banks from the consequences of the business risks they had taken in making loans in East Asia; such bailouts were not available to the domestic banks though. Clearly there was a duality in the approach adopted by the IMF in its dealings as between foreign and domestic banks.[15] Contractionary policies in one country, besides reducing economic activity there, also impacted negatively on neighbors. Unemployment rates shot up, ten-fold in Indonesia, four-fold in Korea, and three-fold in Thailand. Urban poverty tripled in Korea, with a quarter of the population falling below poverty line. Thus IMF created deep recessions in the best performing region.[16]

China and Malaysia did better than others because the two countries chose not to have IMF programs. Malaysia decided not to raise interest rates and in September 1998, as mentioned above, it also imposed capital controls. Controls facilitated lower interest rates, and as a result there were fewer bankruptcies and less public borrowing. Foreign investment increased as well. Predictions that Malaysian policies of imposing capital controls would lead to disaster, including by the then US Treasury Secretary Rubin and the Fed Chair Greenspan, were not borne out. The Malaysian controls were lifted after one year as had been promised at the time of imposition. China on the other hand already had capital controls in place at the time of the crisis. In the downturn it responded with an expansionary macroeconomic program and invested in infrastructure, quite the opposite of the IMF prescription of contractionary macroeconomic policies. In the event its GDP growth was around 8 percent.[17] In addition, it is argued that Korea recovered faster than Thailand because it was selective in accepting IMF counsel, keeping exchange rates low and not closing down the banks.[18]

The IMF perspective on the crisis

In contrast to the East Asian version of the crisis discussed above, a succinct and well articulated version of the IMF view is found in Janet Yellen's account of the crisis, recounted in 2007 some ten years after the event, and just ahead of the global financial crisis of 2008.[19] Yellen was the chair of President Clinton's Council of Economic Advisers at the time, and saw the crisis from close up as a key cabinet official of United States, the country that is the major shareholder in the International Monetary Fund and the only one with a veto. She continues to see the causes of the crisis as local and country specific, not systemic; and writing in February 2007, makes the point as follows.

> I should note that the subject is not really a single Asian crisis, but rather several crises. The afflicted countries obviously differ very much from one another, both in terms of their levels of development and their institutional features. Therefore the causes of the crisis and, likewise, the policy reforms that have been adopted in the last ten years are not uniform for the region as a whole. Nonetheless, there are some overarching themes in these developments.[20]

Surprisingly the country specific aspects, which may help in understanding that there were several crises and not just one, are not mentioned further by Yellen, but she identifies a fair number of "overarching themes" instead, and these are as follows. First is the common policy factor that attracted capital inflows: seeing that East Asia was a rapidly growing region, the "international community" encouraged the regional countries to open their economies to foreign capital and liberalize the financial sector. No sooner had this been done that foreign capital flooded in, chiefly in the form of "short-term loans to banks." A second common factor that furthered the inflow of foreign capital was that in the judgment of foreign investors the governments were in a position to intervene and forestall any bank failures. The third common factor was one that caused the outflow: "foreign investors may have lost confidence" in the "fundamental soundness" of the East Asian economies, "perhaps because of the news about failure of Korean chaebols Hanbo and Sammi Steel, as well as of Thai non-bank financial institutions." A fourth common factor, also negative, was the problems with the quality of supervision and regulation of the financial sector, which, when combined with "relationship lending,"[21] led to "the pursuit of risky lending practices by financial intermediaries." Fifth were the pegged exchange rate regimes, common to the afflicted countries, and such exchange rate regimes are "subject to speculative attacks if markets perceive that the true value of the currency is misaligned with its pegged value," and it was just such a perception rooted in concerns about the possible bailouts of the banks by the government that drove down the exchange rates. The sixth factor that characterized the region once the crisis became evident, was "contagion": speculative attacks spread from one market to another, and from one country to another. Seventh, currency depreciation impacted adversely because of currency mismatches to increase the share of non-performing loans in the region.[22] The puzzle is that Yellen's account eschews the country specific causes she alludes to, and relies instead on the very same factors, with the one exception of the addition of the "crony capitalism" charge, as Stiglitz does in his narration in explaining how the crisis came about.

Yellen notes that her "deep concern" was "about how big the impact would be on the US economy, and the markets certainly were jittery: that October the Dow Jones Industrial Average plunged 500 points."[23] Though Yellen's account does not explain why the markets were "jittery," one might conjecture that it was the fear of the potential losses for the US banks involved in the region that must have figured prominently in the markets' calculus, and thus the problem for the US administration may at least have been as much about saving the American banks as it was about saving the afflicted countries.

Writing just before the onset of the global financial crisis of 2008, Yellen finds that the East Asian recovery after the crisis was much faster than expected. But she notes that even ten years after the crisis, the East Asian countries "still manage their exchange rates to some extent," and when that doesn't quite work, they resort to controls on capital flows. Korea, Malaysia, Thailand and Indonesia "have also moved to improve banking supervision and regulation and to introduce more market discipline since the crisis," but "there are still weaknesses in enforcement." The reserves build up in the region may be "motivated by memories of the crisis."[24]

Yellen gives reasons why China escaped the Asian crisis. Its capital account was closed so it did not have to face the problem of private capital flows. In addition, much of the foreign investment in China was not short-term loans but direct investment, which in many cases involved actual plants and factories."[25] One might point out that the capital flows could well have taken the foreign direct investment route to China, precisely because China had capital controls in place, and capital controls ruled out the quick return, speculative trades in currencies. Thus in explaining why China did not suffer the crisis, Yellen implicitly also offers a version of the appropriate policies to avoid such crises and that version does not differ from that offered by East Asians.

The lesson from the Asian crisis for the IMF, as Yellen sees the matter, is that "its adjustment programs should be tailored to individual nations' characteristics." These country specific "characteristics" are again not mentioned, making it difficult if not impossible to meaningfully evaluate her advice, and she remains silent on how this principle might have been applied in the context of the East Asian crisis (or crises as Yellen asserts), or the difference its application might have made in the circumstances apart from noting the following:

> . . . some critics have charged that while the austerity measures it (IMF) advocated may have worked well in other financial crises, in the case of Asia they may have actually exacerbated the downturn.[26]

Again, no comment is offered on the relevance of the above view attributed to "some critics," but in what might serve as an example of a *non sequitur*, Yellen concludes that the experience with the Asian crisis or crises, firstly, established the importance of "sound financial policies" and "sound macroeconomic policies," and secondly, it points to continued vigilance to prevent future crises and to ensure that reforms are not scaled back.[27]

Looking to the future, and, again, this is in February 2007 just before the global financial crisis of 2008 set in, Yellen does not rule out a future crisis in East Asian economies and judges that there will always be some residual risk of systemic crisis there.[28] She also sees China at risk:

> . . . despite China's recent successes, it still shares some of the vulnerabilities faced by the Asia crisis countries in the 1990s. For example, although it has made significant progress in reforming its banking sector through reducing nonperforming loans, the government still has a degree of influence in Chinese bank lending decisions, and some have expressed continuing concern over the health of the banking sector. Commenting on the challenges China faces in its corporate governance and accounting standards, Chairman Bernanke noted recently that progress has been made in these areas, but large benefits could be achieved from further concentration on these issues.[29]

In the event the next crisis, that of 2008, would originate in United States, thus pointing to the limited capabilities of the economics profession to bring an unbiased mindset in its focus on critical developments, or perhaps the intellectual paucity of economics itself as a serious academic discipline of any value.

Table 2.3. East Asia: Afflicted economies: GDP growth over the crisis period.

	Annual percentage change					Per capita GDP in US dollars			
	1986-95	1996	1997	1998	1999	1996	1997	1998	1999
Indonesia	6.8	8.0	4.5	-13.1	0.8	1264	1184	516	746
Korea	8.5	7.0	4.7	-6.9	9.5	12258	11474	7528	9558
Malaysia	8.2	10.0	7.3	-7.4	6.1	4764	4623	3254	3485
Thailand	9.5	5.9	-1.4	-10.5	4.4	3038	2496	1829	1985
Memo: China	9.9	9.6	8.8	7.8	7.1	699	771	817	861

Source: International Monetary Fund, World Economic Outlook, April 2004, (IMF, Washington DC, 2004), and Asian Development Bank.

An assessment of the two different views on the crisis

Thus we have two different perspectives on the crisis. Seen as perceived by the East Asia, as described above, the Asian financial crisis presents a situation of considerable adversity, created by liberalization of the capital account on the prodding of IMF, which was made much worse by a misdiagnosis of the situation by the IMF and by the latter's insistence on policies that were quite inappropriate to the problem at hand.

Good economic performance in the region was not sufficiently recognized and instead given a bad press. East Asian understanding of the causes was not accepted at the time and neither were the proposals of the afflicted economies on how to deal with the crisis, even though in time East Asians saw their point of view vindicated. The region lost considerably in the bargain, and it would be some years before the East Asians again enjoyed the pre-crisis per capita incomes, as table 2.3 below indicates.

The experience of the crisis severely shook region's sense of self-confidence in its capabilities.

> After more than three decades of prosperity and stability, the East Asia region witnessed riots, looting and student demonstrations in Indonesia, strikes against layoffs in South Korea and public protests against IMF conditionality in Thailand. Ultimately new governments emerged in Indonesia, South Korea and Thailand, whilst the political leadership in Malaysia became split. As the crisis grew deeper, it soon became clear that the costs of the crisis on the less socially privileged were the most severe. High inflation, unemployment and disruption of social services due to budget cuts had a severe impact on the poor.[30]

A number of informed assessments shortly after the crisis saw an uncertain, if not altogether bleak, future for the region.[31]

Yellen's account on the other hand, composed some ten years after the crisis, leaves us with a view that though the capital account had been liberalized at the behest of the "international community" to facilitate investment in the rapidly growing East Asian economies, the crisis occurred because of the pegged exchange rate regimes and weak financial sectors. And as a key official of the major shareholder in the IMF at the time, her concern was how the crisis and the whole related set of developments would affect the US economy; to judge this matter she seemed to be monitoring the US financial indicators, in particular the stock market. Her concerns were about developments on Wall Street, possibly the financial health of the American banks active in East Asia, in contrast with the Asian concerns about the very fabric of their societies.

The two views from different vantage points seem to differ much on the causes of the crisis as well as the solutions. They differ on the role of the government in the economy, the desirability of capital controls, and the policies to be pursued in a financial crisis. The views also seem to differ on the critical indicators to watch in a crisis.

In fairness, it must be said that the IMF eventually accepted that it had made mistakes in its fiscal policy recommendations, but "it has not admitted to mistakes in its monetary policy, nor has it sought to explain why its models failed to predict the course of events so miserably." Independent Evaluation Office's reports issued well after the crisis seem to confirm the problem with fiscal measures, and leave a question mark in respect of monetary policy.[32] In due course the IMF also quietly reversed its position on capital controls.

III: THE REGIONAL RESPONSES TO THE ASIAN FINANCIAL CRISIS

The nature of the problem

The nature of the problem that the East Asians faced was two-fold. To reiterate, firstly, the East Asians saw the crisis as an outcome of speculative forces working in a globalized financial system. The critical element in the Asian financial situation that turned it into a crisis for the East Asians was the speculators indulging in currency trading. The speculators judged that on balance a particular government would not be in a position to defend the pegged rate of exchange for its currency. The government's plight was being foretold by the increase in the short-term foreign debt vis-à-vis its foreign exchange reserves. This was in contrast to the understanding of the "major advanced economies" and the multilateral financial institutions who saw the crisis as a result solely of domestic causes: a combination of crony capitalism in the region and East Asia's lack of financial sophistication.

Secondly, there were the IMF conditionalities that the East Asians judged as inappropriate and contributing to a worsening of the crisis. The only option for the government seeking funds during the crisis was recourse to the IMF; this did bring funds, but only at an inordinate socioeconomic cost. The IMF assistance took time, and the economic doctrine it was to apply to the afflicted East Asian economies was different from the one that these economies considered appropriate. The East Asians also felt that the policies being advocated by the IMF were less accommodating of their concerns than had been the case in IMF's dealings with Mexico and other Latin American economies suffering variously from crises in the 1980s and 1990s. The IMF also had multiple objectives, if not conflicting objectives, needing to also secure the interests of its principal shareholder. In the event even obtaining the coveted IMF's "seal of approval" was not enough, the markets ignored the IMF programme, and speculation continued.

Nothing in the experience of East Asian economies had prepared them for such a world. The crisis had proved to be disruptive of East Asian development effort. It had caused a set back to growth. East Asia felt driven to initiate measures to protect itself from such events in the future, and also from the consequential economic and financial instability that ensues. More worryingly and contrary to expectations in the region, the United States, having made its priorities clear as the crisis had unfolded, was disinterested, and APEC too had proved to be an utter disappointment for the East Asians in the course of the crisis. To take one instance, US vice president Al Gore in an APEC meeting in 1998 did not focus in his central message on how APEC under American "leadership" could see the region through the crisis, but chose to emphasize instead what he perceived to be the political and social shortcomings of the Malaysian government.

> The American vice president expressed support for "Calls for democracy, calls for reform . . . we hear them today—right here, right now—among the brave people of Malaysia."[33]

Hence the crisis was important in bringing to the surface the differences between the "major advanced economies" and the multilateral financial institutions on the one hand, and the East Asians on the other, on the basic functioning of a globalized world economy and its financial system. Even in midst of the crisis, the regional economies could only look to regional solutions.

The East Asian approach to a solution: AMF, ASEAN+3 and CMIM

The first regional response to resolving the Asian financial crisis came from Japan, at the time the world's second largest economy and also then seen as a "leader" in East Asia. In course of the Asian financial crisis a new regional mechanism for intermediating regional savings was put forth, publicly in September 1997 at the annual IMF-World Bank meetings in Hong Kong: Japan proposed a fund of 100 billion dollars towards an Asian Monetary Fund to finance the economic assistance packages for the afflicted economies.[34] The detailed reasons why this did not materialize vary but the broad thrust is that the United States did not wish it. One view is that America was unwilling because the proposed Asian Monetary Fund pointedly excluded the IMF and its principal shareholder the United States, arguably because Japan wished to insulate East Asia from "a perceived US agenda of liberalisation and globalisation that primarily benefited American commercial interests."[35] Stiglitz's account, which is generally supportive of this point of view of why the Asian Monetary Fund did not materialize, is as follows.[36]

> In 1997 Japan offered $100 billion to create an Asian Monetary Fund, in order to finance the required stimulative actions. But (United States) Treasury did everything to squelch the idea. The IMF joined in. The reason for the IMF's position was clear: While the IMF was a strong advocate of competition in markets, it did not want competition in its own domain, and the Asian Monetary Fund would provide that. The US Treasury's motivations were similar. As the only shareholder of the IMF with veto power, the United States had considerable say in IMF policies. It was widely known that Japan disagreed strongly with IMF actions—I had repeated meetings with senior Japanese officials in which they expressed misgivings about IMF policies that were almost identical to my own. With Japan, and possibly China, as likely major

> contributors to the Asian Monetary Fund, their voices would predominate, providing a real challenge to American "leadership"—and control.

On encountering American resistance to the idea, Japan scaled down its offer to US$30 billion. But the United States insisted that the funds not be used for stimulating the economy through fiscal measures. It sought that the money be used instead for "corporate and financial restructuring—effectively to bail out American and other foreign banks and creditors." Perhaps because of these conditions, Japan did not come through with the funds.[37] The critical element in denying Japan's initiative seemed to be not the quantum of funds but, arguably, differences on policy. Thus the Japanese move to create an Asian Monetary Fund and the United States refusal to contemplate it pointed to deep differences on policies between the United States and East Asia. One additional complication, a hypothetical one raised by Andrew Sheng, might have been China's participation, if Taiwan was also going to contribute to this fund, but we shall never know, as the Asian Monetary Fund never took off.[38]

Thus efforts reflecting the Japanese initiative to set up an Asian Monetary Fund that could provide assistance on conditions more nearly in tune with the thinking of the regional economies did not come to fruition. The United States did not seem to be agreeable to independent Japanese-led financial primacy in Asia. Japan's standing as a "leader" in Asia was compromised by its failure to break free of the United States and set up its proposed Asian Monetary Fund. The ASEAN+3 process came next. It was Dr Mahatir, *l'enfant terrible* of the West, who then convened the first ASEAN+3 summit of ASEAN and the other major East Asian economies in Kuala Lumpur in December 1998, bringing together East Asia as he conceived it to be, almost in a reflex action to the difficulties facing the region, and thus stumbled upon the ASEAN+3 format.[39] This ASEAN+3 process has continued.[40]

A meeting of finance ministers of ASEAN+3 held in Chiang Mai in May 2000, on the sidelines of an Asian Development Bank meeting, considered a transfer enabling mechanism.[41] In the course of the Asian financial crisis, the lack of a regional mechanism for transferring funds from savers to those who were in need was deeply felt. The only such facility in existence at the time of the crisis was the ASEAN swap arrangement, and this at US$200 million looked hopelessly inadequate as a deterrent against speculative trading in currencies.[42]

The apparent paradox for the region was that East Asian economies were high savings economies and as such East Asia was an important source of funds for the world. If this was the case then how could East Asia face such a paucity of funds just when the region's needs seemed critical? The answer to the seeming paradox lay in the fact that the East Asian savings were being intermediated to a considerable degree by the foreign banks, which is to say by institutions outside the region:[43] if a government or corporation in East Asia wished to borrow, it would approach a major foreign bank and that bank would advance the funds, essentially recycling the savings within the same economy or the savings from another East Asian economy, but adding on its fees and mark-ups. And, importantly, the lending foreign bank would also impose its terms and conditions on the borrower.

The rather rudimentary facility actually agreed upon at the ASEAN+3 meeting in Chiang Mai in May 2000, referred to as the Chiang Mai Initiative (CMI for short), permitted a participating country to borrow from another participating country's foreign exchange reserves for a period that could be extended for up to two years. This Chiang Mai Initiative initially comprised of two elements: the earlier ASEAN currency swap arrangement of US$200 million—the new CMI arrangement could be seen as building further on this existing embryonic structure—and a network of sixteen bilateral currency swap arrangements. The CMI, amounting to some US$40 billion and in place by 2003, presented a need-based and pragmatic arrangement among the economies of the region, and one that offered greater stability in case of another financial shock in the region.[44] Arguably, it seemed to affirm an implicit lack of faith by the participants in the self-correcting nature of the free markets. In this latter aspect it was not so much a substitute for the IMF, which at the time subscribed unequivocally to the belief in self-correcting nature of the free markets, but also reflective of a different understanding of how economies worked. The Asian financial crisis of 1997 was therefore influential in determining both the course that the East Asia's economies were to take towards regional economic and financial cooperation, and in the region's approach to its interaction with the world economy.

This original CMI, a compendium of relatively modest bilateral swap agreements, has since advanced and been multilateralized to CMIM. Country contributions, voting procedures and mechanics for assisting countries in need have been established. The funds at the disposal of this agreement now amount to US$120 billion, having last increased from US$80 billion in face of the global financial crisis of 2008, and these are to be used to address balance of payments and short-term liquidity difficulties of its members, and to supplement the existing international financial arrangements in such cases. A permanent, independent monitoring and surveillance unit, namely "ASEAN+3 Macroeconomic Research Office" and AMRO for short, has been recently established in Singapore to support the implementation of CMIM. The task of this new AMRO is to "monitor and analyze regional economies" so as to assist in "early detection of risks, swift implementation of remedial actions, and effective decision-making of the CMIM."[45] These developments are the outcome of deliberations over the past many years in the meetings of ASEAN+3 finance ministers and have been implemented in incremental steps. CMIM is now seen as an institution that "played a positive role in safeguarding regional financial stability," and hence in countering adverse developments in course of the global financial crisis of 2008. Future plans for CMIM importantly include the possibility of a crisis prevention function, involving collaboration with IMF in this regard.[46] The CMIM resources can arguably be increased further should the signatories so desire, as an enabling legal framework is in place.

One operational aspect of the CMIM is that access to assistance exceeding 20 percent of the total entitlement remains conditional on IMF's approval of a country program. Critics of East Asian regional cooperation see this feature as pointing to the inability of East Asians to be able to develop mechanisms independent of existing multilateral institutions. Some critics in turn explain this inability as a necessary outcome of East Asia's rivalry with the United States, as well as a consequence of an alleged China-Japan rivalry.[47] The critique, besides suffering from the internal contradiction of admitting a united East Asia poised against the United States, whilst simultaneously positing a divided East Asia where the two major regional economies are pitched against each other in a Japan-China contest, as explanations for the same phenomenon, also seems to miss the fact that CMIM is an evolutionary process. CMIM has developed in a brick by brick manner over several years.[48] It needs bearing in mind that the CMIM has not been put to use thus far in a situation of financially assisting a signatory country, and it may well be that once CMIM gains experience, this IMF link that subjects 80 percent of CMI's assistance to a member country in crisis to the prior existence of an IMF adjustment program may well disappear.

But the CMIM's IMF link may also be seen in a more ambiguous light on two counts. A more experienced and therefore confident CMIM (that is one with actual experience of provision and monitoring of economic assistance to a member economy) could perhaps alter the calculus by severing this link between the CMIM and the IMF. Hence the existence of the link and the possibility of its severance may serve to bring IMF closer to the East Asian understanding of regional economies, if IMF wishes to ensure its continuing involvement in East Asia. The second aspect is that the IMF itself is changing, and, for various reasons, has over time moved much closer to the East Asian point of view regarding the policy conditionalities it imposes on the borrowing country. IMF's approach has become more eclectic, admitting a mix of policies hitherto avoided in its country assistance programs, including capital controls and policies promoting macroeconomic expansion, in the assistance provided in response to the global financial crisis and the more recent Eurozone crisis. These are the very measures that were denied to the afflicted East Asian economies by the IMF in their worst hour in 1997-98. Furthermore, with the recent addition of a reportedly articulate and knowledgeable deputy managing director from China, East Asia may have found effective representation at the top of this organization.[49]

Critics also cite the utilization of a swap line to the tune of approximately US$16 billion from the United States Fed by the Bank of Korea in the course of the global financial crisis of 2008, as an instance of CMIM's inadequacy.[50] This criticism seems to overlook the fact that the basic crisis in 2008 was a crisis of the American banking system and the dollar, that the CMIM was not constructed to provide for such an eventuality, and it is a *non sequitur* to argue that CMIM should have solved a problem it was not designed for.

The CMIM signatories are reported to have diverse views on the existing link between CMIM and the IMF. Malaysia and Thailand are reported to be publicly for eliminating the link, and would also like to increase the immediate access to swap funds to 50 percent of the amount committed by a member country, thus reducing the need for recourse to the IMF, whilst others such as Indonesia and Philippines are said to be of the view that IMF's continuing involvement is helpful in deterring speculators.[51] Interviews with the relevant officials of the ASEAN+3 Secretariat however do not bear out this thinking, and present a picture in which the ASEAN economies are generally desirous of eliminating the 20 percent ceiling but Japan in particular among others points to the situation of moral hazard which would arise in absence of a ceiling.

Reviewing the CMI instance of regional cooperation we get a picture of cooperation process being developed and being built up further gradually over the years in response to an actual threat to economic and financial instability. It is a focused effort and an incremental process, albeit not a neat one.

The build up of foreign exchange reserves

For any swap arrangements such as the CMIM to be credible, most of the participating member countries must have something to lend or offer in a swap, which is to say that they ought to have reasonable levels of foreign exchange reserves. This is the obvious linkage between the need for credible swap arrangements and the existence of foreign exchange reserves. Access to swap arrangements becomes necessary if the reserves available with a country's central bank are insufficient to give credence to its policies regarding the exchange rate. If there are ample foreign exchange reserves, then these very reserves underpin the credibility of the exchange rate policy, and the need for currency swaps is lessened if not altogether obviated.[52]

Hence one can infer the logic of why foreign exchange reserves were accumulated at a rapid pace by individual afflicted economies even though no such regional policy was announced or formulated; ostensibly, these economies are high savers, and trade surpluses therefore arise almost by default. This rapid build up of dollar reserves was achieved through trade surpluses with "major advanced economies" as well as with China.[53] It is an important aspect of the foreign exchange reserve build up that evidently it did not involve any explicit cooperation among the countries in the region. This build up of reserves helps to guard against speculative behavior in the markets. The table below shows this build up of foreign exchange reserves in the region, and, as may be seen, reserve accumulation climbs steeply after 1997, increasing six-fold in ten years and more than doubling within another three years:

Table 2.4. ASEAN+3: Foreign reserves (in billions of dollars).

	Foreign reserves	Memo: GDP
2011	5614	14243
2008	2352	11036
1997	391	6479
1990	139	4052

Source: IMF, International Financial Statistics database, accessed August 18, 2011.

Thus the creation of swap arrangements, and the evolution of these arrangements into a multilateralized funding arrangement, made credible by the exceptional increase in the foreign exchange reserves in the region, provides considerable room in policy making, and constitutes a definite step in credibly reducing the region's dependence on the multilateral financial institutions and the consequent need to follow their policy advice should a crisis situation recur.

An aspect of the CMIM development that reveals much about the culture of cooperation in East Asia is that the project lacked a "leader" to drive it. In particular, Malaysia in initiating the ASEAN+3 process in December 1998 may have been the prime mover, but it is also a fact that serious negotiations on CMI proposals picked up steam only once China was on board, and China's presence, given the extraordinary quantum of its foreign exchange reserves, lends the present CMIM arrangements exceptional credibility. Grimes notes that "While China has not been the primary innovator in terms of creating and promoting specific regional efforts, it has played a key role as veto player and facilitator." And in context of CMI, Grimes states that "concrete cooperation was nonstarter until Chinese officials decided that it was not a vehicle for Japanese influence. . . . Once China was on board, negotiations proceeded rapidly."[54] Thus the CMIM presents a more broad-based institution than the proposed Asian Monetary Fund, in which Japan was to be the major player. CMIM, which provides some of the facilities that Asian Monetary Fund sought to offer but retains an IMF link—even though the link may only be notional for practical purposes—may also be a reason why the United

States and the IMF have not reacted.[55] These episodes point, firstly, to the assessment that only such cooperation succeeds in East Asia as is pragmatically needed; and cooperation in the region is not necessarily extended to grand schemes that just tend to replicate other institutions and experiences elsewhere. Secondly, the episodes also point to the centrality of China to the success of any region-wide economic arrangements in today's East Asia, even though these arrangements may come about without a visible leader.

IV: FINAL WORDS

East Asia's experience with the Asian financial crisis had shown that there were deep differences with the multilateral institutions and "major advanced economies" on economic policies.[56] These differences, which perhaps date back to the East Asian pursuit of the various manifestations of its development model, as distinct from a more laissez faire approach, were reflected both in an assessment of the causes of the crisis as well as on how best to cope with its fallout.[57] From an East Asian perspective the multilateral financial institutions had not comprehended the problem of speculators in an environment of floating exchange rates and freedom of capital flows, and did not see the immense difficulties and damage the speculators could cause to economies, and were also not forthcoming with a relevant and timely solution to that crisis. As the crisis unfolded, East Asia perceived the causes of the crisis differently from the IMF as well as the "major advanced economies." And as discussions began on policies to manage the crisis and its fallout, East Asia differed greatly with the IMF as well as the "major advanced economies" on the appropriate remedial policies.

As the frenzy generated by the Asian financial crisis subsided, it became clear to the East Asians as well as to other observers that for the lack of a few hundred million dollars, half a dozen economies and their multitudes of several hundred millions had been sent into a tailspin. The East Asians seemed to be learning the hard way the importance of access to unconditional funds in the globalized world economy devoid of capital controls. Looking to the future, it was important for East Asia to avoid a repeat of the economic and social catastrophe it had suffered, and to have such resources in hand as would deter the speculators.

The solution that IMF did provide arguably worsened the economic situation of the afflicted economies, and in any event imposed an inordinate cost on the afflicted economies. Japan's efforts in the midst of the crisis to provide an alternative Asian institution, the Asian Monetary Fund, were stymied. In due course as the Asian financial crisis abated and the dust settled, East Asian countries judged that the IMF and APEC had failed them, and felt the need to develop mechanisms of their own that would not expose them to a similar crisis in the future. The East Asian economies needed to do this on their own because of the deep differences with the multilateral financial institutions in perception and understanding about the functioning of the globalized world economy. Thus in the wake of the Asian financial crisis the East Asian governments moved to meet this need through an effort at developing suitable institutional mechanisms and undertaking other policy measures, which could broadly be subsumed under the rubric of financial cooperation. These efforts gathered strength over time. One line of defense can now be seen in the high levels of individual country specific foreign exchange reserves, to serve as a deterrent against any contemplated speculation in relation to the East Asian currencies.

In its search for solutions, the region was sharply conscious of the lacunae in the international financial system in a number of areas, of which two in particular were critical. Firstly, the region lacked the financial capacity to handle the adverse effects of the system, in particular there was no mechanism to deter or to counter the adverse impact of speculative forces in foreign exchange markets in a milieu of free international capital movements. Secondly, the region also realized the impossibility of obtaining short-term balance of payments finance on terms that match the recipient economy's perception of the best course to further its welfare, and that the thinking on this point in the region differed sharply with that of the multilateral financial and economic institutions. Therefore in its effort to cope better with similar eventualities in the future, East Asia as a region initiated efforts to develop regional institutions to provide balance of payments finance, even as Japan's policymakers discovered their limits in an effort to provide a substitute institution for the IMF. And the region also proceeded to develop defenses against currency speculators. In this manner the Asian financial crisis pushed East Asia of necessity towards regional cooperation.

The Asian financial crisis of 1997 proved to be formative for East Asia in terms of its outlook, international economic policies, and regional cooperation. Perhaps for the first time East Asia became mindful of the negative implications of being a part of the globalized world economy and was forced to explicitly consider the question of how to best deal with it. The efforts at regional cooperation as a solution are circumscribed by economic and financial objectives though. It is therefore a significant aspect of these efforts and related developments that the East Asian endeavors in regional cooperation do not stem from a desire to forge a regional identity per se, or from a political or economic ideology, other than a pragmatic reluctance to accept the laissez faire doctrine of self-correcting markets. These efforts are definitely not the outcome of any grand vision. The East Asians almost "sleepwalked" into regional economic and financial cooperation because of the common difficulties they faced in course of the crisis, the failure of APEC to assist, the counterproductive nature of IMF assistance, and the indifference of the United States to their plight. Faced with a crisis, they had been left to fend for themselves. In course of these efforts the East Asians discovered the ASEAN+3 process.

NOTES

1. See Andrew Sheng, From Asian to global financial crisis (Cambridge: Cambridge University Press, 2010).
2. Some argue that it was China's emergence that caused the problem of export loss, but China's export growth also slowed down in 1996.
3. The issue of capital controls, as is discussed below, is seen as the decisive element in the Asian financial crisis. For a discussion of capital controls in the context of IMF's approach to the crisis see Jeffrey M Chwieroth, Capital ideas, The IMF and the rise of financial liberalization (Princeton: Princeton University Press, 2010), especially pp. 181-225.
4. See Andrew Sheng, From Asian to global financial crisis (Cambridge: Cambridge University Press, 2010), pp. 22, 24 and 26.
5. See William W Grimes, Currency and contest in East Asia (Ithaca: Cornell University Press, 2009), p. 67. Only Japan among the East Asian economies at 5.54 percent had voting power worth mentioning. China had 2.28 percent. Indonesia, Korea, Malaysia and Thailand each had 1.02, 0.56, 0.57 and 0.40 percent of voting power, respectively. See IMF, Annual Report 1997 (Washington DC: IMF, 1997), pp. 215-218.
6. See Andrew Sheng, From Asian to global financial crisis, (Cambridge: Cambridge University Press, 2010), pp. 34, 35 and 37.
7. Joseph Stiglitz, Globalization and its discontents (London: Penguin Allen Lane, 2002), pp. 112 and 117.
8. Mahatir's speech of September 20th, 1997 delivered at the IMF-World Bank annual meeting in Hong Kong, quoted by Andrew Sheng in From Asian to global financial crisis (Cambridge: Cambridge University Press, 2010), pp. 32-33.
9. See Joseph Stiglitz, Globalization and its discontents (London: Penguin Allen Lane, 2002), p. 89 and pp. 99-100. The point about capital flows as the main factor leading to the crisis is also made by others. For example Andrew Sheng writes that "the obvious suspect for the currency turmoil was the large capital flows into Asia." See Andrew Sheng, From Asian to global financial crisis (Cambridge: Cambridge University Press, 2010), p. 28.
10. See Joseph Stiglitz, Globalization and its discontents (London: Penguin Allen Lane, 2002), pp. 104-105.
11. Joseph Stiglitz, Globalization and its discontents (London: Penguin Allen Lane, 2002), p. 96.
12. Joseph Stiglitz, Globalization and its discontents (London: Penguin Allen Lane, 2002), pp. 112 and 117.
13. See Joseph Stiglitz, Globalization and its discontents (London: Penguin Allen Lane, 2002), p. 91.
14. See Andrew Sheng, From Asian to global financial crisis (Cambridge: Cambridge University Press, 2010), pp. 30 and 113.
15. Joseph Stiglitz, discussing moral hazard at the IMF in his book Globalization and its discontents, says:

> Moreover, the IMF's behavior should come as no surprise: it approached the problems form the perspectives and ideology of the financial community, and these naturally were closely (though not perfectly) aligned with its interests. As we have noted before many of its key personnel came from the financial community, and many of its key personnel, having served

> these interests well, left to well paying jobs in the financial community. Stan Fischer the deputy managing director who played such a role in the episodes described in this book, went directly from the IMF to become a vice chairman at the Citigroup, the vast financial firm that includes Citibank. . . . One could only ask Was Fischer being richly rewarded for having faithfully executed what he was told to do."

The work for which Stiglitz sees Fischer being "rewarded" was the bailout of the foreign banks in course of the Asian financial crisis. See Joseph Stiglitz, Globalization and its discontents (London: Penguin Allen Lane, 2002), pp. 207-208. Kenneth Rogoff though has questioned the fairness of this assessment by Stiglitz in a critique of the Stiglitz book. Rogoff writes:

> On page 208, you slander former IMF number two, Stan Fischer, implying that Citibank may have dangled a job offer in front of him in return for his cooperation in debt renegotiations. Joe, Stan Fischer is well known to be a person of unimpeachable integrity. Of all the false inferences and innuendos in this book, this is the most outrageous. I'd suggest you should pull this book off the shelves until this slander is corrected.

See Kenneth Rogoff, An open letter, July 2, 2002, http://www.imf.org/external/np/vc/2002/070202.htm.

16. Joseph Stiglitz, Globalization and its discontents (London: Penguin Allen Lane, 2002), pp. 96-97 and p. 109.

17. Joseph Stiglitz, Globalization and its discontents (London: Penguin Allen Lane, 2002), pp. 122-125.

18. Joseph Stiglitz, Globalization and its discontents (London: Penguin Allen Lane, 2002), p. 127.

19. Kenneth Rogoff, economic counselor and director of research at the IMF over 2001-03, wrote a critique of Stiglitz's book shortly after the book appeared, but this critique focused on Stglitz's integrity and did not get into details of specific policies. A subsequent article offered a defense of IMF's general approach to adjustment without getting into the specifics of the Asian crisis. See Kenneth Rogoff, An open letter, July 2, 2002, http://www.imf.org/external/np/vc/2002/070202.htm and Kenneth Rogoff, The IMF strikes back, Foreign Policy January-February 2003.

20. See Janet Yellen, The Asian financial crisis ten years later: Assessing the past and looking to the future, transcript of a speech to Asia Society of Southern California, February 6, 2007, p. 2.

21. "Relationship lending" sometimes substitutes for "crony capitalism." More recently though, with East Asian economies ascendant, "crony capitalism" has been reinterpreted as a model that often helps to ensure the survival of a corporation because of family's loyalty to the firm. See Geoff Owen, Family still has a role to play, Financial Times, August 4, 2010.

22. See Janet Yellen, The Asian financial crisis ten years later: Assessing the past and looking to the future, transcript of a speech to Asia Society of Southern California, February 6, 2007, pp. 3-6.

23. See Janet Yellen, The Asian financial crisis ten years later: Assessing the past and looking to the future, transcript of a speech to Asia Society of Southern California, February 6, 2007, p. 1.

24. See Janet Yellen, The Asian financial crisis ten years later: Assessing the past and looking to the future, transcript of a speech to Asia Society of Southern California, February 6, 2007, pp. 6-10.

25. See Janet Yellen, The Asian financial crisis ten years later: Assessing the past and looking to the future, transcript of a speech to Asia Society of Southern California, February 6, 2007, p. 13.

26. See Janet Yellen, The Asian financial crisis ten years later: Assessing the past and looking to the future, transcript of a speech to Asia Society of Southern California, February 6, 2007, p. 11.

27. See Janet Yellen, The Asian financial crisis ten years later: Assessing the past and looking to the future, transcript of a speech to Asia Society of Southern California, February 6, 2007, p. 14.

28. See Janet Yellen, The Asian financial crisis ten years later: Assessing the past and looking to the future, transcript of a speech to Asia Society of Southern California, February 6, 2007, p. 10.

29. See Janet Yellen, The Asian financial crisis ten years later: Assessing the past and looking to the future, transcript of a speech to Asia Society of Southern California, February 6, 2007, p. 13.

30. See, Andrew Sheng, From Asian to global financial crisis, An Asian regulator's view of unfettered finance in the 1990s and 2000s, (Cambridge University Press, Cambridge, 2009), p. 307.

31. See for example discussion in Richard Robison, Mark Beeson, Kanishka Jayasuriya and Hyuk-Rae Kim, eds., Politics and markets in the wake of the Asian crisis (London: Routledge, 2000), and Pietro P Masina, ed., Rethinking development in East Asia, From illusory miracle to economic crisis (London: Curzon, 2002).

32. Joseph Stiglitz, Globalization and its discontents (London: Penguin Allen Lane, 2002), pp. 128-129. Sheng confirms Stiglitz's reading of IMF's reluctance on this point, noting that the IMF's Independent Evaluation Office's assessment in 2003 says that "the experience of the three countries with monetary policies varies and does not provide a definitive answer to the effectiveness of high interest rates in stabilizing exchange rates." See Andrew Sheng, From Asian to global financial crisis (Cambridge: Cambridge University Press, 2010), p. 118.

33. See Simon S C Tay, Asia Alone (Singapore, Wiley, 2010), pp. 24-25.

34. See, Andrew Sheng, From Asian to global financial crisis, An Asian regulator's view of unfettered finance in the 1990s and 2000s (Cambridge: Cambridge University Press, 2009), pp. 32-33.

35. See William W Grimes, Currency and contest in East Asia (Ithaca: Cornell University Press, 2009), p. 77.

36. Joseph Stiglitz, Globalization and its discontents (London: Penguin Allen Lane, 2002), p. 112.

37. Joseph Stiglitz, Globalization and its discontents (London: Penguin Allen Lane, 2002), p. 113. Andrew Sheng records that Eisuke Sakakibara, the Japanese vice minister for finance indicated to him in November 1997 "that the money might not be forthcoming." See Andrew Sheng, From Asian to global financial crisis, An Asian regulator's view of unfettered finance in the 1990s and 2000s (Cambridge: Cambridge University Press, 2009), p. 39.

38. See Andrew Sheng, From Asian to global financial crisis, An Asian regulator's view of unfettered finance in the 1990s and 2000s (Cambridge: Cambridge University Press, 2009), p. 34.

39. See Simon S C Tay, Asia Alone (Singapore, Wiley, 2010), pp. 26-27.

40. Akiko Fukushima notes that in January 1997 Japanese Prime Minister Hashimoto Ryutaro visited a number of ASEAN countries seeking a Japan + ASEAN summit. Dr Mahatir is said to have counseled that such a summit would make China uneasy, and suggested the ASEAN+3 format for the summit. See Akiko Fukushima, Japan's perspective on Asian regionalism, in Michael J Green and Bates Gill, Asia's new multilateralism (New York: Columbia University Press, 2009), p. 108.

41. See "The Joint Ministerial Statement of the ASEAN+3 Finance Ministers Meeting 6 May 2000, Chiang Mai, Thailand," at http://www.mof.go.jp/jouhou/kokkin/as3_000506e.htm

42. Thailand alone was reported to have spent over US$ 20 billion in its unsuccessful attempt to defend the baht.

43. William W Grimes, in explaining the need regional bond market, writes: "The logic is that that excess savings at home have been exported overseas and then lent back to finance domestic needs in the form of foreign currency-denominated debt."

See William W Grimes, Currency and contest in East Asia (Ithaca: Cornell University Press, 2009), p. 66.

44. Amy Searight, Emerging economic architecture in Asia, in Michael J Green and Bates Gill, Asia's new multilateralism (New York: Columbia University Press, 2009), p. 230.

45. The acronym CMIM stands for Chiang Mai Initiative Multilateralised. Multilateralisation of CMI, which had been under consideration for some years, came into effect on 24 March 2010, and was reported in paragraph 3 of The Joint Ministerial Statement of the 13th ASEAN+3 Finance Ministers' Meeting, held in Tashkent, 2 May 2010. Contributions of Indonesia, Malaysia, Philippines, Singapore and Thailand were also agreed upon in the 13th meeting (paragraph 8 of The Joint Ministerial Statement of the 13th ASEAN+3 Finance Ministers' Meeting, held in Tashkent, 2 May 2010). Approval of operational guidelines for invoking CMIM activation, including in relation to the existence of IMF programs was reported in The Joint Ministerial Statement of the 14th ASEAN+3 Finance Ministers' Meeting, held in Ha Noi, 4 May 2011. Agreement on country contributions, borrowing accessibility and voting procedures was reported in paragraph 7 of The Joint Media Statement of the 12th ASEAN+3 Finance Ministers' Meeting, held in Bali, 3 May 2009, and paragraph 9 of this statement reports admission of Hong Kong, China as a CMIM participant. The objectives of CMI/CMIM were most recently reiterated in paragraph 8 of The Joint Ministerial Statement of the 13th ASEAN+3 Finance Ministers' Meeting, held in Tashkent, 2 May 2010. The current size of the CMIM facility is mentioned at http://www.aseansec.org/19588.htm (ASEAN Finance Ministers Meetings). Establishment of AMRO establishment is reported in paragraph 9 of The Joint Ministerial Statement of the 13th ASEAN+3 Finance Ministers' Meeting, held in Tashkent, 2 May 2010, and future plans for AMRO are mentioned in paragraph 8 of The Joint Ministerial Statement of the 14th ASEAN+3 Finance Ministers' Meeting, held in Ha Noi, 4 May 2011.

46. See paragraphs 2 and 9 of The Joint Ministerial Statement of the 14th ASEAN+3 Finance Ministers' Meeting, held in Ha Noi, 4 May 2011.

47. A narration of such criticism may be read in William W Grimes, The Asian Monetary Fund reborn? Implications of Chiang Mai Initiative Multilateralisation, in Asia Policy, no. 11, January 2011, pp. 79-104.

48. An important element signaling its future development was the road map set out in the ASEAN+3 finance ministers' Istanbul meeting of May 2005: stages to come included "introduction of collective decision-making" and "enhanced surveillance." This meeting also decided to designate one of the three (China, Japan and Korea) as a coordinating country (for each of the sixteen member countries) whose central bank would coordinate and manage assistance in case of need (for a particular member country. It was also decided that the total pool would be doubled to US$80 billion, and the ceiling for immediate access to CMI funds was to be raised from 10 percent to 20 percent of the amount committed by a member country, and this directly quadrupled the quantum of immediately available assistance. In the year to May 2006 mechanics for disbursement of funds were refined and an expert group to improve monitoring and surveillance was also set up. Over 2007-08 agreement was reached that 80 percent of the total size of CMI should come from the "plus-three" countries (China, Japan and Korea), thus making the burden sharing closer to the principle of "from each according to his ability, and to each according to his need." See "The Joint Ministerial Statement of the 8th ASEAN+3 Finance Ministers' Meeting 4 May 2005, Istanbul, Turkey," at http://www.mof.go.jp/english/if/as3_050504.htm, "The Joint Ministerial Statement of the 9th ASEAN+3 Finance Ministers' Meeting 4 May 2006, Hyderabad, India," at http://www.mof.go.jp/english/if/as3_060504.htm, and Masahiro Kawai, The role of an Asian Currency Unit for Asian monetary integration, mimeo, October 2008, pp. 8-13.

49. This is the gist of informal interviews of IMF staff by the authors in August 2011. See also discussion in Ilene Grabel, Not your grandfather's IMF: global crisis, 'productive incoherence' and developmental policy space, Cambridge Journal of Economics, September 2011, vol. 35, no. 5, pp. 805-830; and Keith Cowling and Philip R Tomlin-

son, Post the 'Washington Consensus': economic governance and industrial strategies for the twenty-first century, Cambridge Journal of Economics, September 2011, vol. 35, no. 5, pp. 831-852.

50. Grimes makes this point in William W Grimes, The Asian Monetary Fund reborn? Implications of Chiang Mai Initiative Multilateralisation, in Asia Policy, no. 11, January 2011, pp. 79-104.

51. See William W Grimes, Currency and contest in East Asia (Ithaca: Cornell University Press, 2009), pp. 81-82 and 91.

52. As we mention elsewhere in this chapter, the existence of CMI, and the size of the foreign reserves supporting the CMI, were arguably important factors that helped keep the 2007 global financial crisis out of East Asia. Reserves are extremely helpful in a milieu of speculative finance, and all the more so in the absence of capital controls.

53. An important element in the build up of China's reserves is the difficulties that come up when China wishes to use these reserves to invest in the "major advanced economies." Even Chinese assistance to the developing countries that tends to be unconditional is viewed with some apprehension in the Western media.

54. See William W Grimes, Currency and contest in East Asia (Ithaca: Cornell University Press, 2009), pp. 212-213

55. See William W Grimes, Currency and contest in East Asia (Ithaca: Cornell University Press, 2009), pp. 102-112.

56. The "major advanced economies" nomenclature is used as defined and adopted by the International Monetary Fund. In 2010 this category of "major advanced economies" also included one East Asian economy, that is, Japan. See IMF, World Economic Outlook April 2010 (Washington DC: IMF, 2010). A point to note is that Japan, though a member of the "advanced economies" group, may not share the economic thinking of the transatlantic members of the group; thus when the discussion is about East Asian economies vis-à-vis the "major advanced economies," Japan is generally taken as included in the former group.

57. A fair idea of the debate can be had from Joseph Stiglitz, Some lessons from the East Asian miracle, World Bank Research Observer (1996) vol. 11, no. 2, pp. 151-177; Ha-Joon Chang, The East Asian development experience, The miracle, the crisis and the future (London: Zed Books, 2006); and Alice Amsden, The rise of the rest (Oxford: Oxford University Press, 2001).

THREE

Processed manufacturing and trade cooperation

I: INTRODUCTION

The recovery in East Asia from the Asian financial crisis was much faster than expected, notwithstanding the assessment at the time that East Asia may continue to suffer the effects of the crisis for some time. It was between the Asian financial crisis of 1997 and the global financial crisis of 2008 that the unexpected occurred, East Asia experienced rapid growth, and the economic forces at work in the world economy and East Asian policies helped to transform the organization of production and trade in the region.

In hindsight, the forces at work behind the transformation were threefold. First, the world economy was becoming increasingly globalized, which is to say that barriers to transborder flows of capital, goods and services were in the process of coming down fast. East Asian economies too were pursuing similar policies. A new global economic environment was taking shape. Second, Japan began to experience stagnation and the hitherto primary economic engine for the region began to sputter, the situation made worse by natural calamities, and was quite unable to recover its old heartbeat. Third, China's economic policies and the impact of Chinese economy's rapid growth began to affect the regional economies drawing them in at an increasing pace, and all the more so as the upward surge continued to characterize China's economic performance. Regional economies in their recovery from the crisis and thereafter searched for opportunities in this new and changing regional economic universe.

By the time the global financial crisis struck in 2008, the economic landscape in East Asia had changed decisively. It is the nature of this change that occurred after the Asian financial crisis that is the subject of the present chapter. We consider how over this period production and trade patterns in East Asia shifted from the Japanese *flying geese* orientation, which implied a vertical division of labor and was guided by and centered on Japan, to a Factory Asia network implying a relatively horizontal division of labor with a China orientation, though, and importantly, *sans* Chinese guidance. East Asian economies tended to gravitate around the Japanese economy in 1997. By the time the global financial crisis set in regional economies had developed deep linkages with China. The industrial policy focus had shifted from the *flying geese* concept to one of a networked Factory Asia, a kind of a giant "production and trade industrial zone" that now seems to span the region. Underlying these developments were changes in the organization of production and trade in the region. Deepening of these intra-regional linkages was followed by efforts that sought to formalize the relationships through RTAs and FTAs using an approach that incorporated more general development and cooperation elements as well, and thus differed substantially from the one focused on market access that the United States uses.

In exploring these themes, we next consider the nature of processed manufacturing in the East Asia region, and see how it has impacted on trade and investment relationships in the region. China, now the largest economy in the region, looms large in these developments. Growing intra-regional linkages that arise from processed manufacturing are also one important factor behind the push to achieve trade liberalization agreements in the region, and we try and fathom the sense and current status of these efforts. A concluding section reflects on the discussion in the chapter.

II: PROCESSED MANUFACTURING AND AN INCREASINGLY NETWORKED REGION

East Asia in the aftermath of the Asia financial crisis

East Asia on the eve of the Asian financial crisis could arguably be envisaged as developing within the Japanese conceptual framework of a vertical division of labor between the region's economies, the *flying geese* model, as had been the case in late 1970s and also in the 1980s. The *flying geese* model envisages late comers to industrialization beginning with say the textile industry and moving up the value and technology chain through industries such as steel, popular electronics, automobiles, etc., culminating for example with a HDTV industry.[1] A particular economy's place in the industrialization hierarchy reflects its stage of development; a more developed economy would have the higher technology industries than a less developed one, and the latter would nonetheless be making efforts to move up the technology chain. The validity of the proposition, also very broadly supported by empirical evidence for the period, rested chiefly on Japan's prestige in the region over 1970s, 1980s and, to a lesser extent, the 1990s; and though various reasons are advanced why the *flying geese* concept eventually petered out, the inherent logic of the proposition that a number of countries would continue to observe a given division of labor, even as their economies progressed, was always questionable. In the event economic globalization and China's opening of its economy to the outside world changed the industrialization calculus.

As the Chinese economy began to open up with Deng Xiaoping's 1978 initiative to undertake the necessary economic reforms, China's main asset was a relatively educated and well-disciplined work force willing to work at a low wage. China's approach to policy change had been summed up well in Deng Xiaoping's maxim of crossing a river by groping the stones; suggestive of a cautious one step at a time framework, rather than the erstwhile policies of sweeping changes stemming from a grand ideology. Deng Xiaoping's pragmatic approach combined with his strategy of *3 Ds* that sought to create an enabling environment for economic development, *density* (or the geographic concentration of economic activity to obtain economies of scale), facilitate reduction of *distance* through provision of good transport infrastructure, and elimination of *divisions*, through reducing barriers to movement of goods, helped to develop the coastal regions.[2] Deng Xiaoping had correctly read the opportunities that an increasingly globalized world economy seemed to offer. Overseas Chinese businessmen were consulted in the formulation of policies that led to the creation of the special economic zones.[3] The foreign direct investment that flowed into China in the initial years following the opening up of the economy was predominantly from Hong Kong and Macau, and to a lesser extent Taiwan. A definitive break in the status quo in East Asia came with the Plaza Accord that caused an appreciation of the Japanese yen, making it attractive for the Japanese firms to expand overseas, and Japanese corporations proceeded to set up assembly plants in China.[4] Investment by the transnational corporations came next. The first businesses that were set up in the new zones used cheap labor to assemble imported components or to manufacture from chiefly imported inputs for export to the major advanced economies and elsewhere. This growth based on exports had been the basic idea that had guided the emergence of Japan, Korea, Taiwan, Hong Kong and Singapore, and was then being followed in Southeast Asia as well. As economic activity gathered pace in China's coastal regions, a specialization of the kind that would validate the *flying geese* concept could be seen, and in the 1980s China could conveniently be visualized in this scheme as the lowest flying bird.

Processed manufacturing

The opening up by China timed fortuitously with a shift in economic thinking in the developed economies. This was a shift away from state control of production, trade and money flows. Large global firms were coming forth to manage these, because they needed to do so. In managing these flows, the global firms were guided by "shareholder value," rather than brand, line of business, size, location, employment, etc. Shareholder value meant profits and to maximize this element, the firms sought the low wage locations. Complex organizational forms and financial instruments were invented to enable this, and changes in laws were also successfully sought to facilitate the new approaches. One example of this approach at work was processed manufacturing, the complex production and trade networks that cut across national borders to farm profits even from the barren landscape of sheer poverty—the use of low wage labor. China, opening up at the time and devising policy with an ear to what the corporations were seeking, responded. It responded by creating the infrastructure, and by tailoring the laws and the procedures to facilitate such production. Production was distributed and trade generated across countries. Over time the East Asian region with networked production and trade with China as the hub was the result.

Processed manufacturing splits up the manufacturing process into separate tasks of manufacturing of each of the different constituent components or sub-assemblies, and the work of assembly and packaging, and promotes the location of each activity where costs are the lowest and logistics efficient; and where the foreign corporations responsible for developing the product and organizing the logistics of its production are very likely not directly responsible for labor relations, labor union dealings, plant hazards and pollution. Hence the production of constituent parts of a product and its final assembly, and packaging and distribution tend to be distributed in a number of countries. The high-end, high value added tasks such as research and design, and marketing, may frequently be kept at home (that is, the advanced economies), whilst the developing countries with the most competitive conditions take on the relatively "less-skilled" and relatively low value added work of actual production, that is, fabrication and assembly of goods, and their packaging and distribution. Thus processed manufacturing did not require new skills, only a reorganization of production and trade as the decline in trade barriers and relatively lower tranportation and shipping costs opened up new possibilities.

A large developing country such as China may have workers with differing skills encompassing a spectrum of wage rates, or a developing country may also develop and offer higher skills competitively and could well attract work that was previously confined to the home country.[5] Furthermore, logistical costs are another fundamental consideration in location of industrial activity; the division of labor in processed manufacturing by its very nature promotes trade and transport between the countries involved as components and products are shipped back and forth in the process of producing a good, packaging it, and transporting it to its final destination. The initial division of labor thus need not be a permanent condition. It is just such a dynamic process that took hold in East Asia with China's joining the globalized world economy, and has grown at a rapid pace since. As a result, a range of diverse industries has developed with time, the diversity of these industries cutting across the traditional vertical division of labor centered on the low-wage manual worker, and their inter-linkages and logistics cutting across national borders.

Industry studies as well as aggregate trade statistics exhibit the evolving nature of the East Asia as an economic space, and the centrality of China's economy in this phenomenon. East Asia's HDD industry offers one example where in order to compete in the global market, assemblers try to procure intermediate goods at the lowest price from indigenous suppliers and suppliers in neighboring countries. Most suppliers tend to be located in the neighboring countries of the assembler factory, where the suppliers' engineers are able to easily travel to solve problems arising from defects. The relatively low transportation costs especially encourage the development of international production networks and intermediate trade. Looking at East Asia as a whole, the HDD industry clustered first in Singapore, and then dispersed to Thailand, Malaysia, and then the Philippines due to the supply access effect, and eventually China due to the market access effect, reflecting cost considerations in both cases. HDD assembler factories in Thailand are known to mainly procure components from arm's-length suppliers, who are independent and on an equal footing with the assembler, located in neighboring China, Indonesia, Japan, Malaysia, Philippines, Singapore and Taiwan. Indigenous Malaysian and Singapore firms progressed with time to become regional suppliers and then advanced to become overseas players expanding their production facilities to China. All this activity generates regional trade and production links. The HDD production networks are in turn supported by the Just In Time (JIT) warehouse systems, which exist to ensure the continued availability of intermediate components and sub-assemblies so as to ensure uninterrupted production, and are particularly suited to situations where there are a large number of parts from a variety of sources with differing delivery times.[6]

The organization of the HDD industry in East Asia evolved as China became the largest PC assembler in the world with a large home market. From 1995 onwards PC producers started setting up HDD plants in China, transforming China into the largest HDD producer in the world, with a substantial volume of parts being sourced from Southeast Asia. Hitachi Global Storage Technologies is one of those producers, among China's HDD industry, who currently procure mechanical parts from Southeast

Asia. But several suppliers have been asked by Hitachi Global Storage Technologies in China to begin operations in China, and procurement from domestic suppliers may well increase as a result. This does not necessarily mean that the local content ratio will further increase while international production networks decline because the low transportation costs will continue to encourage network linkage among the separate production blocks.

Currently China is the largest exporter of HDDs with 35 percent of the market share. Thailand, accounting for 17 percent, is in the second place.[7] The nature of HDD industry necessarily involves growth in both intra-regional foreign direct investment as well as in intra-regional trade.

One study that explored regional production networks of Japanese and Korean firms in electronics and automobile industries operating in China again showed substantial imports of parts and components from Japanese and Korean supplier firms. Intra-regional trade grows in the process. A number of these Japanese and Korean supplier firms relocated to China as demand increased.[8] In the case of Taiwan invested enterprises in China (TIEs) a study showed the deep linkages that are developing vis-à-vis the Chinese economy:[9]

> The manufacturing procurement from Taiwan-based companies either in Taiwan or in China was especially prominent in the plastic, electronic and electric sectors. In the plastic sector, around 50% of the manufacturing procurement was from Taiwan and 20% was from the other TIEs in China. In the electronic and electric sectors, almost 46% of the manufacturing procurement was from Taiwan and 20.73% was from the TIEs in China. In the metal sector, the TIEs imported the raw materials and intermediate goods frequently from Taiwan (35.03%) or other foreign firms in China (33.74%). In the chemical sectors, the dependence on the procurement from Taiwan was less clear. Less than 4% was from Taiwan while nearly 90% of the procurement came from other countries.

Other industry specific studies and economy specific studies, as well as a number of region-wide studies on industry and trade and on foreign direct investment, bear out the patterns that may be deduced from the discussion above.[10] Such relocation and other cross-border activity necessarily involve flows of foreign direct investment. The intensity of a network can be expected to vary directly in some correspondence to the level of the value to volume relationship. Processed manufacturing has by its very nature tied the regional economies by linking up production across borders and causing intra-regional trade and investment thereby. The economic interests of the regional economies necessarily get intertwined.

Today's China is a mix of a large peasant population yet to join the industrial labor force and state of the art cities where all kinds of economic and commercial activity seems feasible. The Chinese economy today encompasses regions with significantly different wage and skill levels, some of which can do textiles profitably and other regions that can do HDTV profitably. For all practical purposes today's Chinese economy is several economies, though under a unified political administration, and the structure of Chinese industry naturally reflects this diversity. Industrial diversification rather than industrial specialization seems to characterize the Chinese economy. Again, quite contrary to what the *flying geese* concept would lead one to expect, industrial diversification rather than industrial specialization also seems to be the case in the Korean economy, as a study of manufacturing employment during the period 1990-2005 revealed.[11]

III: THE IMPACT OF PROCESSED MANUFACTURING ON TRADE RELATIONS IN THE REGION

As noted processed manufacturing causes intra-regional trade in intermediate goods to expand. The direction as well as the composition of trade would expectedly be affected. China's centrality in processed manufacturing would necessarily suggest a centrality in intra-regional trade relations as well. Such developments in trade relations would constitute an important element in the shaping of an economic region.

The direction of intra-regional trade: East Asian economies

We begin with a consideration of the direction of trade and note the shift in the direction of trade for the regional economies. An examination of the direction of trade data in respect to the export trade of the East Asian economies with China, Japan, European Union and the United States for the years 1998 and 2010 shows that the exports of the regional economies are directed increasingly at China displacing the shares of Japan, the European Union and the United States. In the case of the larger economies of Japan and Korea almost as much as one-fourth and one-fifth of their exports go to China. For Taiwan and Hong Kong the share of exports going to China is even higher at around 28 and 50 percent. Indonesia, Malaysia and Philippines too send a sizeable portion of exports to China. Only Cambodia, Brunei and Vietnam send less than 10 percent of their exports to China. The table below summarily illustrates this development.

Table 3.1. East Asia: Changing orientation of export trade. Share of Mainland China, Japan and European Union and United States in East Asian exports.

	Mainland China		Japan		EU and US		Export GDP ratio
	1998	2010	1998	2010	1998	2010	
Exporter							
Japan	5.20	19.38	-	-	49.75	36.90	14
Korea	9.01	24.80	9.23	5.98	33.01	21.97	50
Hong Kong	34.45	50.49	5.25	10.17	39.61	22.17	194
Singapore	3.70	10.32	6.57	4.64	36.26	16.46	221
Taiwan	0.76	28.02	8.43	6.56	42.65	21.53	48
Indonesia	3.75	9.94	18.65	16.33	30.94	19.93	24
Malaysia	2.71	18.93	10.50	8.52	38.21	20.06	96
Philippines	1.16	18.46	14.34	12.42	57.59	25.03	32
Thailand	3.14	10.99	13.27	10.45	39.33	21.43	68
Vietnam	4.73	8.96	16.27	10.50	28.42	36.23	68
Brunei d'S	0.43	7.00	47.19	44.94	24.68	0.25	52
Cambodia	4.52	1.16	0.85	1.61	45.12	50.84	60
Lao PDR	1.93	23.06	4.80	1.54	31.26	11.75	32
Myanmar	4.92	13.57	7.14	5.49	28.05	3.02	9

Source: International Monetary Fund, Direction of Trade Statistics, September 2011 and Asian Development Bank, Asian Development Outlook 2011.

As has been widely noted, the East Asian economies in general tend to have high export/GDP ratios, underlying the significance of the export trade for the output growth in these economies.

The share of imports from China in the total imports of the regional economies too has experienced a parallel increase.

Table 3.2. East Asia: Changing orientation of import trade. Share of Mainland China in East Asian imports.

	1998	2003	2008	2010
Japan	13.20	19.73	18.85	22.10
Korea	6.95	12.25	17.67	17.84
Singapore	4.77	8.12	10.54	10.83
Taiwan	3.91	8.61	13.06	14.31
Indonesia	3.31	9.08	11.80	15.05
Malaysia	3.17	8.82	12.80	13.83
Philippines	4.06	4.79	7.55	13.57
Thailand	4.11	8.00	11.17	13.29
Vietnam	4.55	12.42	19.39	25.51
Cambodia	8.47	12.90	14.67	15.26
Laos	3.04	13.35	10.42	14.63
Myanmar	24.85	26.85	31.32	38.93
Brunei	0.43	4.82	5.45	13.02

Source: International Monetary Fund, Direction of Trade Statistics.

The intraregional import trade also conforms to the broad pattern of increasing importance of China as a trading partner for the regional economies without exception and the proportionate increase is greater than that experienced for the exports.

The direction of intra-regional trade: China

We next consider the direction of China's trade, and the bulk of China's trade continues to be with the advanced economies, but the shares are decreasing, and the decline is faster in the case of China's imports than it is for China's exports. As the summary data for 1998 and 2010 in the table below shows developing Asian economies, particularly ASEAN 9, that is excluding Singapore, have increased their shares in China's trade very substantially, but these shares remain relatively small compared to those of advanced economies. Within Asia though, Japan's share in China's exports has fallen more sharply than its share in China's imports. Korea and Singapore present a more mixed picture. This visible differentiation between the trade patterns emerging respectively for China and the other regional economies, which shows a considerably stronger linkage for the region with China than vice versa, underline China's relatively faster rate of output growth as well as the rapid growth in China's share in world trade.

Table 3.3. China: Direction of trade 1998-2008 (as a percentage of total exports and imports).

	Exports			Imports		
	1998	2008	2010	1998	2008	2010
Advanced economies	84.31	71.03	69.95	82.11	59.35	58.96
United States	20.68	17.69	17.95	12.10	7.22	7.31
EU	16.37	20.51	19.71	14.87	11.74	12.08
	37.05	*38.20*	*37.66*	*26.97*	*18.96*	*19.39*
Japan	16.17	8.13	7.61	20.16	13.32	12.64
Korea	3.41	5.17	4.35	10.70	9.91	9.90
Singapore	2.12	2.26	2.05	3.01	1.78	1.74
	21.70	*15.50*	*14.01*	*33.87*	*25.01*	*24.28*
Emerging, developing economies	15.42	28.70	29.61	15.63	32.33	31.89
Developing Asia	5.72	9.08	10.63	7.06	10.57	11.05
ASEAN 9 (less Singapore)	3.89	5.74	6.70	5.97	8.53	9.44
Memo: ASEAN+3	25.59	21.24	20.71	39.84	33.54	33.72

Source: International Monetary Fund, Direction of Trade Statistics, September 2011.

An important aspect of China's trade is that the bulk of this trade is now conducted by "foreign invested enterprises" (the *FIEs*) thus pointing to the growing linkage between trade and processed manufacturing and foreign direct investment, and to the latter two as the driving factors behind the growth in intra-regional trade.

Table 3.4. Foreign invested enterprises: Evolution of shares in China's imports and exports (in percentages).

Year	Imports	Exports	Share in manufacturing output
1986	5.60	1.88	n/a
1988	10.64	5.18	2.28
1993	40.24	27.51	9.14
1998	54.73	44.06	24.34
2003	56.18	54.83	35.87
2008	54.73	55.35	29.74

Source: Investment Promotion Agency of MOFCOM, at: http://www.fdi.gov.cn/pub/FDI_EN/Statistics/AnnualStatisticsData/default.jsp.

It is noteworthy that the FIEs, which accounted for less than 6 percent of imports and less than 2 percent of exports in 1986, had stabilized by 2003 to over 50 percent of China's imports as well as exports.

The composition of trade

A direct and most comprehensive reflection of the impact of processed manufacturing on the composition of trade is evident in China's trade. Exceptionally high levels of China's import and export trade are directly accounted for by the processed manufacturing activity. China's official trade data indicates the extent of such activity by classifying trade flows to show the linkage between imports and exports activities in a processed manufacturing economy. Table 3.5 provides the statistics for 2009 and 2010 to illustrate this aspect.

We see that more than half the exports and a little less than half the imports appear to be related to processed manufacturing, and arguably it is this trade that has propelled China's exports, and its export-led growth. Importantly, the above table also shows that the trade surplus does not arise on account of "ordinary trade" but it results from the trade in categories associated with processed manufacturing.

An indicator of the extent of economic integration of the region is also evident in the summary fact that the share of components and parts in total East Asian trade is more than twice that for the EU 15, and also substantially greater than that for NAFTA. The table below illustrates.

Table 3.5. China's exports and imports, by type of activity, 2009-10 (in billions of US dollars).

	2009		2010	
	Exports	Imports	Exports	Imports
Processing and assembling	93	76	112	99
Processing with imported materials	494	246	628	318
Equipment for processing trade	-	1	-	1
Equipment/materials imported as investment by FIEs	-	15	-	16
Custom warehousing trade	27	54	35	61
Entrepot trade by bonded area	21	64	37	109
Equipment imported into export processing zone	-	2	-	4
Sub-total of the above categories	*635*	*458*	*812*	*608*
Ordinary trade	530	533	721	768
Other categories	33	15	45	19
Total	1202	1006	1578	1395

Source: Government of China Customs website: http://www.customs-info.com; table titled "Imports and exports by customs regime, December 2009." The descriptions are those used on the website.

More generally, the steadily increasing share of manufactures in China's exports, as indicated by the data in table 3.7 below, would appear to affirm the assessment regarding China's emergence as a processed manufacturing economy, and its increasing reliance on manufactured exports.

Table 3.6. Share of components and parts in total trade 2008 (%).

	East Asia	NAFTA	EU15
Exports	47.6	28.8	22.0
Imports	51.7	36.3	22.1

Source: Premachandra Athukorala, East Asia in world trade, ANU, 2009.

The machinery and transport equipment component of manufactured exports in the above table has shown particularly fast growth, more than doubling its share in exports over the period 1995-2009, rising from 21 percent of the total to nearly 50 percent of the total. This development points to both an internationally competitive Chinese economy and a shift over time toward relatively higher value added manufactures. One could plausibly read increasing value addition in exports in the data: the fact that the share of manufactured goods in imports fell over the period, even though that of the manufactured goods in exports increased, makes this point.

Table 3.7. China: Commodity structure of trade (as a percentage of total merchandise exports and imports respectively).

	Exports		Imports	
	1995	2009	1995	2009
All food items	8.3	2.9	7.0	4.5
Agricultural raw materials	1.8	0.5	5.2	3.1
Fuels	3.6	1.7	3.9	12.3
Ores, metals	2.4	1.3	4.6	12.9
Manufactured goods	83.7	93.5	78.7	66.9
Chemicals	6.1	5.2	13.1	10.6
Machinery and transport equipment	21.1	49.2	39.9	38.7
Other manufactured goods	56.5	39.1	25.7	17.6
Total in billions of dollars	148.78	1201.65	132.08	1004.17

Source: UNCTAD, Handbook of Statistics 2010, Table 3.1 Country trade structure by product groups.

The impact of intra-regional trade on economic policies in the region

The increasing centrality of China in East Asia is evident from the above data on the direction of exports for the regional economies, as is its emergence as a processed manufacturing economy. In aggregate terms we note that East Asia's intraregional trade has indeed increased over the years, rising from 37 percent to 42 percent over the 1980-90 period, and to 54 percent in 2008, and the trade in parts and components is the primary driver.[12] Imports from other Asian economies for processing as manufactures for the developed economies, with the active assistance of FIEs, helped China to rapidly expand its trade as well as diversify export capacity. Thus a regional trade and production network with China as its hub has emerged and would likely continue to grow further contingent upon China's continued economic progress. As a processed manufacturing economy, China necessarily imports more from its component-supplying neighbors than it manages to export to them, causing the regional economies to run trade surpluses.[13] ASEAN's trade surpluses with the "major advanced economies" have to a degree been replaced by trade surpluses with China. The East Asian economies now have trade surpluses with China, which in turn has had a trade surplus with the major advanced economies.[14] This shift in the basic trade and investment relationships of East Asian economies has been transformative of the previous trade and investment relationships for these economies. These growing production and trade linkages in the region are arguably one important reason for aligning economic policies and for seeking regional trade accords, a topic that is taken up in one of the following sections.

Though there is little doubt that China's trade links in the region are growing, it is also a fact that China looms much larger in the trade of its neighbors than vice versa, with the possible exception of Japan. The regional economies are increasingly China-centric in production and trade relationships, implying a deeper and stronger linkage in terms of policies with the Chinese economy given the export orientation of these economies, but this relationship is at a first glance somewhat asymmetrical. The relationship appears to be asymmetrical because China accounts for large shares in the East Asian economies trade, whilst its own trade is more diversified and, given the size of its economy, the East Asian economies command only relatively modest shares in China's trade even as China's reliance on advanced economies declines. But this asymmetry belies the critical nature of the East Asian trade links for the Chinese economy:[15]

> It is estimated that around 50% to 60% of China's exports to the U.S. would be at risk to disappear if China could not import parts and components. On average, the real surplus that China gains from trade with the U.S. may account for only one-third of the total value printed on the balance sheet. A lion's share would eventually go to those economies (mainly the other East Asian countries) that supply China with parts and components. In other words, the whole region of East Asia is by far the prime beneficiary of the Sino-US trade surplus rather than China alone.

Policy developments in China would be transmitted to the region via the production and trade networks, and to a degree China's economic policies would be expected to influence the outcome for the regional economies, and vice versa. In formulating policies the regional economies would necessarily take each others economic policies into consideration.

IV: THE DRIVE TO FORMALIZE TRADE RELATIONS

East Asian moves on trade relations after the Asian financial crisis

Formalization of trade relations in East Asia in the post Asian crisis period has been driven by a number of developments. In the aftermath of the Asian financial crisis, it was clear that East Asia needed to address common challenges in the area of trade, besides finance, in order to sustain growth and stability,[16] and a desire in the region for an East Asian community was widely noted.[17] At the end of 1997, about the time the

ASEAN+3 process was initiated, there was not a single bilateral or other regional trade agreement in East Asia with the sole exception of AFTA, which comprises only the ASEAN membership.[18] This reflected the considerable political difficulties in formalizing region-wide trade links in a FTA, chiefly because of the history of relations between the three Northeast Asian economies, that is, China, Japan and Korea, and the public opinion that exists on account of that difficult past. But an ASEAN+3 FTA would be a challenging proposition technically as well. This consideration and the existence of AFTA very much worked to place ASEAN in the driving seat, and that made the task politically easier, and also technically more tractable.[19] A number of trade agreements were pursued with ASEAN as the hub. China-ASEAN, Japan-ASEAN and Korea-ASEAN agreements were negotiated and signed in the years that followed, and are in force now.

But after the Asian crisis, the three Northeast Asian economies, that is, China, Japan, and Korea, also shifted their long-standing policy of "multilateralism-only" approach to trade liberalization to initiation of FTA negotiations with a handful of economies, both within and outside Asia. This development also surely reflected the emerging reality that the East Asian economies seemed to be on a path of becoming an economic space in the organization of production and trade, the Factory Asia. As production and trade linkages deepened in the East Asia region, efforts to reach trade accords also gathered speed. Hence there were bilateral accords as well. In 1998 the first of the bilaterals in the region, that is, FTAs between Korean and Japan, and Thailand and Korea, were proposed.[20] These bilateral agreements tended to be between individual ASEAN economies and chiefly Japan and to a lesser degree with China or Korea. This approach, termed parallel bilateralism, involves a large economy negotiating separate and parallel bilateral deals with a group of countries and then progresses to negotiate a quasi-regional arrangement with that group.[21] The larger economy has superior bargaining power depending on relative sizes. Japan proceeded the farthest in parallel bilateralism and by 2010 it had concluded such agreements with seven individual ASEAN economies. Japan was arguably at an advantage in negotiating these agreements because of its bargaining power vis-à-vis individual ASEAN economies, and by 2010 China and Korea too concluded free trade agreements with individual ASEAN economies: two in China's case and one in Korea's. China also concluded economic cooperation agreements with Hong Kong, Macau and Taiwan.

Today the agreements involving various combinations of economies within the ASEAN+3, Taiwan province and Hong Kong number twenty and another thirteen are contemplated. Besides these agreements, all these economies are also party to a large number of bilateral and plurilateral trade agreements that include at least one participant outside East Asia.

Many years after the Asian financial crisis the Malaysian prime minister was to recall how the ASEAN+3 process, which it may be recalled had its origins in a search for financial cooperation, had progressed from its post Asian financial crisis origins into a collection of arrangements to further economic cooperation:[22]

> The ASEAN+3 cooperation—introduced to enhance regional economic co-operation in the wake of the 1997 economic crisis—is now well-established, with the implementation of many activities aimed at strengthening and enhancing ASEAN's economic ties with China, Japan and Korea. Co-operation is being pursued across a range of areas including trade, investment, industry, agriculture, transport, finance, environment and sustainable development. I also fully support efforts to further strengthen the ASEAN+3 relations through the deepening of economic integration of East Asia involving ASEAN, People's Republic of China, Japan and Korea on a progressive basis.

Though the Asian financial crisis may have provided the first spark, the reasons for this continued mushrooming of agreements within East Asia are various. The perspective of East Asian economies on the balance between the relative usefulness of multilateral approaches vis-à-vis regional approaches to trade continued to shift towards East Asia in the years that followed the Asian financial crisis.[23] Given the evident gains from the growing intraregional trade, caused in turn by the intraregional production networks, regional cooperation in trade seemed to offer means of facilitating existing profitable processes, and this helped to further propel the efforts directed at trade agreements. It is a self-evident proposition that without the boom in intra-regional trade, the tempo of the efforts at trade pacts in the region simply could not have been sustained. And after the inconclusive outcome at Seattle, the stalemate at the WTO with regard to the Doha Round too became a factor arguing for FTAs among the regional economies.[24] East Asia's policymakers increasingly focused their minds on developing and enhancing the potential of regional economic arrangements. East Asian policies on regional economic relations thus arguably reflected the emerging realities. And in 2010 the Taiwanese minister for information expressed a more widely held view in the region, when he explained this increasing tilt towards regional arrangements as follows:[25]

> The global economy is increasingly interdependent. In this new economic environment, lowering trade barriers and finding trading synergies is important. Ideally, the World Trade Organization (WTO) should provide a framework for global economic integration. However, the Doha round of WTO talks is currently at an impasse. As a result, trading partners in the Asia-Pacific are turning to bilateral approaches, like free trade agreements (FTAs) or regional trade agreements (RTAs) to lower trade barriers.

A region-wide FTA remains nonetheless elusive. To negotiate an ASEAN+3 FTA is a daunting task, given both the history of East Asia in the twentieth century and the practical difficulties of negotiating the potentially largest free trade area in the world. No doubt desired by business interests in the region and much as it would dovetail with the intra-regional network of trade and investment, the prospect of an ASEAN+3 FTA would put the East Asian political, diplomatic and technical capabilities to the test. Nonetheless, studies have been undertaken regarding the ASEAN+3 FTA. Recently China and Japan have put forth a proposal for an ASEAN+2 FTA, the two being China and Japan, and ASEAN while welcoming the proposal has committed itself to further studying the matter. The suggestion by China and Japan to form working groups remains to be taken up by ASEAN though, and the Joint Media Statement of ASEAN+3 Economic Ministers noted progress as follows:[26]

> The Ministers welcomed and exchanged views on the joint proposal by China and Japan, "Initiative on Speeding up the Establishment of an East Asia Free Trade Area (EAFTA) and Comprehensive Economic Partnership in East Asia (CEPEA)."
>
> To ensure the economic integration within ASEAN as well as with Dialogue Partners, the Ministers noted that ASEAN is still working on the structure and template for the ASEAN++ FTA, which would include an appropriate institutional mechanism, and is taking into account the joint proposal by China and Japan in developing recommendations by November 2011.
>
> The Ministers look forward to considering the ASEAN proposed structure and template for the ASEAN++ FTA and would also give further consideration to the joint proposal by China and Japan at that time. The Ministers instructed Senior Officials to meet in November 2011 to initially consider these proposals and advise Ministers. The Ministers reiterated the importance of ASEAN centrality in the expanded regional economic integration process.

In the medium run, bilateral trade negotiations between Japan and Korea, and between Korea and China, are on the agenda of the national leaders in these three countries. A particular challenge in any such negotiations for Japan and Korea would be the liberalization of their respective agriculture sector trade; China having liberalized its own agriculture sector in course of its WTO accession. The "plus 3" part of the process also serves as an important tool to keep Japan, China and South Korea engaged, and the by now institutional annual meeting of the three heads of government also affords an opportunity to review and continue with economic cooperation. A Japan-China FTA, or a trilateral Japan-Korea-China FTA, too would require a tremendous effort directed at mobilization of domestic popular opinion, and also political willingness from Japan, and thus remains a rather complicated and uncertain prospect for now. In practice, the "plus 3" part of ASEAN+3 is more likely to materialize through the respective bilateral FTAs of the three with ASEAN.[27]

What may be said is that a new momentum to develop regional trade relations is in evidence. We now turn to examine how the East Asians approach these tasks.

The nature of trade agreements in East Asia

The East Asian approach invariably seeks an economic cooperation and partnership agreement that has clauses on topics in addition to clauses on tariff reduction, rules of origin and other matters directly related to trade. These additional clauses may relate to broader economic cooperation and development activities that do not necessarily directly concern bilateral trade. In addition an agreement in East Asia may come to offer benefits that were not a part of the agreement. The best illustration of this is AFTA, where concessions actually applied may exceed those provided for in the text of the agreement because each member extends to another any benefit that it offers a non-ASEAN partner.[28]

> . . . AFTA was originally designed as a free trade area based on tariff reductions. Because both tariff reduction and the rules of origin were written in a simple format with a clear timeframe, the negotiating parties felt no need for a formal institutional setup to support implementation. In addition, many AFTA members have applied their "preferential" tariff reductions on an MFN basis, which indicates that the implementation exceeds commitments under the original agreement.

An examination of East Asian trade accords shows the multiplicity of considerations in these agreements, and in order to better comprehend the East Asian approach we consider two of these agreements, the China-ASEAN FTA and the China-Taiwan ECFA. We consider these agreements also because the China-ASEAN FTA and the ECFA dynamics, both the format of negotiations and the actual implementation, may help to understand the development of East Asian economic integration, and also the interaction among the three major economies in Northeast Asia. Furthermore, China's efforts with Chinese-ASEAN FTA and China-Taiwan ECFA also serve as examples of diverse considerations in its engagement in the region, and can be seen as a part of China's proactive pursuit of policies to mitigate the widespread but speculative perception of "China threat" in the region and enhance security. In particular the desire for a harmonious external environment may have been at least as important as immediate economic benefits in China's strategic thinking in its dealings with ASEAN and Taiwan.

While the growing intra-regional trade is a singularly important reason for seeking appropriate trade accords in East Asia, one basic aim of Chinese state policy would appear to be to obtain security through a prosperous neighborhood, and to achieve this by enmeshing the region in mutually beneficial economic agreements as quickly as possible. This desire for security with prosperity in its neighborhood may independently guide and reinforce Chinese policy on trade agreements in its neighborhood, that is, the East Asia region. Deng Xiaoping enunciated a well-established domestic consensus when he asserted that a peaceful and harmonious external environment is an important condition for China's economic development and prosperity. Hu Jintao has reaffirmed this consensus when proclaiming that Beijing seeks a harmonious external environment for its long-term peaceful development.[29] More specifically, Chinese leaders use the guidelines of "do good to our neighbors, treat our neighbors as partners" (*yulin weishan, yilin weiban*) and "maintain friendly relations with our neighbors, make them feel secure, and help to make them rich" (*mulin, anlin, fulin*).[30] The fact that a troublesome and uneasy neighborhood can only be a distraction from a focus on economic development is thus recognized: in fact, Chinese government officials admitted that geopolitical considerations for a peaceful neighborhood trump any short-term economic benefit for China, when China is negotiating economic issues with its neighboring countries.[31] A well thought out FTA strategy may therefore also help to assure China's East Asian neighbors of the cooperative aspects of China's "peaceful development," signaling to regional partners the non-predatory and beneficial nature of the country's rapid economic growth and the joint economic gains that FTAs can potentially deliver.[32] It is against such a strategic back drop that we need to assess the two trade agreements, respectively with ASEAN and Taiwan.

The China ASEAN FTA

Consider first the China-ASEAN FTA. China and ASEAN initiated FTA negotiations about the time China joined the WTO in 2001, some three to four years after the Asian financial crisis and about the time that increasing intra-regional trade and investment flows were becoming noticeable. China first proposed a regional trade agreement with ASEAN in November 2001 and signed the agreement in 2002. A point of first importance is that in practical terms the China-ASEAN FTA also marks the beginning of China's formalization of its interest in securing intra-regional trade and investment linkages. Under China-ASEAN FTA, which covers trade in goods, services and investment, a free trade zone will be established among the developed ASEAN countries and China by year 2010, and extended to less developed ASEAN nations by year 2015.[33] At inception, the ASEAN countries visualized that the FTA with China will re-build economic stability and renew growth that was so badly shaken by the Asian financial crisis of 1997.[34] In due course the ASEAN governments also reportedly looked to the China-ASEAN FTA to help offset weak demand in advanced economies after the global financial crisis, thus signifying the importance of the agreement for the ASEAN economies.[35]

After the conclusion of the China-ASEAN FTA, the Mainland Chinese press heralded this agreement in glowing words, and the China Council of Promotion of International Trade (CCPIT) welcomed the agreement:

> The China-ASEAN FTA will form a huge market, with 1.85 billion consumers and a combined gross domestic product of almost US$2.5 trillion. The value of imports and exports of this zone will hopefully exceed that of the NAFTA (North America Free Trade Agreement) by 2010 and its GDP will likely be higher than that in the European Union market. These three, China-ASEAN free trade zones, NAFTA and the EU, will become the three pillars of the world economy.[36]

Such expectations from CAFTA it would seem may well be realized. By 2011, China had become ASEAN's largest trading partner whilst ASEAN was China's third largest trading partner. The trade value between the two sides has grown from $8 billion in 1991 to $292.8 billion in 2010, up 37 times. In the first half of 2011, the trade value between China and ASEAN reached $171.1 billion, up 25 percent year-on-year. In the investment area, the bilateral investment accumulated to $80 billion from twenty years ago until June 2011. And the foreign direct investment of China to ASEAN accumulated to around $13 billion, marking ASEAN as an important destination for Chinese enterprises while enacting their "going out" plans.[37] As a part of the "going out" policy, China was also supporting its cooperation with ASEAN in the field of infrastructure construction. In 2009, China announced $15 billion of credit for ASEAN and decided to establish a $10-billion China-ASEAN Investment Cooperation Fund, which is being used by ASEAN for building infrastructure such as bridges, roads, power plants and a port.[38] There is also specific anecdotal evidence of various businesses gaining from CAFTA.[39]

Table 3.8. Growth in China-ASEAN trade, 1997-2010, shares in percentages.

	China's share in ASEAN trade			ASEAN's share in China's trade		
	Exports	Imports	Total trade	Exports	Imports	Total trade
1997	2.99	3.67	3.34	6.94	8.69	7.71
2001	4.32	5.87	5.05	6.96	9.54	8.19
2005	8.05	10.50	9.21	7.27	11.36	9.17
2010	12.68	14.36	13.49	8.75	11.07	9.84

Source: International Monetary Fund, Direction of Trade Statistics.

China-ASEAN trade has continued to grow since 2007 in the face of the global financial crisis, indicating the robustness of the underlying production and trade linkages in the face of a difficult global economic environment. Once the China-ASEAN FTA was operational, further afield India too felt its impact on its ASEAN trade and sought FTAs of its own with the East Asian economies.[40]

The China Taiwan ECFA.

Taiwan presents a case where the Chinese principle of seeking security through prosperity in its neighborhood, that guides its policy on economic relations with its neighbors, would seem to apply *a fortiori*, and the principle may indeed be seen at work in the terms of China's FTA with Taiwan, the Economic Cooperation and Framework Agreement (ECFA). It is also a fact though that the neighboring economy of Taiwan, which has extensive production and trade linkages with China, was itself drawn into an FTA with China as it feared being left out of the East Asian trade and production loop.[41] With China-ASEAN FTA (sometimes referred to ASEAN+1 FTA) fully operational, Taiwan's President Ma, in his annual address in January 2010, explained this consideration, that is, effectively to consolidate the existing processed manufacturing linkages, as a reason for seeking a FTA arrangement with China:[42]

> Starting this year, as the free trade zone involving the Association of Southeast Asian Nations (ASEAN) and Mainland China has come into effect, affected goods and services from the ten ASEAN member states can enter Mainland China tariff-free. However, Taiwan's competing exports to the mainland are still subject to high import taxes, thus placing us at a disadvantage. We cannot simply sit by and watch this happen. . . .
>
> The trend toward economic integration in Asia is clearly evident, and proceeding at a rapid pace. . . . Facing such a situation, Taiwan must not be marginalized, but make the most of opportunities presented by regional cooperation to expand our market presence. With the ECFA as our starting point, we will fight for a fair international environment to ensure that our enterprises are able to compete on equitable terms. In addition, we will actively pursue FTAs with our other major trading partners. Only through such linkages can we accelerate our involvement in East Asian regional economic integration and remain competitive.

Taiwan also saw an FTA with China as opening "the door for Taiwan to begin FTA talks with ASEAN."[43] "While ASEAN is only one of the competing models for Asia-Pacific regional integration, it signals a trend of bilateral approaches that Taiwan cannot ignore. We must not allow ourselves to become economically marginalized," said Johnny C. Chiang, information office minister for Taiwan.[44] *The Economist* reported that the China-Taiwan FTA would allow domestic Taiwanese companies to increase their market share on the Mainland, the destination for 40 percent of Taiwan's exports even before the pact.[45] Mainland China is Taiwan's biggest trading partner now.[46] *The Economist* also pointed out that Mr. Ma hoped that such a pact would encourage other nations to sign FTAs with Taiwan, noting the fear that the island, already isolated diplomatically, might otherwise become marginalized commercially when the effects of an FTA between China and the ASEAN begin to be felt.[47]

The China-Taiwan FTA, known as ECFA, that is, the Economic Cooperation Framework Agreement, offers a particularly good example of multiplicity of considerations, including cooperation for mutual economic gain, notwithstanding the political differences in the region. In the first instance both parties showed flexibility and the agreement was negotiated and concluded between two "private" organizations, rather than governments, but it is enforced with the assistance of the governments. Furthermore, this agreement represents the first phase in trade liberalization rather than a comprehensive free trade agreement, and has China going the extra mile and doing most of the economic opening initially: China will cut import tariffs across 539 products and services worth $13.84bn in trade, whilst Taiwan will reciprocate with cuts on only $3bn worth of goods. In further concessions to Taiwan, China also agreed not to ask for the opening of agriculture sectors or for Chinese laborers to be allowed to work in Taiwan. By way of contrast, as many as 260,000 jobs are likely to be created in Taiwan as a result of this agreement.[48] The Taiwan business interests welcomed the accord.[49] According to Chinese trade officials further negotiations are likely.[50]

The East Asian approach to trade cooperation in a comparative perspective

China is currently the largest trading nation in East Asia followed by Japan. As we have seen, the Chinese approach to trade pacts generally combines economic objectives with its other strategic policy objectives, and the agreements tend to be in the nature of economic cooperation frameworks.[51] Some of this economic cooperation, such as investments in transportation infrastructure, directly facilitates and furthers the networked production and trade in the region. The agreements differ as between partner countries; invariably with scope for further future development and negotiations. It does also invariably mean that China concedes more in terms of trade and economic benefits than it gets from the other party, as noted earlier. Examples of such accords prominently include the agreements with ASEAN and Taiwan respectively. In both cases the agreements were concluded with relative speed and ease because China conceded much more than it received. Japan too has a similar approach to trade agreements in the region. Development objectives and general economic cooperation are frequently included, and the difficulties faced by partner developing economies also tend to be accommodated.

Thus although the China-ASEAN FTA and the China-Taiwan FTA negotiations and agreements may also be seen justifiably as a part of China's policy that has been variously referred to as a strategy of "smile diplomacy,"[52] and as "China's charm,"[53] with China conceding much more than it received (and that no doubt facilitated the early trouble-free realization of the trade agreement), Japan too shares the Chinese approach to FTAs that cover development cooperation and goals, and its approach is also accommodating of the constraints faced by partner developing economies in the region. The principal difference between the respective Chinese and Japanese policies is that given the interests of its multinational corporations, Japan brings more in way of "commercial regulatory demands" to the negotiating table than does China.[54] Though trade and investment seem to be the most important practical aspect of the relationships between East Asia and China or Japan for now, the policies of China and Japan embrace comprehensive development assistance and also include cultural exchanges, as appropriate. More generally, the East Asian approach to FTAs has been seen as combining economic with other strategic foreign policy objectives, differing between partner countries and often involving follow up negotiations.[55] This East Asian approach to trade pacts marks a departure from the template that forms the basis for trade agreements with the United States in the region, and hence arguably constitutes a difference in approach that helps to better meets the region's preferences.

This East Asian approach contrasts with that of United States. The trade agreements sponsored by the United States tend to focus on trade and are devoid of any development considerations that the partner countries may have. Christopher Dent has made a broad comparison of the East Asian approach to trade relations with that of United States in Asia-Pacific. In context of the American approach, Dent informs us that "a club of ardent free trader nations exists within the Asia-Pacific," and that "what binds these nations is a shared market-liberal approach to trade policy, a competent technocracy willing to take on policy innovation, and *a general deference to US hegemony in the Asia-Pacific's international affairs.*" The "club" sought FTAs "arguably *driven more by geopolitical and economic ideological motives* than by the capture of trade creation gains through their signed agreements," though ostensibly market access has importance. We also learn that excepting United States, "the other club members are relatively small trading powers and relatively insignificant trade partners to each other." Amongst the East Asian economies, there are two members of this club: Singapore, Dent notes, is amongst the "core club members," and South Korea is amongst the "secondary members."[56]

Dent notes that the United States in particular, in its trade agreements, is concerned with market access, and does not enter into advancing economic development in partner economies. The emphasis on market access leads to "behind the border" reforms in the partner economies, and in this respect the agreements mirror regulatory provisions of United States domestic legislation. In this manner the United States uses the agreements "to export its own national commercial regulatory norms and practices overseas," and this "is especially evident in its agreements with other ardent free trader nations."[57] But the motivation for these free trade agreements between United States and others and among the "ardent free trader nations" remain somewhat mixed even if development cooperation is not the diluting factor. Dent goes on to draw a comparison between the East Asian approach and that of the United States.[58]

> While the US model has, then, been more influential in determining the technical policy content, and especially the commercial regulatory aspects, of many FTAs around the region, the Japanese and Chinese models have been arguably just as influential in terms of conceptual approach on FTA formation. This particularly applied to East Asian states, the majority of which have shown a preference for "economic partnership" agreements rather than US-oriented "market access" deals owing to their generally shared developmentalist tradition and their various development capacity needs. Thus, we can expect any emerging East Asia-centered regional agreement to converge on a hybrid Japan–China model rather than the US model. In the meantime, the United States will most likely persist in its endeavors to convince all Asia-Pacific states to converge around its own model of FTA practice.

An important difference that Dent perhaps does not highlight is that the Asian FTAs were initially contemplated against the backdrop of the Asian crisis and gathered momentum as intraregional trade boomed. America's effort in Asia-Pacific is more with ideological friends, even though in some of these cases meaningful trade does not exist.

The current ongoing TPP deliberations offer a fair example of American practice in seeking trade accords. In particular United States efforts "to convince all Asia-Pacific states to converge around its own model of FTA practice" provide the central element in the Trans-Pacific Partnership (TPP). This initiative, which proposes to combine Asia and the Pacific into one free trade area that would cover trade and investment, much like the APEC in its intended geographical scope, has been underway for some years but has yet to reach any recognizable shape. An important aspect is that the approach differs from the East Asian one. But the TPP has had a chequered history. Though the original initiative was floated by United States, it has been in and out of the negotiations—America's tacit support was there even when it absented itself from the negotiations. For the present four members comprise the TPP: Brunei and Singapore from East Asia, and Chile and New Zealand from the "Pacific": this present TPP does not make for a lot of trade between the four partners. From East Asia Malaysia and Vietnam joined negotiations in

October 2010 and December 2010 respectively, whilst from the Pacific, Australia and Peru did so respectively in March 2010 and June 2010. Japan, after announcing its intent to participate in the negotiations, deferred the matter on account of opposition from its business lobby.[59] There is quite a journey ahead, and it is not without hiccups. The lack of actual substantive trade between some of the partners and potential candidates does not help and could reduce the quest to a paper chase for some.[60]

These agreements primarily seek market access and policy reforms in partner countries. The policy reforms sought tend to focus on behind the border measures in partner countries and aim for legislation that mirrors the norms and regulatory provisions of United States domestic laws. Some of the partner countries may not have much in way of intra-trade, but a strong geopolitical and ideological undercurrent regarding United States "leadership" and a "market-liberal" approach exists.[61] Thus while Japan has announced the intent of joining TPP deliberations, it retains a deep interest in the region:

> While announcing last month its plan to join multilateral talks on the Trans-Pacific Partnership Agreement, a U.S.-led free-trade initiative, this month Japan concluded a joint study with China and South Korea on the possibility of signing a tripartite free-trade accord.[62]

Even though trade agreements that involve economies outside the ASEAN+3 are not the subject of this book, it seemed appropriate to mention this one particular and separate initiative to highlight the difference in approach between the intra-East Asia trade initiatives and others. The majority of East Asian economies display a predilection for economic partnership frameworks rather than liberal market access deals.[63] This preference is consistent with the general approach to economic policy in East Asia that sees a useful role for the state in economic development.

VI: CONCLUSIONS

The Asian financial crisis had been a difficult experience from which the region learned. In East Asian perception the multilateral economic institutions had failed the region in its hour of need. The regional institution of APEC too had failed to live up to expectations, echoing in effect the views of the international financial institutions. The United States, hitherto a trusted friend, had not helped either. It was the effort within the region that had helped pull the afflicted economies out of the quagmire of 1997-98. Looking to the future, East Asia somewhat in unison sought self-reliance in the form of regional cooperation in finance and trade.

In the period following the Asian crisis, China in particular continued to pursue a flexible and pragmatic approach of adapting its economic policies to the emerging opportunities, with its economy exhibiting an exceptional flexibility to organize labor resources and infrastructure for the new and diverse tasks. This approach was reflected in the measures adopted by China to attract foreign direct investment, in the further development of special zones on the country's eastern seaboard and in the measures taken to facilitate trade, including its admission to the WTO in 2001. It was a mark of this flexibility that there was perhaps no conceptual straitjacket that disciplined Chinese policies in the manner of the *flying geese* approach that had earlier guided Japanese policies in the region.

It is a unique aspect of the intra-regional economic linkages that they continue to develop in the absence of any grand vision or a master plan, and without the need for "leadership." Indeed, the issue of "leadership" in the traditional sense of a leader country (or countries) providing the blue print for the region's institutions and its future looks increasingly to be a vacuous one in the East Asian context. The regional economic cooperation and integration that is taking place seems to be in response to real issues and opportunities, with business as the prime mover. Processed manufacturing relationships created intra-regional trade and eventually led to trade pacts. What seem to matter more than exhortations about cooperation and leadership, or about ideologies and models, are the policies that maximize the opportunities and thus help shape developments.

NOTES

1. See Justin Yifu Lin, From Flying Geese to Leading Dragons, New Opportunities and Strategies for Structural Transformation in Developing Countries, World Bank Policy Research Working Paper 5702, Washington DC, June 2011.
2. See for example discussion in Yukon Huang, Eye China's coasts, not its currency, Financial Times, August 10, 2010.
3. Li Lanqing for example mentions the importance of drawing on the experience of Chuang Shih-ping, a Hong Kong businessman, in designing the rules for the special economic zones. See Li Lanqing, Breaking through (Oxford: Oxford University Press, 2009), pp. 147-148.
4. There is different version which links China's economic development of the Plaza Accord:

> Asian integration may have been mainly the fortuitous effect of the Plaza Agreement signed in 1985 to help the United States (US) reduce its current account deficit and to facilitate its recovery from a recession. It resulted in the doubling of the Japanese yen's (JPY) value vis-à-vis the US dollar, from JPY250 in 1985 to JPY125 in two years; the precipitous decline of the US dollar was only halted with the 1987 Louvre Accord.
> Faced with increasing costs at home and armed with an appreciated currency, Japanese firms found it attractive to expand their business operations overseas. According to Mr. Sakakibara, deflation in Japan at the turn of the century could have been an offshoot of Japanese outsourcing. Simply put, Japanese firms, as well as other East Asian corporations exported parts and components, assembled them in the region, mainly in the People's Republic of China (PRC), and re-exported the goods back to their respective home

> countries. An international division of labor which is one of the characteristics of production networks in this region has emerged. In fact, intra-regional trade in parts and components is much higher in the Asian region than in the EU and the North American Free Trade Area. East Asia has become the world's factory.

See, Distinguished Speaker Seminar: Eisuke Sakakibara - Market-driven Integration in East Asia, Tokyo, June 24, 2009, at http://www.adbi.org/event/3032.sakakibara.distinguished.speaker.market.integration.east.asia/

5. For example a recent report on the aircraft industry in China noted:

> In trying to catch up with Boeing in China, Airbus has followed a strategy of localizing its operations to a certain extent, assembling A320 aircraft in the northeastern city of Tianjin. Boeing has chosen not to make planes in China, though it notes that it has been the biggest purchaser of made-in-China aviation parts.

See Simon Rabinovitch, China's Comac confronts aircraft duopoly, Financial Times, September 23, 2011.

6. See Daisuke Hiratsuka, Production Networks in Asia: A Case Study from the Hard Disk Drive Industry, ADBI Working Paper 301, Tokyo, July 2011.

7. See Daisuke Hiratsuka, Production Networks in Asia: A Case Study from the Hard Disk Drive Industry, ADBI Working Paper 301, Tokyo, July 2011.

8. See Won Bae Kim, The rise of China and the repositioning of NAEs, Seoul Journal of Economics, vol. 24, no. 2, 2011.

9. See Min-Hua Chiang and Bernard Gerbier, Taiwan and the Transformation of Asia-USA Economic Relationship: From the Triangular Trading Bloc to the Four-Corner Structure, La Chronique des Amériques, Novembre 2008 N°19.

10. See for example discussion on different aspects in H. Lim and F. Kimura, The Internationalization of Small and Medium Enterprises in Regional and Global Value Chains, ADBI Working Paper 231, Tokyo, 2010; Willem Thorbecke, Investigating the Effect of Exchange Rate Changes on the People's Republic of China's Processed Exports, ADBI Working Paper Series No. 202, March 2010; and Yuqing Xing, Processing Trade, Exchange Rates and China's bilateral Trade Balances, mimeo, National Graduate Institute for Policy Studies, Tokyo, January 2011.

11. See Won Bae Kim, The rise of China and the repositioning of NAEs, Seoul Journal of Economics, vol. 24, no. 2, 2011.

12. See Mari Elka Pangestu, The Challenges for Trade Policy in a Dynamic World and Regional Setting: An Indonesian Perspective, ADB Institute, Tokyo, December 14, 2010.

13. See Yuqing Xing, Processing Trade, Exchange Rates and China's bilateral Trade Balances, mimeo, National Graduate Institute for Policy Studies, Tokyo, January 2011.

14. For example Lurong Chen writes:

> On average, the real surplus that China gains from trade with the U.S. may account for only one-third of the total value printed on the balance sheet. A lion's share would eventually go to those economies (mainly the other East Asian countries) that supply China with parts and components. In other words, the whole region of East Asia is by far the prime beneficiary of the Sino-US trade surplus rather than China alone.

See Lurong Chen, Production sharing and East Asian regional trade liberalization, mimeo, p. 9. Also see Yuqing Xing, Processing Trade, Exchange Rates and China's bilateral Trade Balances, mimeo, National Graduate Institute for Policy Studies, Tokyo, January 2011.

15. See Lurong Chen, Production sharing and East Asian regional trade liberalization, mimeo, p. 9.

16. See for example Masahiro Kawai and Ganeshan Wignaraja, eds., East Asia's free trade agreements, How is business responding (Cheltenham, Edward Elgar, 2011), p. 9. Also see discussion in Chapter 2 above.

17. For example John Ravenhill makes the point about the widely shared desire in the region for an East Asian community after the Asian financial crisis. See John Ravenhill, Extending the TPP: The political economy of multilateralization in Asia, mimeo, paper presented at the Asia-Pacific trade economists' conference, Bangkok, November 2009, pp. 20-21.

18. AFTA came into force on 1 January 1993. See Asia Regional Integration database at: http://www.aric.adb.org/fta.php?id=1&ssid=3&title=ASEAN%20Free%20Trade%20Area

19. See IMF, Tubagus Feridhanusetyawan, Preferential Trade Agreements in the Asia-Pacific Region, IMF Working Paper, WP/05/149, July 2005, p. 32.

20. See Christopher Dent, Free trade agreements in the Asia-Pacific a decade on: evaluating the past, looking to the future, International Relations of the Asia-Pacific vol. 10 no. 2, pp.

21. See Christopher Dent, Free trade agreements in the Asia-Pacific a decade on: evaluating the past, looking to the future, International Relations of the Asia-Pacific vol. 10 no. 2, p. 234.

22. Prime Minister Najib Razak of Malaysia speaking at the Malaysia-China Economic, Trade & Investment Cooperation Forum on 28 April 2011. See: http://www.1malaysia.com.my/zh/speeches/malaysia-china-economic-and-trade-cooperation-forum/. Also see chapter 2 above.

23. The Asian financial crisis also affected the region's approach to multilateral financial institutions, and international financial relations. This aspect is explored further in chapters 2 and 4.

24. See Christopher Dent, Free trade agreements in the Asia-Pacific a decade on: evaluating the past, looking to the future, International Relations of the Asia-Pacific vol. 10 no. 2, p. 230; and IMF, Tubagus Feridhanusetyawan, Preferential Trade Agreements in the Asia-Pacific Region, IMF Working Paper, WP/05/149, July 2005, p. 32. Also see ASEAN and Korea a perfect fit, in Bangkok Post, June 27, 2009, at: http://www.bangkokpost.com/tech/mobile/19233/

25. Johnny C. Chiang, information office minister for Taiwan, remarks from a talk at Carnegie Council in New York, July 13 2010, at: http://www.worldpress.org/Asia/3596.cfm

26. See paragraphs 6-8 of the Joint Media Statement of the 14th AEM+3 Consultations, Manado, Indonesia, August 12, 2011

27. At times also referred to as 10+3 or East Asia Free Trade Agreement (EAFTA). The ten and three in 10+3 are the ASEAN 10 plus China, Japan and Korea.

28. See IMF, Tubagus Feridhanusetyawan, Preferential Trade Agreements in the Asia-Pacific Region, IMF Working Paper, WP/05/149, July 2005, p. 28.

29. In response to the widespread discussion of a hypothetical "China threat" and the speculation about China's true intentions, recently China modified its "peaceful rise" proposition to "peaceful development." Thus "China aims to grow and advance without upsetting existing orders. We are trying to rise in a way that benefits our neighbors." See discussion in Yoichi Funabashi, " China's peaceful Ascendancy," *Yale Global*, December 19, 2003. Logically, China's peaceful development posture is only a natural outcome of its highly globalized national economy. China now has a clear stake in preserving the liberal, rule-based global economic system that the United States worked to establish over the past half century.

30. See Robert Sutter and Chin-hao Huang, "China-Southeast Asia Relations: Military Diplomacy and China's Soft Power," in Comparative Connections: A Quarterly E-Journal on East Asian Bilateral Relations, April 2005.

31. Developing regional trade ties is therefore not simply an economic goal, and explains the bemusement of some scholars in their critique of East Asian trade accords as being insufficiently demanding in their trade opening measures.

32. See Katada, Saori N., and Mireya Solís, "Cross-Regional Trade Agreement in East Asia:Findings and Implications," a chapter in Saori N. Katada and Mireya Solís, eds., Cross Regional Trade Agreements: Understanding Permeated Regionalism in East Asia (Berlin, Springer, 2008), pp. 147-159.

33. In Southeast Asia, Indonesia, Malaysia, the Philippines, Singapore and Thailand started a formal framework for economic cooperation in 1967. These five countries were later joined by Brunei, Cambodia, Laos, Myanmar and Vietnam. The ten members share various levels of economic development, uneven natural resource distribution, different size of population and divergent economic development strategies. Thus there existed substantial disagreements among the ten members about if and how trade liberalization should be carried out.

34. "WTO rifts spurs ASEAN to tackle free trade," *South China Morning Post*, October 7, 2003.

35. See Economist Intelligence Unit, Asia's economy: ASEAN's China gamble, EIU Viewswire, August 10, 2010. For the moment though the trade covered by this agreement is reportedly not substantive: John Ravenhill, whilst pointing out the defective nature of the surveys on which he bases his estimates, notes that the "early harvest" provisions cover just one million dollar worth of trade, only 11, 20 and 0.3 percent of 2007 exports in respect of Thailand, Indonesia and China were covered by this agreement. See John Ravenhill, Extending the TPP: The political economy of multilateralization in Asia, mimeo, November 2009, p. 14.

36. Remarks by Wang Jinzhen, spokesman of China Council of Promotion of International Trade (CCPIT), in Xiamen, quoted in Robert Lawrence, "China in the multilateral trading system," KSG working paper, 2006. For the moment China-ASEAN FTA remains the third largest trading bloc in the world. Also see discussion in EIU Viewswire, Asia's economy: ASEAN's China gamble, August 10, 2010.

37. "Going out" policy is discussed in Chapter 4.

38. See Xinhua, August 16, 2011, Commerce minister urges deeper China-ASEAN co-op, at: http://www.gmseb.com/NewsView.aspx?nid=81

39. See China ASEAN FTA in creation of win-win situation, People's Daily, 29 October 2010, at: http://english.peopledaily.com.cn/90001/90778/90861/7181778.html, Xinhua, Yuan Trade Settlement Benefits China-ASEAN FTA, 23 October 2010, at: http://english.cri.cn/6826/2010/10/23/1821s600798.htm, and Xinhua, ASEAN companies eye China for future growth, October 21, 2010, at: http://english.cri.cn/6826/2010/10/21/2681s600611.htm

40. See China-Asean FTA may hit trade balance: Scindia, in Economic Times, April 23, 2010, at:http://articles.economictimes.indiatimes.com/2010-04-23/news/27580373_1_india-asean-fta-asean-members-asean-bloc

41. The fear is a more general one. Like many other WTO members, China and other countries in the region are concerned about the discriminatory effects of being left out of FTA arrangements being forged in the region. For example, the contemplated US-Korea FTA, or the recent US-Taiwan FTA agreement will inevitably affect the trade of other regional economies with South Korea and Taiwan. Such RTAs and FTAs in the region as China and other regional governments are able to conclude should help offset this risk.

42. See President Ma's new year's message, Taiwan News, January 1, 2010, http://www.etaiwannews.com/etn/news_content.php?id=1145660&lang=eng_news

43. Former vice president Lien of Taiwan, cited in "Taiwan aims for Asean FTA," in Bangkok Post of November 10, 2009 at http://www.bangkokpost.com/business/economics/27156/taiwan-aims-for-asean-fta

44. Johnny C. Chiang, information office minister for Taiwan, remarks from a talk at Carnegie Council in New York, July 13, 2010, at: http://www.worldpress.org/Asia/3596.cfm

45. Taiwan-China trade talks, Chinas in a bull session, see The Economist April 19, 2010, at: http://www.economist.com/node/15903164

46. Johnny C. Chiang, information office Minister for Taiwan, remarks from a talk at Carnegie Council in New York, July 13, 2010, at: http://www.worldpress.org/Asia/3596.cfm

47. Taiwan-China trade talks, Chinas in a bull session, see The Economist April 19, 2010, at: http://www.economist.com/node/15903164

48. See Robin Kwong, China and Taiwan sign landmark deal, Financial Times, June 29, 2010. Whilst industrial and commercial interests were pleased with the agreement and saw much opportunity for profit, others perceived mixed motives. In one case the agreement was seen as a part of China's long standing efforts to "draw Taiwan closer for eventual unification," and noting that "It's easy to oppose moving closer to China now, but once people enjoy the economic benefits it would be very hard to reverse [the deal]."

49. Robin Kwong reports that industrial and commercial interests were pleased with the agreement and saw much opportunity for profit. See Robin Kwong, China and Taiwan sign landmark deal, Financial Times, June 29, 2010.

50. A Chinese trade official stated this in an interview with one of the authors in March 2012.

51. See discussion in Agata Antkiewicz and John Whalley, China's new regional trade agreements, NBER Working Paper 10992, December 2004.

52. Attributed to Shi Yinghong at Renmin University, China. See Myrna S. Austria, "East Asian Regional Cooperation: Approaches and Process," Philippine Institute for Development Studies Discussion paper Series No. 2003-02, 2003.

53. Joshua Kurlantzick, China's Charm: Implications of Chinese Soft Power, Carnegie Endowment Policy Brief, no. 47, June 2006.

54. See Christopher Dent, Free trade agreements in the Asia-Pacific a decade on: evaluating the past, looking to the future, International Relations of the Asia-Pacific, vol. 10 no. 2, p. 231.

55. See discussion in Agata Antkiewicz and John Whalley, China's new regional trade agreements, NBER Working Paper 10992, December 2004.

56. See Christopher Dent, Free trade agreements in the Asia-Pacific a decade on: evaluating the past, looking to the future, International Relations of the Asia-Pacific, vol. 10 no. 2, pp. 214-218. Italics added for emphasis.

57. See Christopher Dent, Free trade agreements in the Asia-Pacific a decade on: evaluating the past, looking to the future, International Relations of the Asia-Pacific, vol. 10 no. 2, p. 230.

58. See Christopher Dent, Free trade agreements in the Asia-Pacific a decade on: evaluating the past, looking to the future, International Relations of the Asia-Pacific, vol. 10 no. 2, pp. 230-231.

59. See Japan's warming to TPP poses political and diplomatic conundrums, November 14, 2010, xinhuanet, at: http://news.xinhuanet.com/english2010/indepth/2010-11/14/c_13605713.htm

60. The point has been made that such FTAs are "a distortion of priorities" for the United States. Alan Beattie discusses three separate bilateral FTAs, Colombia, Korea, and Panama, being pushed by the United States administration for approval of the Congress to argue that the gains to the American economy are miniscule (those from the largest of the three FTAs, the one for Korea, would amount to a one-off gain of 0.1 percent of America's GDP spread over several years), while the effort required distracts from more urgent issues. See Alan Beattie, Round two in currency war: A phoney US victory, Financial Times, October 7, 2011.

61. See Christopher Dent, Free trade agreements in the Asia-Pacific a decade on: evaluating the past, looking to the future, International Relations of the Asia-Pacific, vol. 10 no. 2.

62. See Kyodo, Japan pushing bilateral, regional trade talks, Japan Times, December 27, 2011.

63. See Christopher Dent, Free trade agreements in the Asia-Pacific a decade on: evaluating the past, looking to the future, International Relations of the Asia-Pacific, vol. 10 no. 2.

FOUR

The global financial crisis of 2008 and China's response

I: INTRODUCTION

The Asian financial crisis created a certain awareness in East Asia about the need for regional solutions to its problems. It led to some economic and financial cooperation that progressed in the decade that followed. Over this period East Asia successfully developed as an increasingly integrated economic space, with China-centric production and trade networks crisscrossing the region. At the same time China, along with other East Asian economies, accumulated large foreign exchange reserves, with China's being exceptionally so. This accumulation of reserves, though a result of trade surpluses, was in good part a reflection of the experience with the speculators in course of the Asian financial crisis. China was seen with expectation as a rising power. Much of the above has been covered in the two preceding chapters.

By the time the global financial crisis occurred in 2008 both East Asia and China were important elements of a globalized world economy. But for China the global financial crisis came at a time of introspection on policies. A large economy, growing at double-digit rates like China, cannot long stay dependent for its growth on the export of low-wage low-technology manufactures. A large economy that is amongst the leading traders also cannot keep its currency perpetually in a non-convertible state. And a large economy that invests the bulk of its national income cannot continue to do so year after year. Recognizing these imperatives, the 17th Party Congress in 2007 laid out some medium-term policies that could enable China to adapt to the fast changing economic situation in the region as well as in the world at large.[1] With the advent of the global financial crisis in 2008, American economic conditions and prospects for the world economy deteriorated sharply. The combination of trade surpluses, that had enabled the build up of the large quantum of reserves in East Asia, and United States external current account deficit were often described as "global imbalances" in the transatlantic narrative. And as the United States looked for solutions to work itself out of this predicament, it conceived of rectifying the "global imbalances" as a part of the answer, and sought "rebalancing of the world economy."

East Asia and China in particular survived the global financial crisis of 2008 in better shape than the transatlantic economies, causing China and the region to gain greater significance in the world economy, and imparting confidence in the policies that these economies had pursued since the Asian financial crisis. The transatlantic economies had difficulty in navigating their way out of the financial imbroglio and the mass unemployment that the global financial crisis left in its wake. The United States perception of its problems and that of the problems of the world economy differed sharply from that of the East Asians, particularly China. The efforts to deal with the crisis brought out the reality of a disconnect between the emerging global economic and financial problems and the institutions that had been set up to cope, such as the G-7/8 forum and the multilateral institutions of IMF and the World Bank. The G-20, a forum in which the East Asian economies as well as other developing economies have representation, was hauled out in addition. Programs to stimulate the sagging economies, and thereby also the world economy, were jointly undertaken as a result of the G-20 deliberations but these efforts were only partially helpful. As the 2008 crisis persisted with the epicenter shifting to the Eurozone, the ability of the existing mechanisms to cope became all the more evident and the international currency system looked adrift. In this milieu China was frequently called upon to help. China's assistance seemed critical to efforts to salvage the world economy, the euro and the individual Eurozone economies, and hence also the international currency system. China though showed circumspection and restraint in its new calling, perhaps wary that it end up as a part of the problem.

Thus China in the post global financial crisis phase looked central to the smooth functioning of the world economy. China also appeared to be more firmly in authority in the East Asian economic space. The region too had become a relatively stable economic zone more capable of taking care of itself, the economies benefiting as China's continued growth fed through the regional production and trade networks. The renminbi acquired a new authority. Though it is early to judge, the global financial crisis perhaps changed the world for China in a fundamental sense, very likely more so than the Asian financial crisis had done.

This chapter attempts to track aspects of China's policy trajectory from the beginning of the global financial crisis, and any policy shifts that would most certainly have implications for the region. The rest of the chapter is organized as follows. The next section sets out the relative performance of East Asia during the global financial crisis; and the demands made on China, *rebalancing of the world economy* being the operative term, are taken up. The Chinese policy response to these demands in terms of policies on consumption and internationalization of the renminbi is the subject of sections three and four. A fifth and final section concludes the chapter, and draws together the discussion.

II: EAST ASIA AND THE GLOBAL FINANCIAL CRISIS

The Asian financial crisis of 1997 and the global financial one of 2008 impacted very differently in East Asia. Unlike the Asian financial crisis, the global financial crisis had a relatively limited economic impact on the East Asian economies, but the magnitude of the shock and the damage it caused to the banking and finance industry in the transatlantic economies was unprecedented in postwar history.[2] Only sustained socialization of banking losses through the large-scale injection of public funds saved the financial sector, and consequently the transatlantic economies, from what seemed to be an impending economic and financial collapse. The unemployment that followed continues to plague these economies, creating a situation of a crisis characterized in its tenacity by serious social and economic pressures. The oft-reported return to growth has failed to seriously dent the high unemployment levels. The 2008 crisis, besides resulting in more stringent financial conditions, also caused the first dip in world trade since 2001, and world exports as well as imports fell significantly in 2009.

East Asia in 2008 was a robust economic region, having grown year on year since 1998, with deep intraregional linkages of production and trade in place, and with a gradually decreasing reliance on the transatlantic American and European economies as final markets. But it did suffer from the slump in world trade that followed the global financial crisis. An examination of micro-data shows that the fall in the value of trade was chiefly a quantity driven phenomenon in the case of differentiated goods. On the other hand, in the case of non-differentiated goods the fall in value was explained chiefly by a fall in prices. Industrial production in the region suffered as exports plummeted.[3] Besides the fall in export demand, domestic demand in East Asia was also adversely affected. Protectionist tendencies of the "creeping" variety reportedly appeared on the increase in some of the "major advanced economies," and, consequently, possibilities of "deglobalization" were mooted.[4] Bank flows to Asia fell as reporting banks reduced their leverage, and external bond issuance also slowed down sharply in the second half of 2008. Each of the East Asian economies was sufficiently resourceful though to be able to cope adequately with the varying impact of the global financial crisis of 2008, and, unlike the earlier Asian financial crisis, this one did not give rise to a need for any emergency collective action in the region.

Table 4.1. Global financial crisis, selected indicators: World and East Asia (annual percent change).

	2007	2008	2009	2010
World GDP	5.4	2.8	-0.7	5.1
World exports	6.5	2.0	-12.0	14.0
World imports	6.0	2.0	-13.0	13.5
GDP growth				
United States	1.9	-0.3	-3.5	3.0
Eurozone	3.0	0.4	-4.3	1.8
China	14.2	9.6	9.2	10.3
Japan	2.4	-1.2	-6.3	4.0
Korea	5.1	2.3	0.3	6.2
Taipei	6.0	0.7	-1.9	10.8
Indonesia	6.3	6.0	4.6	6.1
Malaysia	6.5	4.8	-1.6	7.2
Philippines	6.6	4.2	1.1	7.6
Singapore	8.8	1.5	-0.8	14.5
Thailand	5.0	2.5	-2.3	7.8
Vietnam	8.5	6.3	5.3	6.8

Sources: IMF International Financial Statistics database, and WTO, International Trade Statistics 2011, (WTO, Geneva, 2011).

In the post Asian financial crisis phase in 1997-98, it was chiefly the export industry interests that had guided economic policy in East Asia, including in the case of China. But by 2008 China had emerged as a major player in world trade and was running record surpluses on the external current account. In particular sustained economic growth had catapulted China to a size that vied with that of the United States economy by some measures,[5] and to a size that now dictated a multiplicity of interests extending beyond regional concerns. A wide ranging spectrum of industry interests, a rapidly growing financial sector, increasing defense interests, assertive provincial governments with interests impinging on foreign policy, the growing need for energy and other critical resources, had made China's interests more diverse and also more firmly global; no longer was Chinese policy focused on chiefly regional concerns or the concerns of export industry and trade.

By 2009 both domestic demand as well as exports had rebounded in East Asia, though a restocking of inventories was the major factor that helped to jump start the quick turnaround in the export sector. An increase in the region's market share also contributed to the recovery of its exports. Global financial conditions too began to ease as credit spreads narrowed and equity flows resumed. Notwithstanding the shocks emanating from the global financial crisis, the East Asia region survived the crisis in good shape, returning to robust growth by 2010, and on this occasion presented a significantly better economic performance in terms of output than the transatlantic economies.[6]

A significant aspect of the global financial crisis of 2008 was that the usual mechanisms for oversight of the world economy and necessary international policy coordination, that is, the G-7/8 forums and multilateral financial institutions, proved quite inadequate to cope with the 2008 global financial crisis. One reason was that economies that were relatively unaffected by the crisis, and had the resources to be of assistance in coping with it, were not a part of G-7/8 and neither did they carry meaningful weight in multilateral institutions of the IMF and the World Bank. China was the most prominent among these economies. The G-20 forum, which brings together some of the larger Asian and other developing countries, including China, India and Indonesia, with some of the larger "advanced economies," was therefore mobilized for the purpose of tackling the global financial crisis, thus highlighting issues in suitability of existing structures of global governance for managing current economic conditions. With four of the G-20 members from Asia, and three of the four from East Asia (not counting Japan), the region seemed to acquire a new authority in global governance. In responding to the crisis, the initial consensus among the G-20 members settled on simultaneous pursuit of policies of fiscal stimulus and monetary easing—East Asia was quick to respond and its fiscal response to the crisis was substantial and larger than for the average G-20 member. But this G-20 stance and the identity of views that had brought it about fell apart by 2010 as the differing impact of the crisis among the "major advanced economies" as well as others became evident. One problem was that the reflationary measures taken by United States and some other economies failed to make much of a dent in the high unemployment rate in respectively the United States, the world's largest economy, and the other affected transatlantic economies. Further complications in maintaining any semblance of unity surfaced as the crisis spread to the Eurozone. Faced with such difficulties, and perplexed by the intransigence of the real economy to respond to traditional expansionary policy measures, the G-20 could be seen shifting its stance between its quarterly meetings, even though the facts did not change much qualitatively, thereby suggesting that the group was truly at sea with neither a compass nor a rudder to help steer course through this crisis.[7] As protest movements took root, the economic crisis looked set to become a visible social crisis as well. All this intensified the feeling of a deep and continuing socio-economic crisis in some of the "advanced economies" as well as a lack of a suitable global forum to effectively and adequately identify and address the issues.

In the wake of the global financial crisis policy measures were sought by the "major advanced economies" from China in particular, given its economic size, its sustained growth, and its external surpluses and mounting reserves. Specifically, action by China was sought by the United States, acting bilaterally as well as via the G-20 mechanism and via the pronouncements from the multilateral financial institutions. The arguable purpose of these demands on China was to help moderate the impact of the 2008 crisis on the world economy, and in particular the United States. The proposed policies would work towards the newly introduced concept of "rebalancing of the world economy" so as to help resolve the issue of "global imbalances." "Rebalancing" meant that the countries in external current account surplus, particularly China and to a lesser extent Germany, would institute expansionary policies to reduce their surpluses and countries with current account deficits, particularly United States but also others such as the United Kingdom, would undertake measures to reduce the deficits. Countries with a trade surplus would increase domestic demand and countries running trade deficits would contract domestic demand. A notable aspect was that the United States seemed to accept in principle some of the burden of adjustment and talked of improving the fiscal balance and reducing domestic expenditure. Perhaps this course had become unavoidable. In the event Germany did not judge demand expansion to be a prudent course of action, and the United States found it politically difficult to significantly reduce expenditure.[8]

In China's case the policy implications of "rebalancing" also required an appreciation of the renminbi vis-à-vis the dollar besides the increase in domestic consumption; together the two measures would help facilitate the switch from an export-oriented economy to one relying on domestic demand and thus lower China's external current account surplus. The appreciation of the renminbi had been a long-standing demand on the part of the United States.[9] Indeed thus far appreciation of renminbi had been accompanied by rising Chinese trade surpluses, more so vis-à-vis the United States, an aspect that is discussed further below. Others besides the United States such as Brazil, India, and Singapore have also on occasion sought an appreciation of the renminbi.[10]

Another development also impinged upon East Asia's thinking on economic policies in the context of a global slowdown: the United States contentiously sees China's trade policies as an important cause of the global financial crisis, arguing that the flood of cheap credit in the United States that caused the global financial crisis had its source in China's trade surpluses and, by implication, in China's exchange rate policies. On this point China's analysis of the global financial crisis differs very sharply, but these and other differences on economic policies are the subject of a separate chapter.

III: CHINA'S RESPONSE: SHARING THE BURDEN OF ADJUSTMENT

The economic policies that had propelled China's growth from a relatively small size for the past many years did not appear sustainable in 2008, as it vied in size with Japan to become the second largest economy in the world. The bedrock of the economy's growth was the processed manufacturing with a strong orientation towards increasing exports. Though consumption had been increasing in absolute terms, its share in national income had been falling, and wages had been stagnant for some years. The share of investment in national income had been increasing. Such a situation was unsustainable and warranted adjustment. Renminbi remained a non-convertible currency with capital controls in place. This situation too was untenable given the size of China's external sector. Finally, the growing foreign exchange reserves, a result of the growth in net exports and which had reached record levels, were for the most part in dollars, exposing China to a currency risk in an uncertain global environment. The pace of China's development had been unprecedented and the rapidity with which the changes had taken place had possibly added to the difficulty of devising any immediate but well thought out policy response to address these concerns arising precisely because of China's rapid economic development. Efforts were underway to address these issues when the global financial crisis unfolded.

The demands made on China in the G-20 deliberations, and particularly by the United States, were in context of resolving the global imbalances and rebalancing of the world economy, and involved expansionary policies to enhance domestic consumption, thereby implying a reorientation of the economy away from exports and also implying a restructuring of industry on account of higher wages. A further implication was that the higher wage would likely cause prices to rise and in turn call forth anti-inflationary policies. United States emphasized the appreciation of the renminbi as a key element. But the direction of policy implicit in these demands did not differ much from what China itself had decided at the time. Improved infrastructure, higher consumption and consequently higher wages were prominent amongst the policy goals laid down by the 17th Party Congress in 2007. We consider in turn the policies and the developments relating to consumption and to the renminbi.

"Rebalancing": consumption, the "stimulus package" and higher wages

We begin with a look at consumption trends, follow that with a review of the stimulus package adopted in response to the global financial crisis, then consider wages and increase in wages, and finally how the higher wages might impact on the economy and the region.

Consumption in China had lagged well behind the overall economic growth for some time, whilst the share of investment in GDP had risen. In particular China experienced a substantial fall in the share of wages in national income over the long term. The "proportion of the country's GDP that makes up wages and salaries (had) peaked at 56.5 percent in 1983 and dropped to 36.7 percent in 2005," and had "not changed too much since then."[11] Wages for migrant workers increased by only 2-5 percent over 2001-2003, and by around 7 percent over 2004-2007.[12] Consequently, the share of private consumption in China's GDP has experienced a secular decline as the table below shows:

Table 4.2. China: Share of private consumption in GDP.

Year	Share (in percent)	Year	Share (in percent)
2001	45.34	2006	36.94
2002	44.04	2007	35.97
2003	42.19	2008	35.12
2004	40.56	2009	34.98
2005	38.82	2010	33.80

Source: IMF, International Financial Statistics database.

Thinking on a policy response to correct this unsustainable trend of declining consumption was visible in 2007, before the advent of the global financial crisis. The 17th Party Congress pronounced on wages as well as consumption quite explicitly. Sustained wage increase became a part of declared policy goals: "Vigorous efforts will be made to . . . gradually increase . . . the minimum wage, and set up a mechanism of regular pay increases for enterprise employees. . ."[13] The policy set out at the 17th Party Congress also emphasized the need for an increase in consumption, and looked to an increase in urban numbers over the five years, any such increase in urban population itself being a harbinger of higher consumption:

> The ratio of consumption to GDP will increase steadily, and consumption, investment and export will be coordinated to boost economic growth. . . . The proportion of urban residents will notably increase.[14]

The demands for "rebalancing" by increasing domestic consumption that resulted from the G-20 policy response to the global financial crisis thus synchronized well with China's own policy shift, from reliance on exports to an increased emphasis on domestic consumption. A major upward push in wages nonetheless did not manifest itself until 2009 and the increase in the minimum wage had to wait until well into 2011.

In its immediate response to the global financial crisis and the G-20 discussions that followed, China launched a large stimulus program of US$602 billion, giving the domestic expenditure a large boost. The program focused on infrastructure: US$226 billion was to be utilized in transportation infrastructure projects, US$60 billion was for low-income housing and US$32 billion went to energy saving and environment. Another US$56 billion was to support development of rural areas including infrastructure, and US$151 billion went into reconstruction of rural areas affected by natural disasters. US$32 billion was to be utilized in education and health.[15] Given a record of fiscal prudence, the stimulus program did not present a fiscal problem for China. The large injection of expenditure did however add to domestic expenditure and also to the inflationary pressures in the economy.

Wage increases when they came were rapid; initially these wage increases were in response to threats of industrial action, and unfolded as follows. In 2009, the wages for migrant workers jumped up by 16 percent.[16] Then early in 2010 reports of labor shortages being experienced in Guangdong province, which accounts for one-third of China's exports and is the world's tenth largest exporter, began to mushroom.[17] Coming from the world's most populous country the news was something of a surprise. Employers responded as worker dissatisfaction to the stagnancy in wages became evident. In a large number of cases, some well-publicized, assertive workers obtained substantial wage increases through industrial action. As industrial action spread, wage increases became more frequent, the wage doubling in one case.[18] And the surge in wages continued through 2010 and into 2011 on the back of strident demands for increases by workers. The government too increased wages significantly. By September 2011, twenty-one of China's thirty provincial governments had increased the minimum wage by 21.7 percent.[19] This upward movement in wages is expected to continue for now, and looking to the future, industry managers foresee wage increases of 20 percent every year.[20]

Demographics of the one-child policy, China's population will begin to age from 2015, are also a part of the explanation.[21] The cohort of young workers entering the workforce is declining every year, and the ratio of the male entrants is increasing. Factory owners in southern China report the ratio of factory male/female workers is now 60:40, whereas the labor force used to be predominantly female. This shift in the male/female ratio may arguably be traced back to a preference for boys in a one-child policy world, with reportedly some selective female fetus abortions.[22]

Implications of higher wages and the stimulus program

Wage increases arguably have a two-fold effect. Firstly, wage increases directly confer enhanced purchasing power on the worker, and given the worker's presumed relatively low propensity to save, higher wages translate into an increase in consumption and thus in aggregate demand, albeit over a period as workers take time to adjust consumption patterns to higher incomes. The shift to a consumption driven economy is thereby furthered. The increase in aggregate demand may arguably be expected to reduce the export surplus as some of that production meant for exports would now likely be consumed locally. Should the workers' consumption pattern include imports, there would also be an increase in imports as workers' incomes rise.[23] A wage increase is perhaps the most efficient instrument for maximizing benefits to the worker, but China as a society may not necessarily encourage "consumerism" of the Western variety, seeing it a source of mounting household debt and economic problems, and this may moderate the impact of wage increases on aggregate demand.[24] The wage increases are very recent, and it may be some time before one can be definitive about the impact of the wage increases on consumption in China.

Secondly, any wage increase also directly increases the cost of production, and the affected industry may respond in any one of at least four ways. One possibility is that the industry may absorb the additional wage costs thereby reducing its profits. Another outcome is that the industry may relocate to a lower wage location thus maintaining its profits whilst leaving the product prices unchanged, and, as we discuss below, this also falls neatly within the policy goals enunciated at the 17th Party Congress. Or the industry may choose to pass on the higher wage costs to the final customer in the form of higher prices. Finally, the manufacturing industry may decide to shift to higher value added activity, which is also one the goals set out by the 17th Party Congress. Various combinations can also occur, and all of these possibilities seem to be in evidence in the case of China.

In industries where wage costs account for only a small proportion of total costs, the preferred approach may be to absorb the additional wage and thus maintain competitiveness. For example the wage cost is reported to be as low as 3-5 percent of the overall cost in the case of the PC industry, and a 10 percent increase in wages such a situation would not be a significant amount in terms of the total product cost.[25] More generally, survey evidence for the manufacturing sector as a whole shows "that wages make up just 10-15 percent of factory overheads," and the industry managers believe that it should be possible to manage wage increases of up to 10 percent within the existing product prices.[26]

Relocation to a relatively labor abundant, low-wage area is not always an option because of the networked nature of certain industries.[27] Where relocation to a low-wage area is feasible, it may be the natural choice for an industry facing higher wages. Such moves may also dovetail in instances with China's regional policy as set out at the 17th Party Congress.[28]

> Following the general strategy for regional development, we will continue to carry out large-scale development of the western region, rejuvenate northeast China and other old industrial bases in an all-round way, boost the development of the central region and support the eastern region in taking the lead in development.

The relatively labor abundant, low-wage areas in China would be its relatively less industrialized provinces in the west and southwest, away from the eastern seaboard, underscoring the point that given its size and economic diversity, China provides a variety of locations in terms of labor and transport costs, infrastructure, etc.[29] Thus when working on possibilities of relocation, firms are said to consider provinces such as Sichuan, Inner Mongolia and the vast city of Chongqing, egged on in such efforts by aggressive city and provincial governments and also encouraged by Beijing.[30] Wage increase therefore may well cause relocation of some of the economic activity to areas where government has invested much in housing, transportation and communication infrastructure. Thus, some of the affected industry has been relocating to western and southwestern provinces, and has also been making efforts to raise the skill levels and productivity of the work force.[31] The global sourcing company Li & Fung, which sources for Wal-Mart as well as Toys 'R' Us among other western retailers, found that the volume of production by its suppliers in China actually grew by 30 percent in the first half of 2011, with more suppliers moving to lower-cost interior provinces. Its chief executive, quipped that the answer to "what next in global manufacturing—is China."[32] A factor that encourages firms to stay in China is its increasingly first world infrastructure and its supply of higher productivity, skilled labor; factors that are perceived to remain unmatched for the foreseeable future, say, the next five to ten years.[33]

Though most relocation is within China,[34] relocation to other economies outside Mainland China is also taking place, and the fall in the share of light manufacturing from 50 percent to 48 for the first half of 2011 would seem to indicate just that. Judging from exports to the United States, the tentative gainers in the region include Vietnam and Indonesia, and further afield Bangladesh and Turkey too have gained.[35] But these gains remain tentative for now and are by no means secure. For example, in the case of Vietnam, manufacturing units there are increasingly facing industrial action and rapidly increasing wages that are a reflection of rising prices. High interest rates are another factor that eats into the profits.[36] The reportedly "high reject rate" in the apparel industry in India for example, a natural destination for relocation, discourages moves to that country. Philippines, another low-wage country, too has not benefited at least yet.[37] Poor infrastructure in other developing countries, including India, is often seen as a major hurdle by industry wishing to relocate from China, and the problems with infrastructure are serious enough to erase any advantage from a lower wage.[38] Finally, there is also speculation of "reshoring," jobs moving back to United States and Western Europe.[39]

Next, there are situations where higher wages may very likely result in higher output prices and these increased prices may help offset wage increases, even though wage is only a minor component of costs. A strong likelihood of a corresponding increase in export prices exists in cases where wage increases may be granted by a number of manufacturers across an industry.[40] For example, in conceding a wage increase recently, Foxconn, a major supplier of electronics, made sure that the increase was sufficiently large so that the competitors would be forced to raise wages as well. In the bargain its customers would also see the logic of higher output prices,[41] and of a corresponding increase in export prices.[42] Rising inflation in China suggests that wage increases may indeed have been passed on in higher prices for end products in a number of cases.

It is also the government policy to encourage a move to a more skill and technology intensive, and low pollution industry, and wage increases combined with skills and good infrastructure may help China shift out of low technology or high pollution industries. In this respect the 17th Congress had once again formulated some policy goals.

> We need to vigorously push forward strategic economic restructuring and make greater efforts to improve China's capacity for independent innovation as well as energy and environmental conservation . . .
> Accelerate . . . the transition from relying heavily on increased consumption of material resources to relying mainly on advances in science and technology, improvement in the quality of the workforce and innovation in management.
> We will develop a modern industrial system, . . . and eliminate outdated production capacities. We will upgrade new- and high-technology industries and develop information, biotechnology, new materials, aerospace, marine and other industries.[43]

Thus the migration of low paid jobs from Guangdong, China's most industrialized and wealthiest province, is what the provincial government has been seeking for some time. Hang Hua, the province's governor and Wang Yang, the Communist party secretary of Guangdong, have repeatedly stressed the need for polluting industries to move out of the province in favor of more technology intensive industries.[44] Enforcement of the policy to achieve higher industry standards in environment could be seen most vividly in the closure of the plant that produced casings for Apple notebooks on account of pollution. The quest for higher industry standards was equally evident in penalization of Walmart for violation of food safety standards. The booking of globally recognized names for industry standard violations serves to put on notice all industry about the seriousness of the government's resolve.[45] Wage increases may also importantly work to "nudge exporters up the value chain."[46]

To sum up, relocation and absorption of higher wage costs by the producers may help to moderate the impact of higher wages on exports and the trade balance. On the other hand higher wages may result in increased consumption by wage earners, and that in turn may cause higher imports as well as a reduction in the goods available for export. The stimulus program, which provided a one-time boost to the economy, and the specific program components sought to create new infrastructure, would have a similar impact on consumption.

Higher export prices could also moderate the demand for the respective goods overseas. On the other hand, according to the management of China's export industry, increase in wages in China's manufacturing sector is unlikely to materially affect China's international competitiveness in its key exports.[47] The net effect of wage increase in export industries on China's export performance thus appears to be ambiguous for now,[48] but any increase in export prices would *ceteris paribus* lead to an appreciation of the real renminbi/dollar exchange rate.[49] Any appreciation in the real exchange rate should in principle act to reduce China's trade surplus.

To conclude, we can see that the "rebalancing," as it relates to growth in consumption, has fortuitously combined with a situation of labor shortages and ensuing wage pressures in parts of the Chinese economy, and with private sector initiatives that aim to increase wages. Such wage increases would seem to contribute in resolving the "rebalancing" issue in one of the most advantageous ways for China, meeting at the same time a number of policy goals laid down by the 17th Congress.[50] Should these developments lead to a shift away from export orientation, as seems likely from recent developments, China may as a result be less dependent on its export markets in the "major advanced economies."[51] The intra-regional linkages may be less affected and may continue to grow as domestic demand increases and causes a rise in imports both as final consumption goods and as industry inputs. Regional economies may also benefit from any relocation of industry from China. Any increase in wages implies "currency appreciation," an appreciation of the renminbi in real terms, which may have a salutary effect on the trade balance. China could therefore once again work to its advantage an adverse external development, the 2008 global financial crisis in the present instance, to help achieve its domestic as well as external policy goals, very much as it did at the time of the Asian financial crisis, but it is early to judge.

IV: CHINA'S RESPONSE: SHARING THE BURDEN OF ADJUSTMENT: THE CURRENCY ISSUE

"Rebalancing": the imperatives of trade and going out policies for the renminbi

Turning now to the currency issue, we see that for some years preceding the global financial crisis of 2008, China had been quite conscious of the implications for the renminbi of the size of its growing economy, its rapidly expanding trade and of its fast expanding overseas economic and financial presence, the latter owing to its "going out" policy. We consider these aspects below.

The significance of using a particular currency in actual trade has to be seen in context of China's growing external trade and the growing importance of this trade, in the East Asia region, as well as globally; the value of trade in renminbi seems to be growing rapidly.[52] Thus about 9 percent of China's trade was being settled in renminbi by November 2011, up from almost zero two years earlier.[53] Exchange rate fluctuations involving multiple currencies introduce great uncertainty in costs of imported raw materials and other inputs that are a necessary requirement for the typical processed manufacturing network of the kind that now permeates the region. Keeping costs under control and predictable is essential for competitive production. China is the leading trading partner for most of the East Asian economies. The use of renminbi in such intra-regional trade transactions would help to answer a specific need as this trade volume is both large and growing in an organic manner: using renminbi as a tool to better manage risks arising from exchange rate fluctuations. In this intra-regional trade, China is a net importer from most of the trading partners in the East Asian region, and regional exports to China have expanded at record rates over the past twenty years; the implication being that the regional surplus economies may eventually accumulate renminbi balances from their trade surpluses with China, substituting them to some degree for dollar ones. And as the renminbi's use is generally restricted to trade transactions, it cannot be subjected to speculation. Trade flows and production costs are thus somewhat shielded from some of the worst aspects of the existing international monetary arrangements.[54]

Most of the above considerations also apply to furthering the use of renminbi in rest of the world. China's prominence in global trade is established and growing, and in the case of a fair number of countries China is now the major trading partner. To the extent that trade transactions between China and its trade partners are in renminbi, uncertainty relating to fluctuations in exchange rates is reduced considerably for all concerned, protecting the parties from fluctuations in the value of the dollar. This may perhaps be one of the reasons that motivate an increasing number of Chinese companies to ask their foreign trading partners to accept renminbi as payment.[55]

China's "going out" policy also raises the need for wider acceptability of its currency.[56] This "going out" strategy appears to aim also at "reserve diversification in a broader sense."[57] Over the next decade, China is expected to undertake foreign direct investment (FDI) to the tune of US$2 trillion.[58] Though China's existing outward FDI has been quite modest until very recently, the outward FDI flows for 2009 amounted to only US$57 billion[59] and the overseas FDI stock being a unassuming US$230 billion (just marginally ahead of tiny Singapore's US$213 billion), considerable scope for growth exists with a ten year target of US$2 trillion. China's development finance operations too have been building up recently, and at an increasing pace. Chinese financial assistance to developing countries exceeded that of the World Bank for the three years 2008-10. The overseas operations of Chinese banking sector too are expanding.[60] Financial assistance was provided by Chinese banks at concessional rates, invariably lower than those offered by the World Bank, to undertake infrastructure and resource related projects in the developing economies of Asia, Africa and Latin America.[61] The Eurozone governments have also eagerly sought portfolio investment and other financial help from China in the Eurozone crisis.[62] With the advent of the global financial crisis, Premier Wen Jiabao was reported as saying that China should hasten the implementation of its "going out" strategy and combine the utilization of foreign exchange reserves with the "going out" of its enterprises.[63]

The projected foreign direct investment and the likely development assistance activities both necessitate a credible and widely acceptable renminbi and thus compel the internationalization of the currency.[64]

China's currency policy on the eve of the 2008 global financial crisis

Thus China's currency policy on the eve of the global financial crisis was directed chiefly at widening its international usage and circulation, and at making the renminbi convertible. Measures to gradually increase the relevance and use of its currency overseas had been afoot for some years, and the need for systematic work on a larger role for the renminbi was explicitly recognized at the 17th Party Congress. As a step in this direction, the strategic goal of achieving convertibility of the renminbi "under capital controls" was announced by President Hu before the global financial crisis had quite set in.[65]

> We will improve the RMB exchange rate regime and gradually make the RMB convertible under capital controls.

It is important to note that the policy did not seek to do away with capital controls. More recently a PBoC official, the head of its statistics section, writing in a newspaper put forth proposals for making the renminbi convertible.[66]

President Hu Jintao's work report to the 17th Congress also underlined the implementation of the "going out" strategy. The policy on "going out" had also figured prominently in the President's work report to the 17th Party Congress:

> We will make innovations in our way of overseas investment and cooperation, support domestic enterprises in carrying out international operations of R&D, production and marketing, and accelerate the growth of Chinese multinational corporations and Chinese brand names in the world market.[67]

The 17th Party Congress was only recognizing the ongoing policy on the renminbi, and emphasizing the implementation of that policy, rather than defining a new direction. Chinese efforts to gradually further the greater international use of renminbi and to implement its going out policy had not quite factored in the severity of the global financial crisis of 2008, or the ensuing problems with the United States economy and the Eurozone economy, and hence the dollar's and the euro's credibility as world currencies.

The 2008 crisis and "rebalancing": appreciation of the renminbi

Arguably, in China's policy thinking, the issue of appreciation of the renminbi vis-à-vis the dollar was a different one and of a different order than the internationalization of the renminbi. Whilst for China the renminbi exchange rate represented a balance between the interests of the export producers amongst the Chinese industry and the interests of the domestic producers for the domestic market, for the United States the issue was pivotal in its understanding of global imbalances and the rebalancing efforts that followed the 2008 global financial crisis: it were thus the persistent United States external trade deficits that lay behind the American demand for appreciation of the renminbi. United States has been running trade deficits with China for many years, climbing steadily from US$6 million in 1985 to US$33.8 billion in 1995 and US$202.3 billion in 2005; after a small hiccup in 2009, when world trade fell sharply, the deficit attained a peak of US$295.5 billion in 2011.[68] An American demand on China, stemming from this persisting deficit, and one that well predated the 2008 global financial crisis as well, was that China ought to appreciate its currency, the renminbi. The basic reasoning was that if the renminbi were to be made dearer vis-à-vis the dollar, America would import fewer Chinese goods as these would be more expensive in dollar terms, and China would import more of American goods as these would be cheaper in renminbi, and thereby the United States balance of trade with China would improve. The charge of currency manipulation frequently made by American officials in their dealings with China, and often discussed by American academics and media, is a particular

American version of this narrative. To facilitate some understanding of this proposition, the relevant parameters are set out in the table below.

Table 4.3. Renminbi /Dollar exchange rate and United States-China trade account.

	Renminbi exchange rate		Foreign trade balance			
	Nominal RMB/USD	Real effective exchange rate	United States deficit	China's surplus	US-China component	
	per unit	index	percent	percent	$ billion	percent
2005	8.070	100.00	6.18	5.78	202.28	25.91
2006	7.809	101.60	6.25	8.18	234.10	28.01
2007	7.305	105.68	5.84	9.72	258.51	31.57
2008	6.828	115.41	5.81	8.94	268.04	32.29
2009	6.828	119.19	3.63	5.15	226.88	44.84
2010	6.623	118.70	4.45	5.13	273.06	42.28

Source: IMF eLibrary Data, International Financial Statistics, Direction of Trade Statistics and United States Bureau of Census, Foreign trade data. Notes: United States trade deficit and China's trade surplus relate to trade in goods and are shown as a percentage of GDP. The United States-China component refers to the percentage of the United States trade in goods deficit accounted for by trade in goods with China.

The above table makes the point that the renminbi has appreciated since 2005 and China's global trade surplus as a quotient of its GDP has declined significantly since its high water mark in 2007. The relationship between currency appreciation and a declining trade balance would thus seem to hold. But the United States on the other hand continues to be in deficit in its bilateral trade with China, and this deficit does not appear to be susceptible to any feasible appreciation of the renminbi/dollar exchange rate. It may be noted though that the United States global trade deficit has fallen appreciably since 2006. The bilateral American trade deficit with China thus shows a remarkable resilience to the appreciation of the renminbi. The predicament of a continuing deficit in face of renminbi appreciation parallels the US-Japanese experience with the revaluation of the yen in context of the Plaza Accord in 1985. The yen appreciated against the dollar substantially but this appreciation had virtually no effect on the United States-Japan balance of trade and Japanese surpluses in its bilateral trade with the United States continued.

In the Chinese perspective its continuing trade surpluses with the United States are a necessary outcome of the international currency system that is based on the dollar. Such an analysis of the problem, that is radically different from the American understanding, is considered in chapter 5 below.

The 2008 crisis and the internationalization of the renminbi

China's efforts with furthering the overseas acceptance and use of the renminbi and of the implementation of its going out strategy picked up steam with the onset of the global financial crisis. Though China had presented a profitable investment opportunity for investors on account of the sustained growth of its economy, the crisis made it more attractive as the transatlantic economies entered a period of uncertainty. The economic prospects continued to look unfavorable for the United States as it suffered a downgrade of its credit rating in 2011, three years after the global financial crisis began, and the Eurozone too faced a deepening of its financial crisis later that year with no clear resolution in sight. The Chinese economy and its financial assets became more attractive as investment propositions. There was a demand for renminbi and related assets both by overseas official agencies and by the international banking and investment community. These developments combined to promote the renminbi, causing its internationalization to speed up beyond perhaps the intent of the original policy.

From modest beginnings in 2004, that is, permitting the use of renminbi by some specified categories of Hong Kong enterprises, the international role of the renminbi has grown at an increasingly rapid pace, making quantum leaps from December 2008 onwards. It now involves international currency swap arrangements and the use of renminbi in foreign exchange reserves by some countries, besides emergence of certain international financial centers as hubs for renminbi business.

Consider first the growing use of renminbi in international banking transactions. The official use of renminbi outside the Mainland was initiated in Hong Kong in 2004 in a small way, being limited to designated Hong Kong businesses in specified commercial transactions. As deposits built up, the arrangement was marginally broadened in 2007 to include issue of renminbi bonds in Hong Kong by designated Mainland enterprises. Since then the global financial crisis and China's rapidly increasing role in the world economy seem to have speeded up developments considerably, and the scope of the project appears to have expanded greatly since 2009 in a number of ways. First, Mainland subsidiaries of Hong Kong banks were also included amongst institutions that could issue renminbi bonds in Hong Kong. Second, a pilot scheme was initiated whereby some of the Hong Kong arrangements were extended to ASEAN economies for designated enterprises there as well as to designated enterprises on the Mainland.[69] In July 2009, China extended the use of renminbi for trade related transactions to external trade with five cities on the Mainland. By 2010 the scheme had been extended to twenty Chinese provinces.[70] These arrangements were further extended to a larger number of Mainland enterprises.[71] In August 2011 the scheme was extended to the whole of China.[72] Third, in July 2010 offshore banks were permitted to transfer renminbi amongst them,[73] and renminbi accounts in Hong Kong were permitted to almost anyone wishing to open one.[74] Renminbi deposits in Hong Kong had surged to Rmb 408 bn (US$62bn) by February 2011, up more than eightfold from two years ago, before climbing on to Rmb 627 bn (US$99bn) by November 2011.[75] Fourth, in August 2010 offshore banks and foreign central banks were permitted to invest in China's interbank bond market, and the first foreign non-financial company was permitted to issue renminbi bonds.[76] Renminbi bonds help the issuer to raise renminbi to buy dollars, or help avoid dollar inflows aimed at purchasing renminbi, and transactions of this nature work to diversify and moderate the risk from China's increasing holdings of dollars and dollar denominated securities.[77] In March 2012 China agreed to work on setting up a BRICS development bank, which "could be an important tool for China, . . . in its quest to promote the renminbi."[78] Limited convertibility of renminbi on the capital account too is being tested out.[79]

Bilateral currency swap arrangements have built up rapidly between China and neighboring countries as well as further afield. The swap funds may be drawn upon for any reason, and though the swap agreements help establish the credibility of renminbi as a settlement currency, they may also further its wider acceptability. Thus we see that "currency swap agreements with Uzbekistan, Singapore, New Zealand, Mongolia, Malaysia, Kazakhstan, Indonesia and Argentina are mainly used for bilateral business and trade settlements; currency swap with South Korea is mainly to facilitate the financing of Korean firms in China, and expansion is planned; currency swap with Hong Kong is mainly to satisfy supply of funds; and currency swaps with Belarus and Iceland aim to turn renminbi into a reserve currency."[80] Besides reducing financial risk as well as financing costs, such swap agreements are also helpful in promoting bilateral trade. In the words of Zhang Yansheng, the head of the International Economic Research Institute under the National Development and Reform Commission:[81]

> Conducting currency swaps with other countries shows China's fulfillment its responsibility amid the global crisis and its contribution to a stable regional currency system. China's trading partners have been confident about the stability of both the yuan and China's economy.

All the above swap arrangements were signed from December 2008 onwards, and yet others, such as the one with Turkey, are being negotiated. An arrangement with Brazil that permits the use of the Brazilian real and the renminbi in bilateral trade, instead of the dollar, is planned.[82] China is also reported to have offered loans to the other BRICS countries.[83]

Given that China is the main trading partner in the case of most of the Southeast Asian economies, the renminbi has a large weight in their respective currency baskets, and these currencies now tend to move in tandem with the renminbi's fluctuations.[84] With the establishment of the China-ASEAN FTA, the scope of the Renminbi Trade Settlement Service has naturally increased.[85] Some of the East Asia economies also wish to see renminbi take on a regional role. China now plans to sign an agreement with the ten-member Association of South East Asian Nations (ASEAN) to settle trade in renminbi, and this is expected to lay the foundation for the renminbi to become a regional currency, and a renminbi settlement service has been started in Malaysia.[86] The ASEAN economies are perhaps motivated by their large bilateral trade and investment flows as well as substantial bilateral current account balances with China. These economies are perhaps also motivated by a desire to hedge their bets vis-à-vis the dollar and the euro because of the relative uncertainty that characterizes the dollar and the performance of the United States economy as well as the euro and the performance of some of the Eurozone economies. The renminbi is perceived as a relatively stable currency, and for that reason costs are more predictable enabling better control over production and trade when China and Southeast Asian businessmen settle their transactions in renminbi.[87] The Malaysian deputy finance minister has argued that "a unified currency in Asia, where most countries are emerging economies that might easily attract hot money inflows from industrialized nations, could help diminish the risk of exchange rate fluctuations and help boost the region's trade" and that China's participation in such an effort is fundamental.[88] It is claimed that the recent addition of renminbi and renminbi denominated bonds to Malaysia's foreign exchange reserves has raised "renminbi's credibility to a whole new level" in international banking, and other economies in the region are likely to follow this example in a "domino effect."[89] In some of Southeast Asian countries, China's currency is becoming acceptable as a universal method of exchange, a development that some expect would likely extend to ASEAN+3New.[90] Korea too is reported to be seeking to invest its foreign exchange reserves in renminbi and renminbi securities.[91] The role of the renminbi in the East Asian economies is a rapidly evolving one.

Given sustained high growth of the Chinese economy and its large reserves, countries outside the region have also been attracted to the renminbi and keen to use it as a reserve currency as well as to float renminbi bonds:[92]

> The renminbi is winning the popularity contest against the greenback. The debt problems of the US as well as those of other western govern-

> ments continue to encourage investors to gain exposure to the redback in a bid to profit from its likely appreciation.
> The downgrading of the US's credit rating from triple A by Standard & Poor's earlier in the year adds to the uncertainty swirling around the US dollar and suggests the renminbi could eventually be elevated to a reserve currency. If this comes to pass, central banks—which hold no renminbi—will be forced to purchase the currency.

Nigeria recently announced plans to diversify its foreign exchange reserves and invest 10 percent of the US$35 billion in renminbi; its central bank governor explained:

> Confidence in China doesn't mean lack of confidence in America. Europe and America will continue to be important parts of the world. Having said that, it will be almost living in a dream world to ignore China. It's the second-largest economy in the world and it's *well-managed*.
> . . . There's no reason, based on history, why we cannot for instance receive renminbi for our sales of oil to China.[93]

As the renminbi's international usage increases, the scope for financial intermediation and investment services related to the offshore renminbi too grows. Hong Kong has become a financial center for renminbi transactions. Renminbi business in Hong Kong has expanded gradually from personal deposits for Hong Kong residents, when its use was first allowed in 2004, to bonds and then to trade credit. Singapore seeks to become the second renminbi clearing center outside the Mainland, after Hong Kong.[94] China has also agreed to support the development of London as an offshore trading center for the renminbi that has been sought by the United Kingdom.[95] Taipei too is keenly looking for renminbi business.[96] Taiwan authorities also report "a 'tacit understanding' with Beijing to begin talks within this year to establish a renminbi clearing and settlement mechanism." In Taiwan's case an important consideration is that its export receipts are chiefly in US dollars while its imports from China, being a large part of its costs, are in renminbi. With the renminbi appreciating vis-à-vis the US dollar, Taiwan needs hedging options.[97] According to the announced CCP policy, in the longer term China also plans to develop Shanghai as an international financial center by 2020, and turn it in to a global renminbi trading center by 2015.[98] But continuing economic growth on the Mainland is fundamental to the growth of Hong Kong as a renminbi offshore center, and to Shanghai's emergence as one.

Yet others such as the international banking community see much profit in pushing an internationalized renminbi.[99] The private sector financial institutions, that is, the international banking and investor community, are keen to profit from China's exceptional growth and a number of renminbi investment funds and instruments have been launched or are planned. To meet a growing demand from Western investors for renminbi investments, private funds that invest in offshore renminbi bonds have been opened up recently and more are planned in the near future by leading investment houses, including Barclays, Blackstone, Carlyle, Goldman Sachs and Morgan Stanley.[100]

A policy of delinking the renminbi from the dollar to more nearly a free float is also being simultaneously implemented albeit in a measured fashion.[101] But there seems to be an evident reluctance to move any faster on appreciation of the renminbi than plan and prudence would seem to permit, notwithstanding repeated exhortations and threats of "currency manipulation" legislation from the United States.[102] It needs mentioning here that the American demand for appreciation of the renminbi touches on policy debates in China. One such debate is arguably between export interests on the one hand, and interests oriented more towards domestic demand on the other, and this debate parallels a potential structural shift in the economy. The other currency debate raises concerns about problems with the working of the dollar based international currency system, and in this respect China also put forth proposals for systemic reform. This aspect is discussed further in chapter 5.[103]

V: CONCLUSIONS

East Asia's external economic policies are guided and informed by the domestic considerations of the individual economies, and, indeed, this is not much different from the general case that obtains elsewhere. China's past experience is often interpreted though as offering a good example of leveraging major external developments to China's national advantage to achieve its domestic policy goals. For example, it is claimed that China's WTO accession was used to effect widespread and substantive change in domestic policies to further pro-market reform. It is also claimed that the earlier Asian financial crisis of 1997 proved "helpful" in furthering pro-market reform in China as well as more generally in East Asia.[104]

The priorities laid down by the 17th Party Congress reveal an awareness in China, well before the advent of the global financial crisis of 2008, to raise domestic consumption and wages, and also to internationalize the renminbi and to strengthen the "going out" policy. These efforts gathered pace as the 2008 crisis set in. The rise in wages is impacting on the location and structure of industry as well as on its competitiveness, and on China's earlier plans that intended a shift to technology-intensive non-polluting industry. Separately a stimulus program, undertaken in response to the 2008 crisis, provided an opportunity to develop infrastructure, to improve healthcare and to reduce the incidence of poverty.

The global financial crisis of 2008 also seems to have provided justification that is grounded in global welfare for these policies. The global financial crisis brought demands from the G-20 and in particular from the United States, for China to institute policies to boost domestic consumption and for the appreciation of the renminbi. Thus these demands made by the United States via the G-20 and the multilateral institutions seemed to jive well with China's own policy goals.[105] The result has been that China continued on its earlier policy, albeit at a faster pace, and in the case of the renminbi with support from some other countries as well as some in the international banking and investment community.

The low wage, light manufacturing, industry may shift out of the eastern seaboard because of higher wages in the latter location and the ensuing wage differentials, and also because such industry is no longer welcomed by the local authorities. The shift to other low wage economies or to China's interior would assist in the development of those areas.

The global financial crisis of 2008 could also arguably prove "helpful" to the region, and to China in particular, as its major export markets in the United States and European Union appeared to falter as a result of the crisis and no longer presented a robust prospect in the medium term. For China, the rapid growth of its economy was already making an export-based growth strategy untenable, and the crisis provided an opportunity to counter the pressures from the reputedly strong export interests in the country,[106] and to restructure its economy to a more domestic orientation in demand, and thus to further reduce the reliance on the external demand stemming from the export markets of Europe and the United States. Such a shift could be expected to help China to better meet long-term domestic policy goals, such as improvements in the living standards of the average citizen, relocation of activity to western provinces, strengthening regional economic linkages in East Asia, etc. The differences between China and the United States with regard to rebalancing of the world economy would thus appear to a considerable extent to be over the quantum and speed of any adjustments and policy shifts, rather than the direction of change. China seems to live up to the famously ambiguous meaning of the Chinese equivalent of the word crisis; a crisis is also an opportunity.

Though an uncertain and tentative global economic environment greatly complicates the task of economic policy for East Asia, it strongly advances the case for guiding a largely externally oriented region to one geared relatively more towards increasing the domestic and regional components in the economy.

A summing up and the outlook on renminbi

China's approach to internationalizing the renminbi too presents a case of domestic considerations guiding economic policy and the global financial crisis of 2008 being taken as a reason for accelerating an earlier policy. The policy on the renminbi has been problem oriented such as how to reduce its growing exposure to the dollar, or focused on a particular purpose or task such as the financing of its growing trade transactions, rather than a generalized, across the board move based on theory or ideology. In particular any policy measure that could create possibilities of speculative trades in renminbi instruments seems to have been avoided thus far. The word *internationalization* has been preferred to *liberalization* to describe the process.

Taken as a whole, the gradual application of measures adopted to give renminbi wider international usage also appear to be in line with China's practice of applying any new policy in a piecemeal fashion to specific areas or situations, and on the basis of the experience gained, to further refine the policy and its implementation before generalizing the application and implementation to other areas.[107] Based on the past experience with China's approach to policy formulation and implementation, one may hazard the conjecture that it appears most likely that the use of renminbi may gradually be extended further in trade relations, thus providing increasing protection against exchange rate fluctuations whilst avoiding the risk associated with speculative capital flows and, at the same time, reducing the potential dollar balances and reserve accumulation on account of intraregional and international trade.

The effort at regionalizing the renminbi in East Asia, a modest but a rapidly growing and evolving one, serves to reduce the role of traditional reserve currencies, for China as well as for some of its trading partners, and lends a new significance to the renminbi in the region.[108] The fact that China is the production hub in East Asia helps in the regional use of renminbi: growth in China's regional trade and the growing regionalization of renminbi are interdependent processes. The extension of the renminbi scheme to Southeast Asia and Hong Kong and Macao implies that potentially 40 to 50 percent of China's imports and 20 to 30 percent of its exports could be invoiced in renminbi.[109]

The sum of China's currency moves would seem to be to gradually increase the overseas use of renminbi in "non-speculative" transactions, increasing the coverage in terms of types of transactions permitted, and in terms of authorized businesses, financial institutions and economies, moving in this manner towards renminbi convertibility and its eventual status as a reserve currency.[110] Private foreign banks and other financial institutions too are gearing up to develop business in renminbi, and in these efforts they seem to have full support of Peoples Bank of China.[111]

The experience with the Eurodollar market in the 1960s before the dollar became freely convertible offers an example in support of Beijing's approach of internationalizing the renminbi through a growing volume of offshore transactions: in that period the dollar too was being used in offshore transactions even though the United States had not fully liberalized its capital account.[112] The renminbi's sustained appreciation against the dollar and the euro lend the currency credibility, notwithstanding that the lack of convertibility restricts its use as an international currency. China's buying power in relation to commodities may also assert itself in carving a role for the renminbi.[113]

One potential impediment in Chinese foreign direct investment destined for the United States is the puzzling nature of the CFIUS scrutiny and it is argued "that as the scale of Chinese ambitions increases, the CFIUS will have to work harder to demonstrate it is subject to due process and oversight and convince investors it is 'not being used as a tool for protectionism'."[114] Otherwise, continued CFIUS intransigence would amount to an impediment in the "rebalancing" process.

To sum up, the steps taken so far are very much an embodiment of Lao Tzu's words that "A journey of a thousand miles, Starts from beneath one's feet,"[115] but the pace is ever faster and the efforts are gathering momentum, as the dollar's position becomes hostage to the continuing weakness of the American economy and the euro's authority falters in the face of structural flaws in the architecture of the Eurozone.

NOTES

1. See President Hu Jintao's statement at Communist Party of China's 17th Congress at http://www.china.org.cn/english/congress/229611.htm#2
2. The term transatlantic economies is used to refer to the economies of North America, chiefly the United States, and Europe, excepting some of the Scandinavian countries. Also the severity of the impact was relatively less for Germany and Switzerland.
3. See Gita Gopinath, Oleg Itskhoki and Brent Neiman, Trade prices and the global trade collapse, NBER working paper no.: 17594, November 2011.
4. See discussion of protectionist tendencies that seem to be gathering strength in Fredrik Erixon and Razeen Sally, Trade, globalisation and emerging protectionism since the crisis, ECIPE working paper no.: 02/2010.
5. Arvind Subramanian asserts that by PPP measures, the size of the Chinese economy exceeds that of the United States. See Arvind Subramanian, Eclipse (Washington, DC: PIIE, 2011).
6. See David Pilling, Asia: more self-contained, Financial Times, August 10, 2010. Also see discussion in the following chapter.
7. See for example discussion in Alan Beattie, International economy: a display of disunity, Financial Times, October 22, 2010.
8. An important element in "rebalancing," an issue that predates the present demand, has been that the average Chinese should save less, and that a good social security system including good healthcare facilities would bring that about. Such an argument has been made by a number of authors, for example by Olivier Blanchard and Francesco Giavazzi. But the proposition elides the empirical fact that East Asian socieites with good social security and healthcare systems such as Japan and Singapore continue to have high savings rates. Clearly demographics as well as cultural factors count, and cannot be ignored. See Olivier Blanchard and Francesco Giavazzi, Rebalancing growth in China: A three-handed approach, MIT Det of Economics working paper 05-32, November 25, 2005.
9. See discussion below.
10. See Geoff Dyer, Brazil and India add to pressure on China, Financial Times, April 21, 2010.

11. See Jin Zhu, China's wage proportion decreases for 22 years, China Daily, May 13, 2010.

12. Geoff Dyer cites Cai Fang, a researcher at the Chinese Academy of Social Sciences who has written at length about labor issues as the source for this data. See Geoff Dyer, End looms for era of cheap Chinese labour, Financial Times, June 3, 2010.

13. See Hu Jintao's report at the 17th Party Congress, VIII. Accelerating Social Development with the Focus on Improving People's Livelihood, paragraph 3 at http://www.china.org.cn/english/congress/229611.htm#2

14. See Hu Jintao's report at the 17th Party Congress, IV New Requirements for Attaining the Goal of Building a Moderately Prosperous Society in All Respects at http://www.china.org.cn/english/congress/229611.htm#2

15. See discussion in People's Daily, China's 4 trillion yuan stimulus package at farewell platform, People's Daily, November 24, 2010. Also see discussion in Kevin Brown and Geoff Dyer, Hu defends China's role in global recovery, Financial Times, November 13, 2009

16. Cai Feng cited in Geoff Dyer, End looms for era of cheap Chinese labour, Financial Times, June 3, 2010.

17. These reports, based on interviews with industry managers and bankers in the region, stated that the labor shortages were very much in evidence, specifically in the electrical goods, electronics, and medical goods industries. See Tom Mitchell, Labour shortage hits China export recovery, Financial Times, February 25, 2010, and Tom Mitchell, No place like home for migrant workers, Financial Times, February 25, 2010.

18. Strikes at Foxconn and Honda have been widely publicized and are best known, and have resulted in doubling of wage in the former, and an offer of 24 percent increase in the latter. See Geoff Dyer, End looms for era of cheap Chinese labour, Financial Times, June 3, 2010. Foxconn is a Taiwan based producer of electronic goods and employs 1.2 million workers in its factories in China. Furthermore, "In announcing the wage increase late Sunday, the company (Foxconn), a unit of Taiwan's Hon Hai Precision Industry Company, said that within three months the basic salaries of many of its 800,000 workers in China could reach nearly $300 a month, about double what many were earning a few weeks ago." See David Barboza, Foxconn Increases Size of Raise in Chinese Factories, New York Times, June 6, 2010.

19. Recent instances of worker unrest leading to wage increases have been reported at Yum brands, which runs KFC and Pizza Hut, and which granted a 33 percent wage increase to workers in Shenyang; at Foshan Fengfu autoparts, which granted a 24-33 percent wage increase to its work force; and at Merry Electronics, a manufacturer of audio equipment, where the management, when faced with a strike, said that it "had decided at the beginning of the year to raise wages 10 percent by July 1, but had never announced this to the staff." See Tom Mitchell, Justine Lau, and Robin Kwong, Unrest spreads among Chinese workers, Financial Times, June 9, 2010. Also see Simon Rabinovitch, China's labour costs soar as wages rise 22%, Financial Times, October 25, 2011.

20. See Rahul Jacob, China wage rises brings shift in production, Financial Times, September 6, 2011. Also Robin Kwong cites Joseph Hsu, chairman and chief executive of Micro-Star International, a maker of products such as motherboards and netbooks, as saying that "Salaries will probably increase 20 percent year-on-year from now on [because] living costs in China are also getting much higher." This assessment has been borne out by the subsequent announcement of a 20 percent increase in the minimum wage. See Robin Kwong, China confident of electronics role, Financial Times, June 3, 2010. The most recent incident is that of the auditor's report on Foxconn with the latter committing to yet another increase in wages as well as a reduction in working hours. See Charles Duhigg and Steven Greenhouse, Electronic giant vowing reforms in China plants, New York Times, March 30, 2012.

21. Reported in the Financial Times editorial of March 14, 2010, The return of Chinese inflation.

22. See Rahul Jacob, China wage rises brings shift in production, Financial Times, September 6, 2011.

23. Some recent data indicates that China's export growth has slowed down, whilst the growth in China's imports is accelerating. See Simon Rabinovitch, China export growth dips as EU slows, Financial Times, November 10, 2011.

24. Wang Yuanfeng, Western countries should rethink consumerism, Peoples Daily, September 2, 2011.

25. In the case of the PC industry, even a 30 percent increase in wages implies an increase of one percent in the total product cost. See Robin Kwong, China confident of electronics role, Financial Times, June, 3 2010.

26. Josh Noble cites a survey of manufacturing industries in Guangdong earlier this year about wages by Standard Chartered Bank. The majority of those asked said they were expecting pay to rise by around 10 percent. And while a few Chinese firms and multinationals have tentatively started to peer over the borders into Vietnam, Thailand or across to Indonesia, most companies thought that any relocation would be within China. See Josh Noble, Higher wages in China: good news for the economy, Financial Times, June 3, 2010.

27. Discussing whether the enthusiasm of foreign investors would wane on account of industrial action being experienced in Guangdong province, David Pilling writes: "Yet few are likely to pull out. That is because China has ceased to be merely a low-cost production centre. For many companies, it is also becoming an important market and an integral part of their global supply chain. Walmart sources $30bn worth of goods from China each year. Japanese car manufacturers, such as Honda, have brought with them a network of components makers, and built ties with Chinese parts suppliers. What goes for cars goes for iPads, mobile phones, digital cameras and colour photocopiers. Such a clustering effect makes it almost impossible for manufacturers to pick up sticks and start afresh elsewhere." See David Pilling, Change is finally afoot for China's workers, Financial Times, June 2, 2010.

28. See Hu Jintao's report at the 17th Party Congress, Section V. Promoting sound and rapid development of the National economy, paragraph 5. See http://www.china.org.cn/english/congress/229611.htm#5

29. See Tom Mitchell, No place like home for migrant workers, Financial Times, February 25, 2010. Such relocation moves are said to be encouraged by aggressive local governments and as well as by authorities in Beijing. See Josh Noble, Higher wages in China: good news for the economy, Financial Times, June 3, 2010. There are also reports that good infrastructure has been developed outside the eastern provinces, and these new towns now await residents. See Geoff Dyer, China: No one home, Financial Times, February 21, 2010.

30. See Josh Noble, Higher wages in China: good news for the economy, Financial Times, June 3, 2010. There are also reports that good infrastructure has been developed outside the eastern provinces, and these new towns now await residents. See Geoff Dyer, China: No one home, Financial Times, February 21, 2010.

31. Tom Mitchell, No place like home for migrant workers, Financial Times, February 25, 2010. Any increase in economic activity in the western provinces would also likely be a strong and direct poverty reduction measure, given that poverty incidence is considerably worse in those areas.

32. See Rahul Jacob, China wage rises brings shift in production, Financial Times, September 6, 2011.

33. Joseph Hsu, chairman and chief executive of Micro-Star International, a maker of products such as motherboards and netbooks, which employs 30,000 workers at its plant outside Shanghai, is reported as saying that said few other countries in Asia could rival China's combination of extensive infrastructure and still relatively low-cost environment. He said "the whole infrastructure [for the industry] is now in place . . . over the next five to 10 years, I can't see any other countries that could compare with that." See Robin Kwong, China confident of electronics role, Financial Times, June 3, 2010.

34. See Josh Noble, Higher wages in China: good news for the economy, Financial Times, June 3, 2010.

35. See Rahul Jacob, China wage rises brings shift in production, Financial Times, September 6, 2011.
36. See Ben Bland, Vietnam: A question of balance, Financial Times, November 24, 2011.
37. See Rahul Jacob, China wage rises brings shift in production, Financial Times, September 6, 2011.
38. See Rahul Jacob, China factories eye cheaper labour overseas, Financial Times, November 8, 2011.
39. See Tim Leunig, 'Reshoring' jobs from China won't happen, Financial Times, October 30, 2011.
40. See David Barboza, As China's wages rise, export prices could follow, the New York Times, June 7, 2010.
41. See Kathrin Hille and Robin Kwong, Foxconn wants clients to share wages burden, Financial Times, June 7, 2010. Also see Robin Kwong, Second Foxconn wage hike marks wider change in strategy, in Robin Kwong's blog in Financial Times, June 7, 2010. David Barboza reporting on Foxconn's wage increase notes:

> In announcing the wage increase late Sunday, the company, a unit of Taiwan's Hon Hai Precision Industry Company, said that within three months the basic salaries of many of its 800,000 workers in China could reach nearly $300 a month, about double what many were earning a few weeks ago.

See David Barboza, Foxconn increases size of raise in Chinese factories, New York Times, June 6, 2010.
42. See David Barboza, As China's wages rise, export prices could follow, New York Times, June 7, 2010.
43. See Hu Jintao's report at the 17th Party Congress, V. Promoting sound and rapid development of the national economy, http://www.china.org.cn/english/congress/229611.htm#2
44. See Rahul Jacob, China wage rises brings shift in production, Financial Times, September 6, 2011.
45. See Robin Kwong, Apple supplier ordered to shut China plant on environmental concerns, and Financial Times, October 17, 2011. Also see Rahul Jacob, Patti and Waldmeir Barney Jobson, Walmart presents irresistible target, Financial Times, October 20, 2011.
46. See Simon Rabinovitch, China's labour costs soar as wages rise 22%, Financial Times, October 25, 2011.
47. On the other hand continued growth at high rates in China and the resulting growth in consumption has generated inflationary pressures and the impact of such inflation is being felt by China's trade partners in the form of higher import prices. See David Barboza, Inflation in China poses big threat to global trade, New York Times, April 17, 2011.
48. Some recent data indicates that China's export growth has slowed down, whilst the growth in China's imports is accelerating. See Simon Rabinovitch, China export growth dips as EU slows, Financial Times, November 10, 2011.
49. Continued growth at high rates in China and the resulting growth in consumption has generated inflationary pressures and the impact of such inflation is being felt by China's trade partners in the form of higher import prices. See David Barboza, Inflation in China poses big threat to global trade, New York Times, April 17, 2011.
50. It is very likely though that the workers may save some of the additional income, given the traditional needs of medicare and welfare of the family including childcare and old age requirements.
51. Some recent data indicates that China's export growth has slowed down, whilst the growth in China's imports is accelerating. See Simon Rabinovitch, China export growth dips as EU slows, Financial Times, November 10, 2011.
52. See Jamil Anderlini, Beijing looks to broaden renminbi use, Financial Times, August 17, 2010, and also see Keiko Yoshioka, Moves afoot to give renminbi greater

international play, AJW The Asahi Shimbun, August 26, 2011, at: http://ajw.asahi.com/article/asia/china/AJ201108267944

53. See The rise of renminbi, China Economic Review, March 2012, vol. 23 no. 3, pp. 32-37. Also see Kevin Brown and Robert Cookson, Singapore aims to be renminbi hub, Financial Times, April 19, 2011; and Keiko Yoshioka, Moves afoot to give renminbi greater international play, AJW The Asahi Shimbun, August 26, 2011, at: http://ajw.asahi.com/article/asia/china/AJ201108267944

54. These considerations are also raised in David Pilling, Long march to renminbi convertibility, Financial Times, August 25, 2010.

55. Carmen Ling, Hong Kong Head of global transaction services at Citi, cited in Robert Cookson, Banks back switch to renminbi trade, Financial Times, August 26, 2010.

56. The "going out" strategy refers to China's overseas development assistance, its direct foreign investment policy, and includes efforts of the larger state-owned industrial groups such as Petro China, Chinalco, and China Telecom to operate and invest overseas.

57. Remarks made by the chief economist, HSBC, cited in Jamil Anderlini, China to deploy foreign reserves, Financial Times, July 21, 2009.

58. See David Barboza, As China invests US could lose, New York Times, May 4, 2011; David Pilling, China's spending spree deserves three cheers, Financial Times, May 11, 2011; Richard McGregor, Chinese offshore investment set to take-off, Financial Times, May 4, 2011; and Daniel H. Rosen and Thilo Hanemann, An American open door? Maximising the benefits of Chinese direct foreign investment, Asia Society, May 2011.

59. See UNCTAD, Global Investment Trends Monitor no. 6, April 27, 2011.

60. Bank of China reportedly has 800 plus subsidiaries in 29 countries. See Wang Yuan Long, A geological and functional "three-step strategy" for renminbi's internationalization, in China Economist, November-December 2009, pp. 83-85.

61. See Geoff Dyer, Jamil Anderlini, and Henny Sender, China's lending hits new heights, Financial Times, January 17, 2011. Also see Geoff Dyer, David Pilling, and Henny Sender, A strategy to straddle the planet, Financial Times January 17, 2011.

62. See Stefan Wagstyl, Europe to China: please chip in, Financial Times, October 28, 2011.

63. See Jamil Anderlini, China to deploy foreign reserves, Financial Times, July 21, 2009. Also see for a specific example, Justine Lau and Geoff Dyer, CNPC boosts war chest with $30bn loan, Financial Times, September 9, 2009.

64. See UNCTAD, World Investment Report 2010 (Geneva, UNCTAD, 2010).

65. See Hu Jintao's report at the 17th Party Congress, Section V. Promoting sound and rapid development of the national economy, paragraph 7. See http://www.china.org.cn/english/congress/229611.htm#2 Renminbi had been temporarily pegged to the dollar in the middle of 2008 to help cope with the global financial crisis. This temporary pegging was ended on June 19, 2010. See China's renminbi regime, Financial Times, June 20, 2010. Also see Hu Xiaolian, A Managed floating exchange rate regime is an established policy, July 15, 2010 at: http://www.pbc.gov.cn/publish/english/956/2010/20100727144152118668062/20100727144152118668062_.html

66. See Simon Rabinovitch and Robert Cookson, China outlines plan to loosen capital controls, Financial Times, February 23, 2012.

67. See Hu Jintao's report at the 17th Party Congress, Section V. Promoting sound and rapid development of the national economy, paragraph 8. See http://www.china.org.cn/english/congress/229611.htm#2

68. The figures stated refer to the deficit in trade in goods. See U.S. Census Bureau, Trade in goods with China, at: http://www.census.gov/foreign-trade/balance/c5700.html

69. See "Renminbi trade settlement pilot scheme," in Hong Kong Monetary Authority Quarterly Bulletin, September 2009. Also see Richard McGregor, China to allow

Renminbi trade payments, Financial Times, July 2, 2009; and Michael Hudson, Washington cannot call all the shots, Financial Times, June 14, 2009.

70. See Kevin Brown and Robert Cookson, Singapore aims to be renminbi hub, Financial Times, April 19, 2011.

71. See, for example, discussion in Gerard Lyons, China is undermining the dollar by the back door, Financial Times, April 27, 2010.

72. Keiko Yoshioka, Moves afoot to give renminbi greater international play, AJW The Asahi Shimbun, August 26, 2011, at: http://ajw.asahi.com/article/asia/china/AJ201108267944

73. See David Pilling, Long march to renminbi convertibility, Financial Times, August 25, 2010.

74. See Robert Cookson, China revs up renminbi expansion, Financial Times, July 28, 2010.

75. See Kevin Brown and Robert Cookson, Singapore aims to be renminbi hub, Financial Times, April 19, 2011; and The rise of renminbi, China Economic Review, March 2012, vol, 23 no. 3, pp. 32-37.

76. See David Pilling, Long march to renminbi convertibility, Financial Times, August 25, 2010; Lex, McDonald's renminbi bonds, Financial Times, August 20, 2010; and Jamil Anderlini, Beijing looks to broaden renminbi use, Financial Times, August 17, 2010.

77. From February 2010 Hong Kong based corporations have been allowed to issue renminbi bonds. David Barboza cites cases of Caterpillar and McDonald corporations as having issued renminbi bonds. Of the Caterpillar Corporation, Barboza writes:
"Richard Lavin, a group president at Caterpillar, said his company's $150 million Hong Kong offering last November was less expensive than taking out a loan in China or raising the money in dollars and then converting those dollars into renminbi. The bonds were issued to help finance Caterpillar's equipment leasing business in China. "This was a successful issue," Mr. Lavin said. "Before, we were funding our operations by bringing in dollars and changing them to RMB.'" See David Barboza, In China, tentative steps towards global currency, New York Times, February 11, 2011.

78. See Stefan Wagstyl, Brics: missed opportunity II, Financial Times, March 29, 2012, and also see Joe Leahy and James Lamont, Brics to discuss common development bank, Financial Times, March 19, 2012.

79. Instances of substantial increases in quotas under the qualified institutional investor (QFII) schemes that allow foreign institutions to invest in China's securities markets are noted in an EIU report. See EIU Viewswire, China economy: Reform push, April 18, 2012, at: http://viewswire.eiu.com/index.asp?layout=VWArticleVW3&article_id=488969233&region_id=420000442&country_id=1800000180&refm=vwCtry&page_title=Latest analysis&fs=true&mkt_tok=3RkMMJWWfF9wsRokvaTIZKXonjHpfsX97uwlW6Wg38431UFwdcjKPmjr1YACT8B0dvycMRAVFZl5nQlRh

80. See Wang Yuan Long, A geological and functional "three-step strategy" for renminbi's internationalization, in China Economist, November-December 2009; Pam Kwan Yuk, Who's who in the yuan trading club, Financial Times, June 13, 2011; and Isabel Gorst, Kazakhstan and China agree $1bn currency swap, Financial Times, June 13, 2011.

81. See Xinhua, China Focus: Who's next to swap currency with China? February 16, 2009.

82. China replaced US as Brazil's largest trading partner in April 2009. The first cross-border renminbi trade settlement took place in November 2009. One may surmise that the operational plan may be similar to that adopted in the ASEAN+1 context. See discussion in China, Brazil seek to boost strategic partnership, People's Daily Online, November 6, 2009. Also see Jonathan Wheatley, Brazil and China eye plan to axe dollar, Financial Times, May 18, 2009.

83. Henny Sender and Joe Leahy, China offers other Brics renminbi loans, Financial Times, March 7, 2012.

84. See Takatoshi Ito, RMB as number one: When will the Chinese RMB become a regional currency? mimeo, University of Tokyo, April 10, 2011, pp. 2 and 14.

85. Xinhua News Agency, "China-ASEAN FTA to enhance China-Malaysia ties," December 12, 2009, http://news.xinhuanet.com/english/2009-12/26/content_12706177.htm

86. See Reuters, Exclusive: China to step up ASEAN yuan trade settlement, October 20, 2011, and Xinhua, Malaysian central bank unveils onshore RMB settlement service, March 21, 2012, at: http://news.xinhuanet.com/english/business/2012-03/21/c_131480848.htm

87. See Xinhua, Malaysian central bank unveils onshore RMB settlement service, March 21, 2012, at: http://news.xinhuanet.com/english/business/2012-03/21/c_131480848.htm

88. Lim Siang Chai, Malaysia's deputy finance minister's interview reported in China Daily. See Zhou Yan, China should lead over single currency, China Daily, April 28, 2011.

89. Kevin Brown, Robert Cookson and Geoff Dyer, Malaysian bond boost for renminbi, Financial Times, September 19, 2010. Also see Lim Siang Chai, Malaysia's deputy finance minister's interview reported in China Daily; see Zhou Yan, China should lead over single currency, China Daily, April 28, 2011.

90. See Yung Chul Park and Chi Young Song, RMB Internationalization: Prospects and Implications for Economic Integration in East Asia, Asian Economic Papers, Fall 2011, vol. 10, no. 3, pp. 42-72. ASEAN+3New stands for China, Hong Kong SAR, and Taiwan.

91. China's financial markets are closed to foreigners except under the Qualified Foreign Investors Program (QFII), which allows foreigners to buy equities and bonds on the Mainland. Thus far Beijing has granted quotas totaling US$21 billion to around 100 foreign investors, including the central banks of Malaysia and Hong Kong. The Korean central bank also expects to get a quota. See Song Jung-a and Robert Cookson, South Korea seeks to shift reserves to China, Financial Times, May 4, 2011.

92. See Ellen Kelleher, Renminbi outshines dollar amid investor demand, Financial Times, October 9, 2011.

93. See Fion Li and Sophie Leung, Sanusi says Nigeria plans to get yuan to 10% of reserves soon as possible, Bloomberg, September 7, 2011. Emphasis added. http://www.bloomberg.com/news/2011-09-07/sanusi-says-nigeria-plans-to-get-yuan-to-10-of-reserves-soon-as-possible.html

94. See Kevin Brown and Robert Cookson, Singapore aims to be renminbi hub, Financial Times, April 19, 2011.

95. See James Blitz, Britain and China strengthen relations, Financial Times, September 8, 2011.

96. See BEA's Taiwan offshore banking unit launches renminbi services, news release dated October 26, 2011, at: http://www.hkbea.com/FileManager/EN/Content_2396/20111026e.pdf

97. See Robin Kwong, Why can't we be an RMB hub? Financial Times, August 18, 2011.

98. See Rob Minto, Shanghai: moving up a league? Financial Times, January 30, 2012; and Reuters, Highlights - Key points from Shanghai's global yuan hub plan, January 30, 2012.

99. Wall Street institutions such as Goldman Sachs, Blackstone, Carlyle, etc., have sought to set up renminbi funds in China. See Jamil Anderlini, Wall St banks to launch renminbi funds, Financial Times, May 12, 2011, and Kathrin Hill, Renminbi fund to support overseas expansion, Financial Times, March 14, 2011.

100. See Ellen Kelleher, Renminbi outshines dollar amid investor demand, Financial Times, October 9, 2011.

101. See for example discussion in Michael Pettis, Do not overreact to China's currency delays, Financial Times, October 13, 2010.

102. See Alan Beattie, Joshua Chaffin, and Kevin Brown, Wen warns against renminbi pressure, Financial Times, October 6, 2010. http://www.ft.com/intl/cms/s/0/f92d794e-d16d-11df-96d1-00144feabdc0.html -axzz1b1Aqi7uq

103. For a discussion on aspects of the currency issue see Jean-Marc F. Blanchard, "China's Grand Strategy and Money Muscle: The Potentialities and Pratfalls of China's Sovereign Wealth Fund and Renminbi Policies," Chinese Journal of International Politics, vol. 4, no. 1 (Spring 2011), pp. 31-53.

104. Edward Steinfeld argues that China used its WTO accession agreement as a fait accompli to push through a domestic policy agenda placing the responsibility for this on "outsiders or 'objective' market pressures." See Edward Steinfeld, The capitalist embrace, in Andrew MacIntyre, T. J. Pempel, and John Ravenhill, eds., Crisis as catalyst, pp.192-193, (Ithaca: Cornell University Press, 2008). Also see Andrew MacIntyre, T. J. Pempel, and John Ravenhill, East Asia in the wake of the financial crisis in Andrew MacIntyre, T. J. Pempel, and John Ravenhill, eds., Crisis as catalyst, (Ithaca: Cornell University Press, 2008), and Bo Qu, Dynamic engagement: China's preference to the international monetary cooperation, paper presented at the Second GLF Colloquium, May 3, 2010, Woodrow Wilson School, Princeton University.

105. Increase in domestic consumption is one important objective of China's 12th Five Year Plan 2011-2015, finalized in March 2011. See Nicholas Stern, The prize, perils and price of China's plan, Financial Times, April 28, 2011. The goal, a freely convertible renminbi was announced by the 17th National Congress of the CPC in October 2007.

106. See discussion in Geoff Dyer and Edward Luce, Renminbi dispute looks set to haunt Sino-US economic talks, Financial Times, September 3, 2010.

107. See discussion in previous chapter.

108. The addition of renminbi denominated bonds to Malaysia's official reserves mentioned earlier may be recalled.

109. See Paola Subacchi, 'One currency, two systems': China's renminbi strategy, Chatham House briefing paper, October 2010, pp. 6-7.

110. Analysts from various foreign banks are cited in drawing this conclusion. Those mentioned voicing this opinion include Frances Cheung of Credit Agricole, Donna Kwok of HSBC, Wang Tao of UBS. See Jamil Anderlini, Beijing looks to broaden renminbi use, Financial Times, August 17, 2010, and Robert Cookson, China revs up renminbi expansion, Financial Times, July 28, 2010.

111. See Robert Cookson, Banks back switch to renminbi trade, Financial Times, August 26, 2010.

112. See Dong He and Robert N. McCauley, Offshore markets for domestic currency: Monetary and financial stability issues, HKMA working paper 2010.

113. See Jack Farchy, LME eyes renminbi move for metals, Financial Times, April 16, 2012, and Leslie Hook, Rmb internationalisation: first steel then the world, Financial Times, July 8, 2011.

114. Recently, a renminbi index for iron ore and steel prices has been launched. See David Pilling, China's spending spree deserves three cheers, Financial Times May 11, 2011.

115. The verse reads as follows:

> A tree that can fill the span of a man's arms
> Grows from a downy tip;
> A terrace nine stories high
> Rises from a few hodfuls of earth;
> A journey of a thousand miles
> Starts from beneath one's feet

From Lao Tzu, Tao Te Ching, LXIV, p. 71, translation by D. C. Lau (London: Penguin, 1963).

FIVE

East Asian perspectives on economic policies

I: INTRODUCTION

The previous chapters discussed the Asian financial crisis, the emergence of networked economic space in East Asia, the trade pacts with China increasingly as a hub, and the global financial crisis and China's response to that crisis. The issue of policy differences between East Asian economies and the major advanced economies and the multilateral financial institutions surfaced frequently. These policy differences, which reflect the facts of East Asia's own development experience, its experience of coping with the Asian financial crisis and the 2008 global financial crisis, and working with a region-wide production and trading system, are explored in this chapter. These differences lie chiefly in three areas: the respective roles of the state and the market in economic management, differences over the approach to a production and trading system that became evident in the mushrooming of trade agreements in East Asia and are now being highlighted in the Trans-Pacific Partnership dialogue, and further problems with the international currency system, which were raised first by Japan in the 1980s, then surfaced again in course of the Asian financial crisis in 1997 only to resurface chiefly vis-à-vis China with the global financial crisis of 2008.

In all cases the differences relate to the existing systems for global economic management, the origins of which date back to the arrangements following the end of the Second World War and were laid down chiefly by a United States that was the victor and accounted for 50 percent of the world's output at the time. These arrangements were modified over the years with American initiative, drive and support. As East Asian economies emerged these rules seemed discordant given the reality of their own development experience and of their interaction in the region as well as with the larger world economy, and were found wanting. East Asians seemed to challenge these rules in some cases and resist them in other instances.

The chapter is organized as follows. The next section considers the differences on development policy between the East Asians and the multilateral financial institutions, which are managed chiefly by the advanced economies, beginning with the East Asian Miracle study at the World Bank that was published in 1993 and discusses how the issues evolved in course of the Asian financial crisis in 1997. The global financial crisis of 2008 brought into focus the dollar-based international currency system. The third section explains how East Asia views this system, and discusses the East Asian proposals for its reform.

II: THE ROLE OF THE STATE IN ECONOMIC POLICY

A global shift in policies

Until late 1970s the developing countries had been pursuing such economic policies as each considered appropriate to its circumstances. As a result, a policy mix that combined an active state and reliance on market forces to varying degrees determined outcomes obtained in developing economies. In the aftermath of the second oil shock in 1979, the developed market economies led by the United States and the Washington-based multilateral economic and financial institutions began advising a uniform set of policies of universal applicability, which differed from the earlier practices, and they proceeded to do so with some firmness. In particular these practices sought to rule out an active role for the state in the economy and at the same time also sought to considerably enlarge the freedoms for private enterprise across national borders.

The policies promoted were founded on a laissez faire approach that held axiomatically that the free working of the markets is the only approach to successful development and that any "interference" by the state in the working of the market only impedes and distorts development. The critics though saw these policies as "based on a simplistic model of the market economy" in which "there is no need for government—that is free unfettered markets work perfectly," and the policies were often referred to as "neoliberal," being based on "market fundamentalism."[1] This new formulation was popularly described as the Washington Consensus, a term attributed to John Williamson. The word "Consensus" referred to a commonality in the thinking on policies between the IMF, the World Bank and the US Treasury, the three being Washington-based institutions, whereby the use of the word "Washington." More specifically these prescribed policies included market determined interest rates and exchange rates, privatization and deregulation, and liberalization of international trade and of inward foreign direct investment.[2] The provision of economic and financial assistance to the developing economies by the World Bank and the IMF, and in time by others as well, was made conditional on the pursuit of such policies, and the Washington Consensus policy prescriptions became deeply entrenched in the conditionalities that the two Bretton Woods institutions imposed on their developing country clients as the only viable and non-negotiable course, certainly from the early 1980s if not earlier. The Washington Consensus gained much traction with the fall of the Berlin wall and from the subsequent coming apart of the Soviet Union. The end of socialism increased its claim to legitimacy, notwithstanding the shock therapy debacle that followed its application in Russia as well as its rather ambiguous record in Latin America and elsewhere over the years.[3] The coming of the WTO in 1994 further strengthened the validity of these policies. The imposition of such policies had to be accepted in situations where finance was sought from the multilateral financial institutions or from developed market economies or, once the WTO had been established, because of the membership of WTO.

The East Asian perspective

The Washington Consensus firmly ruled out the much trodden traditional path to industrialization with state support and with protectionist measures in place that had historically been followed by today's advanced economies. And by thus raising the bar for the late industrializers among the developing countries, it presented a problem for the East Asian economies that relied on an active state for economic management in their process of industrialization. Thus East Asia found it difficult to accept as universally valid a set of propositions such as the Washington Consensus that so obviously belied its own industrial development experience, and also ran counter to the industrial development phase of today's advanced economies, which the East Asians saw as a clearly state directed effort and not an outcome of laissez faire policies.[4]

Historically, economies that were industrializing had indulged in state interventions in market processes on a grand scale. They had been protective of their nascent or infant industry from foreign competition, because the newly emerging industry could not have developed in the face of foreign competition and in the absence of protection. The state therefore afforded it such protection through some mix of restrictions on competing imports, including tariffs, and some financial support. Once a country succeeded in acquiring a strong and competitive industrial base, it would then make sense to do away with protection and to seek free and unrestricted trade in relation to the industry in which the country was strong and competitive: a policy reversal would follow thereafter to enable the competitive industry to exploit world markets.

Thus Robert Walpole's reforms of 1721, close in spirit to the East Asian policies, made Britain the first country to use industrial policies, and thus protect its domestic woolen textiles industry at the time by stemming the competing imports of woolen cloth from Holland. Similarly Alexander Hamilton of the United States was perhaps one of the trailblazers of organized and systematic protection and theorized on the subject, leading the United States into a situation of protection that lasted until the end of World War II. German industry in its initial decades sold its products labeled for a good part as "Made in England" until such time as its industry became competitive enough to be recognized in its own right. Such protectionist policies were also followed among the early industrializing countries of East Asia in the postwar period, and by the newly independent developing countries of the post Second World War world that sought to industrialize in the 1960s and 1970s.

In this perspective East Asia did not see its industrialization as a unique experience in historical terms but rather saw itself as drawing on the historical pattern of state-led economic development as the normal practice for all successful industrialization and development. Japan's postwar state-led economic development, and by implication that which followed in much of East Asia, too, could only be normal.[5] Japan and other East Asians therefore claimed that state-led economic development was the normal practice for all successful late industrializers. In this respect it was the developed economies that in the process of exalting the Washington Consensus as the only course disowned their historical experience relating to their industrialization and development.

Having industrialized with the benefit of a state organized effort and with protection against foreign competition in place, Japan saw its industrialization phase in the 1950s and 1960s as no different from the earlier industrialization of Western Europe and North America. The experience of Korea and Taiwan also supported the proposition that the generalities of the Washington Consensus based approach were quite inappropriate for industrialization and development, and that state-led industrialization and economic development was the norm established over long experience. In an effort to incorporate the East Asia region in a larger scheme of foreign direct investment, trade and industrialization, Japan generalized its own development experience in a model of state supported industrialization across regional economies at different stages of development. This was described as the flying geese model, the flight of geese providing the imagery for countries developing together albeit at different levels of industrialization in time, and the concepts were applied to Southeast and East Asia.[6] In this manner a generalization of Japan's own development experience, combined with the dynamic comparative advantage of different regional economies to the benefit of all, which did not draw on laissez faire thought, provided the basis for an early formal conceptualization of a regional approach to development policy for East Asia.

China's development, following Japan and Korea in time, viewed the situation as one of each country forging and pursuing a development path that best served its interests and was best suited to its endowments and circumstances, thus modifying the Japanese flying geese concept that seemed to imply an East Asian model of coordinated industrialization in which economies industrialized in sequence, including a sequencing between different industries within an economy. In China's perspective an economy's experience reflected its history, culture and resources, and the opportunities that the world economy offered at the time of industrialization.[7] Development policies could thus be seen as economy and time specific. The seriousness attached to this issue in East Asia is also reflected in the fact that on the eve of his 2011 visit to the United States, President Hu Jintao formally announced that United States and China should "respect each other's choice of development path."[8] Chinese Premier Wen Jiabao amplified this point by saying that "China never sees its development as a model," that all countries can have their own development paths which are suitable for their own national conditions, and "we respect the choice of their people."[9] East Asia's industrialization seemed to comprise a set of experiences that varied in terms of the choice and phasing of the specific protectionist measures pursued and the manner and the degree of support extended by the state, and this perspective could not be more different from the Washington Consensus one size fits all recipe.

The policy differences in play

Japan requested the World Bank in the early 1990s to examine the nature of East Asian industrialization and development experience.[10] In making its case and that for East Asian experience, Japan was in fact challenging the credibility of the Washington Consensus, the new orthodoxy that had been put in place chiefly by the United States. The outcome of the project was the World Bank's East Asian Miracle study in 1993.[11] The findings of the study showed that a proactive role of state was indeed fundamental in East Asia's successful economic and social development. The East Asian experience thus called into question the neoclassical paradigm for development but, according to Joseph Stiglitz who as World Bank's chief economist supervised the research and publication, it was also the case that in the published study this finding was toned down at the insistence of the World Bank hierarchy so as to sustain the official World Bank ideology of market friendly policies, that is, the Washington Consensus.[12]

These differences on the role of the state in the economy came to a head when the East Asian economies affected by the Asian financial crisis of 1997 sought financial assistance and support from the multilateral institutions and in particular the IMF. As discussed in an earlier chapter, the IMF made this assistance conditional upon a set of prescribed policy measures that conformed to the Washington Consensus model. In East Asian perception these IMF prescribed conditionalities could only make matters worse. Indeed some in East Asia saw the crisis as being caused precisely by the pursuit of laissez faire policies in the financial sector. Apart from the fact that the IMF policy conditionalities ran quite counter to the East Asia's own policy experience, the record of similar IMF sponsored structural adjustment programs in Latin America and elsewhere had been widely seen as counterproductive.[13] This rather mixed record as well as East Asia's own experience were important elements in questioning the narrative of the Washington Consensus. East Asians, contrary to the IMF prescription, were of the view that a proactive state implementing capital controls and expansionary policies was necessary in order to recover from the crisis.

The IMF in a rather nuanced assessment saw the East Asian development policies as an example of "crony capitalism," thus "normatively, if not empirically, delegitimating the Asian model while normatively, if not empirically, privileging the market-based processes and outcomes."[14] The East Asians on the other hand saw the crisis as the outcome of speculative forces taking advantage of a situation where capital flows had been liberalized in pursuance of the laissez faire thinking. This latter argument gained strength from the fact that the one country that had not liberalized its capital account, that is, China, did not suffer the crisis. The argument also gained strength from the fact that the first country from amongst the affected ones to impose controls on its capital account, that is, Malaysia, suffered less than others.

Japan was East Asia's economic hub and the world's second largest economy at the time of the Asian financial crisis, and its concern about the evident adverse impact of this crisis on the region caused it to look for solutions. Initially, but only very briefly, Japan seemed on board with the IMF supported assistance to Thailand and the implied set of policy conditionalities, and the IMF's Thailand operation was finally agreed upon on August 11, 1997.

Following on these discussions, Japan sprung a surprise on the United States as well as the others and proposed the creation of an Asia only Asian Monetary Fund at the September 1997 annual meetings of the World Bank and the IMF, that is, within a month of the Thailand IMF agreement to which Japan was a party. But it would seem that Japan, steeped in the lessons of the East Asian Miracle, had serious reservations about the appropriateness of IMF diagnosis of the causes of the crisis and the relevance of its policy conditionality to revive the afflicted economies.

Even as the IMF deliberations on Thailand were underway, Japan's vice minister, Mr. Sakakibara, was secretly canvassing support in Southeast Asia to set up a source for financial assistance, an Asian Monetary Fund.[15] In this manner the IMF funding and the associated policy conditionalities could be avoided. Japan now proposed to provide the finances to this Asian Monetary Fund, which in its turn would be expected to assist with the relief and recovery of the crisis afflicted East Asian economies, but expectedly with policies that were closer to the Asian development experience and the region's diagnosis of the crisis. Such an institution would by definition exclude the United States. The reason for exclusion was inherent in the reasons for the proposal: the Asian Monetary Fund was premised on a particular diagnosis of the crisis and the validity of policies that the United States, a believer in the contrarian Washington Consensus, was not prepared to accept. But the United States did not wish to be left out from what it saw as a possibly new economic bloc centered on Japan.[16] An Asian Monetary Fund would also be a competitor for the IMF, and the latter was an institution that the United States dominated by virtue of its exceptional voting power. Andrew Sheng records that Larry Summers, then deputy secretary at the US Treasury, on hearing the news made a midnight call to Mr. Sakakibara to protest angrily.[17] In the event the Asian Monetary Fund project faltered chiefly because Japan found itself unable to carry the idea in the face of strong American opposition.

Express exclusion of the United States by Japan in an East Asian organization such as the proposed Asian Monetary Fund and the earlier Japan funded East Asian Miracle study arguably reflects the seriousness with which Japan considers this economic policy aspect. In the case of Japan, it is an important fact that the Asian Monetary Fund is the only attempt by Japan to exclude the US from a regional or multilateral organization, and may be seen as reflective of the importance to Japan of its development experience and its geography. Yong Wook Lee is of the view that this factor seems to have arguably trumped Japan's "rational" interests, that is, the prospect of foreseeable economic gains, that could perhaps be best served by discarding its own mercantilist past, much as other advanced economies such as France, Germany, and the United States had done. Indeed, business interests from export sectors expressed doubts about the wisdom of setting up an Asian Monetary Fund.[18]

Plausible as it sounds Yong Wook Lee's thesis rests on an important supposition, that Japan wished to assert "leadership" in East Asia vis-à-vis the United States. If it were so then it was surely strategically important to have the confidence of China and Korea among other East Asian economies in making such a move. It is also difficult to square Japan's desire to assert itself vis-à-vis the United States with the fact that Japan has looked to the United States for the whole of the postwar period for its security, and that continues to be the case today.

The 2008 global financial crisis and the Washington Consensus

Faced with a financial crisis on an unprecedented scale in 2008, the state in the transatlantic economies of North America and Western Europe intervened substantively with a certain firmness, making extensive use of its political and financial resources to salvage the private financial sector. In the process the state shifted the burden of crisis from the private sector financial institutions to the public sector, took over the ownership of the assets of a number of private financial sector institutions and also directed the policies of some of these institutions for a time. All these actions, quite contrary to the policies enforced by the IMF with full support of the United States during the Asian financial crisis in the afflicted East Asian economies, were carried out under the rubric of *too big to fail*, and, strangely, the sub-text was that the neoliberal laissez faire doctrine has been salvaged and therefore the Washington Consensus remains intact even though the actions taken in course of the 2008 crisis and thereafter were anathema to that very doctrine.[19] Thus intervention by the state in the economy pursued during the 2008 crisis did not lead to the expected shift in the basic neoliberal ideology of self-correcting free markets at the policy level in those economies or at the multilateral institutions, and that ideology continues to be applied *a fortiori* to the developing economies by these institutions.[20] In this manner the underlying assumptions of the globalized market economy continue to underpin the discussions at the G-7/8 and at the G-20, even though a number of developing countries are a part of the latter grouping.[21]

Nonetheless, notwithstanding the rhetoric, the policies adopted by the transatlantic economies to survive the global financial crisis could be seen as validating East Asia's view of the appropriate policy stance in course of the Asian financial crisis. In practice the transatlantic economies responded to the global financial crisis in a non-doctrinaire manner, the response comprising state-led interventions in the economy, very much consistent with the approach that had been argued by the East Asians in course of the Asian financial crisis but was much derided and ridiculed at the time. Déjà vu came for East Asia with the global financial crisis of 2008.

The suffering and the policy response between the two crises provided a study in contrast. East Asia suffered much on account of the imposition of the Washington Consensus. Interest rates spiked up sharply and this in itself was enough to send most businesses into the bankruptcy courts, at one point the numbers rising to hundreds per week. Countries devalued rather steeply. Hence in those cases where loans had been contracted in say dollars, survival was truly impossible. Some afflicted countries undertook massive cuts in budget deficits that along with a slack in private sector demand led to economic contraction. The only business that thrived was of those helping with bankruptcy. By contrast in the 2008 global financial crisis, budget deficits reached 12 to 15 percent per annum in United States, United Kingdom and Ireland, to counter the fall in private sector demand. Interest rates hovered around zero, and beyond that was the various rounds of "quantitative easing." Unlike the Asian financial crisis, where a large number of local banks in East Asian economies had failed because the IMF did not permit a bailout by the government or other state support, in the 2008 crisis the financial institutions were generally bailed out by the state through injection of public funds on a large scale and in some cases also nationalized. At the end of the year, the management of these banks awarded substantial bonuses to themselves!

In particular the approach to coping with the two crises (the Asian one in 1997 and the global one in 2008) by the multilateral financial institutions showed the use of remarkably contradictory measures between the two events, and one of the two different sets of policies had to be mistaken.

The consequences of applying the Washington Consensus in East Asia

The East Asians did not believe that the policies imposed by the multilateral institutions with United States support during the Asian financial crisis helped in overcoming the crisis, and felt that the imposition of IMF policy conditionalities had caused much damage instead. As noted earlier, what followed the Asian financial crisis was an effort to avoid any future possibility of another recourse to the IMF.

The shared experience of adversity resulting from the Asian financial crisis combined with the shared resentment of the US-led policy response to the crisis: "Most Asians . . . [felt] . . . that they were both let down and put down by the West."[22] These feelings lent some impetus to the concept of regional cooperation in East Asia. The Thai deputy prime minister at the time said that one could not "rely on the World Bank or the IMF but we must rely on regional cooperation." The South Korean president voiced the opinion as to why Asia "alone among the 'three poles' of the global economy, not have its own grouping." The Japanese finance minister visualized the "need to form some type of regional cooperation of our own."[23] The emergence of an economically successful Asia and the policies pursued to achieve that and safeguard it through regional cooperation seemed to offer a promising prospect.

Unless a consensus obtains on the basics, there cannot be fruitful organizational forms that include parties with contrary, non-negotiable positions that may talk past each other. Inclusion of the United States in Asian organizations would arguably make it difficult for such organizations to pursue policies from an East Asian perspective or policies that did not conform to the neoliberal view. Thus Japan's decision to put forth the Asian Monetary Fund proposal *sans* the United States, even though unsuccessful, advanced the concept of new Asian regionalism that excludes by an important step.[24] With the Asian Monetary Fund proposal, East Asia indicated a shift to a new reality in its understanding of regional cooperation where its economic policy perceptions and therefore its economic interests differed clearly from those of the United States. The practice of exclusion demarcates the "new" from "old" Asian regionalism, of which the United States was a part (for example, APEC), and a perception of the region having moved on to a higher stage of regionalism exists in post Asian financial crisis Asia. This perception gains strength from the post crisis dialogue among the East Asian economies.

The ASEAN+3 meeting in 1997 was the first step towards the post crisis exclusionary practice. This meeting may indeed have been the seed event for the regional economic and financial cooperation that seems to be emerging gradually, and, as noted earlier, has been visibly successful in finance. The Tokyo meeting between Japan and the ten ASEAN countries in December 2003, and the heads of government meeting in Malaysia of ASEAN+3 in December 2005 to consider how to implement the concept of an Asian community, without bringing in Asia-Pacific into the discourse, followed.[25] The ASEAN+3 process became institutionalized with the aim of financial cooperation in the region to avert any recourse to the IMF again serving as a galvanizing factor. The Chiang Mai Initiative can plausibly be seen as the pursuit of the Asian Monetary Fund concept under a different organizational form, or the pursuit of that concept by other means. As noted earlier, the Chiang Mai Initiative in facilitating unconditional short-term liquidity support for a member economy offers what IMF does not.

Thus we see that the Asian financial crisis led East Asia to question the market friendly laissez faire paradigm, also known as the Washington Consensus. East Asia though was unable to convince the United States, the IMF and the World Bank of its point of view at the time and the region suffered the socio-economic consequences of having to implement their advice. The result was East Asia moving to develop regional mechanisms for economic and financial cooperation. As if to emphasize its basis in policy differences, this "new" Asian regionalism was summed up by some in the region as "bringing the state back in, keeping the (United) States out."[26]

III: GLOBAL IMBALANCES AND THE INTERNATIONAL CURRENCY SYSTEM

Nature of the problem

The global financial crisis of 2008 served to add a new urgency to the resolution of "global imbalances," a reference to relative external current account positions of different countries, highlighting in particular the differences between United States and China on the causes as well as the remedies. At the time of the 2008 global financial crisis and also thereafter, it was Germany and the East Asian economies, China and Japan by far the most prominent among the latter by absolute size, which were running trade surpluses (and thereby external current account surpluses) of note. The counterpart deficits obtained chiefly in the United States, United Kingdom, and some other European economies. This phenomenon that some countries were persistently in surplus on the external current account whilst some others were persistently in deficit was not entirely novel.[27] The manner of financing the deficits was also a part of the "global imbalances" discussion. Though the United States had been running external current account deficits for many years and the problem was evidently multilateral, the phenomenon in context of China dates only from 2004, the post 2008 global financial crisis discussion of the issue proceeded for most part in a bilateral context between the United States and China. As mentioned in chapter 4 above, it was not for the first time that the United States saw this as an issue in misaligned exchange rates. China in this instance though perceived the problem as one relating to the architecture and the working of the international monetary system, as the "other" party had invariably done in times past.[28]

An East Asian assessment of the international currency system

In the East Asian context global imbalances first surfaced as a prominent policy issue in the 1980s as Japan's trade surpluses grew, and these expanding surpluses found recognizable correspondence in America's growing debt to Japan. At the time the angst amongst the American liberal establishment was palpable. The caption of an article by Peter G Peterson read: "America has let its infrastructure crumble, its foreign markets decline, its productivity dwindle, its savings evaporate and its budget and borrowings burgeon. And now the day of reckoning is at hand."[29] With some irony, Fred Bergsten at the time summed up the matter as follows: "We finally understand the true meaning of supply side economics. Foreigners supply most of the goods and all of the money."[30] In the event "the day of reckoning" never came, and the answer was an unwilling Japan being "guided" to undertake a revaluation of the yen in a floating rate regime, and, through this mechanism, also accept an implied write-off in yen terms of the American dollar liabilities owed to Japan. In this manner, and notwithstanding Japanese arguments to the contrary, the burden of adjustment was successfully shifted to Japan. The American criticism of Japanese trade surpluses abated thereafter, even though the Japanese economy continued to record surpluses, and America's deficits, notwithstanding the stronger yen. Indeed; it now seemed to be China's turn to "supply most of the goods and all of the money."

For the East Asians the Asian financial crisis had been a learning experience, and a follow up measure agreed upon in one of the ASEAN+3 meetings was the setting up of a monitoring mechanism for watching critical macroeconomic indicators. This proposed monitoring mechanism was to serve as a part of an early warning mechanism to cope with the likelihood of financial crises in the future.[31] In this context America's deteriorating macroeconomic indicators and their impact on the dollar based international currency system were seen as a source of concern in East Asia well ahead of the global financial crisis of 2008; as early as 2003 Li Ruogu had called upon the IMF to tighten its surveillance of macroeconomic policies of "major industrial countries": the East Asians seemed to be a step ahead of the multilateral institutions. As the 2008 global financial crisis set in, without any forewarnings from the multilateral financial institutions and with these institutions failing to offer any credible solution in the face of the crisis, the international monetary system stood exposed. In Li Ruogu's words the 2008 global financial crisis "let us see how unreasonable the current international monetary system is."[32]

As China's trade surpluses gained in prominence from 2005, the United States sought a realignment of currencies, much as it had done in the case of Japan, and shortly after the onset of the 2008 global financial crisis it charged China with "currency manipulation" in a voice that was louder than ever before. In the new "unipolar world," the angst and introspection of 1987 were missing on the part of the Americans: even though "the foreigners" continued to "supply most of the goods and all of the money," Bergsten now saw the problem with China's currency policy instead.[33] Whilst the renminbi appreciated against the dollar, the American bilateral surplus did not decline and the rhetoric of currency manipulation continued, albeit with a varying tone and volume dependent upon the different exigencies at any given moment in a complex China-United States relationship.[34]

Writing in *China Daily* amid of the 2008 financial crisis, Zhou Xiaochuan (the current governor, People's Bank of China) offered his "personal view" of the problems that had arisen on account of the international currency system, and about the linkage between financial crises and the international currency system.[35] The argument was broadly as follows. The existing system used the dollar, a national currency, in international transactions, and the problem with the use of a national currency as an international currency is that "the issuing countries of reserve currencies cannot maintain the value of the reserve currencies while providing liquidity to the world."[36] Therefore the issuing country "may either fail to adequately meet the demand of a growing global economy for liquidity as . . . (it tries) . . . to ease inflation pressures at home, or create excess liquidity in the global markets by overly stimulating domestic demand." The dollar-based international currency system had an inherent tendency to cause imbalances, and it lacked a credible adjustment mechanism to resolve such imbalances.[37]

Lack of an effective international check on the issue of dollars had resulted in excess liquidity. In a reference to various "bubbles," Zhou Xiaochuan argued that this excess liquidity had in turn "led to a situation where boom-bust cycles in asset prices have become the norm." Even though the global financial "crisis may not necessarily be an intended result of the issuing authorities, it is an inevitable outcome of the institutional flaws" noted the article, and the "frequency and increasing intensity of financial crises following the collapse of the Bretton Woods system suggests the costs of such a system to the world may have exceeded its benefits." The article drew attention to the fact that in any event the "acceptance of credit-based national currencies as major international reserve currencies, as is the case in the current system, is a rare special case in history."[38]

Zhou Xiaochuan's analysis had much in common with the earlier analyses of the working of the dollar based international currency system. The tendency for the international currency system to encourage consumption in the United States and avoid any correction of the resulting deficits had been noted early, from 1960s onwards, and the critiques of Nicholas Kaldor, both a leading Cambridge academic and a one time economic advisor to the United Kingdom government, and Jacques Rueff, a leading French economist of his time and President Charles de Gaulle's economic advisor, had anticipated much of what Zhou Xiaochuan was now saying. Nicholas Kaldor, writing in the midst of the Vietnam War, noted the potential for an increasing drift towards debt-based consumption on the part of the United States:

> So long as countries preferred the benefits of fast growth and increasing competitiveness to the cost of part-financing the United States deficit (or what comes to the same thing, preferred selling more goods even if they received nothing more than bits of paper in return), and so long as a reasonable level of prosperity in the United States (in terms of employment levels and increases in real income) could be made consistent with the increasing uncompetitiveness of United States goods in relation to European or Japanese goods, there was no reason why any major participant should wish to disturb these arrangements . . .
>
> . . . [But] as the products of American industry are increasingly displaced by others, both in American and foreign markets, maintaining prosperity requires ever-rising budgetary and balance of payments deficits, which makes it steadily less attractive as a method of economic management.
>
> If continued long enough it would involve transforming a nation of creative producers into a community of rentiers increasingly living on others, seeking gratification in ever more useless consumption, with all the debilitating effects of the bread and circuses of Imperial Rome.[39]

Jacques Rueff for his part had perceived the political difficulty in adjustment on the part of the United States to its growing external deficit. Rueff had argued that the United States would not be in a position to accept the burden of adjustment raised by its external current account deficits that were a consequence of the dollar based international currency system:

> And they (the United States) have had for five years an enormous deficit in their balance of payments. If they have not done by credit policy what the gold standard would have done by automatically restricting purchasing power, it is proof that it is not possible. And why is it not possible? I cannot imagine any parliamentary country with a democratic regime in which you could do such a difficult thing.[40]

What Rueff was saying was that it was not politically feasible for an elected American government to undertake the required reduction in consumption and other expenditure that any adjustment directed at eradicating the deficit would entail.

The East Asian perspective was therefore not unique or unprecedented, but crucially it differed from that of the United States. A nation's monetary policies would naturally address its own national objectives but these monetary policies would also impact globally if its currency were to be used internationally. Thus the use of the dollar as international currency subjected the world to the vicissitudes of American global objectives and domestic politics. The American proclivity to spend more than its income had gone unchecked, because to check it was a course difficult to advocate for politicians seeking the popular vote. Faced with a deficit the United States, unlike other countries, could easily borrow abroad in its own currency. That indeed was what had happened and was continuing.[41] Hence America had been running deficits and creating counterpart surpluses. The most competitive export economies, which tended to be East Asian, naturally had the largest of these surpluses.

In East Asian perception the fundamental problem was therefore not about an "artificially low" renminbi or currency manipulation: it was the fact of the existing international currency arrangements centered on the dollar, a national currency, which was leading to creation of excess liquidity and it was these excessive quantities of dollars that were contributing to the occurrence of financial crises and global imbalances. Thus East Asia arguably saw the global imbalances and the global financial crisis as a result of the use of a national currency as an international currency. Much like Kaldor and Rueff, the East Asians seemed to be saying that the time had come to review the balance of advantage from continuing with such a crisis prone system.

The East Asians also voiced a separate and particular worry about the security and safety of their dollar denominated assets, that is to say their foreign exchange reserves, and the specific threat here could be visualized as the possibility of the United States inflating or devaluing its way out of its debt; China's prime minister Wen Jiabao publicly aired his reservations on this point.[42] Such a development would severely affect the real value of East Asia's dollar based reserves. The discussion suggested that East Asians were raising a demand for an alternative and more stable reserve asset.

Inherent tendency of the international currency system to create "imbalances"

More generally, the perception that the "global imbalances" may be "built in" to the existing international currency system, which centers on the United States dollar as the world's currency, is widely shared.[43] And three structural features of the dollar based international currency system are of relevance. Firstly, it creates a universal need for the dollar in its role as the world's currency, and the United States has to meet that demand; secondly, the dollar balances held abroad need to be invested, and that is possible only in United States; and thirdly, the United States wishes to pursue a "strong dollar" policy. These three features do not necessarily work out in sync. They are considered below in turn.

Taking up first the use of the dollar as the world currency, it is evident that there would necessarily be a demand for dollars, from individuals to nations. Apart from general transactional needs, countries feel they need to prepare for the eventuality of a financial crisis, for the possibility of speculative attacks on their currencies, and for the possibility of the reversal of capital flows. For these reasons countries need to build up reserves as large as their circumstances permit, so that they may cope better with difficulties as they arise.

There are not many ways of building up reserves. Dollars are earned via exports, and export earnings help to augment reserves. Hence an export-oriented growth policy for economies other than the United States is built in to the international currency system. A competitive exchange rate is a sine qua non for countries seeking to earn export surpluses.

The only sources for the supply of dollars though are United States government and the banking system. The United States, by providing the world with its currency, is effectively "borrowing" those sums free of cost and need never repay the "loan," but a counterpart deficit is created.[44] It is a widely held perception that America has indulged itself in such "borrowing" in a measure more than could be considered prudent.[45]

The dollar foreign exchange reserves of other countries, and the overseas dollar balances of corporations and individuals, would need to be "returned" to the United States to be reinvested there in dollar assets such as securities and other earning assets. For this reason there would be continuous capital inflows of dollars into the United States to enable purchases of American financial assets. In this manner the dollars held outside the United States would find their way back to American banks, and such capital inflows into the American banking and financial system would *ceteris paribus* imply corresponding credit creation in the American economy. Hence the availability of credit in the United States would necessarily increase, causing downward pressure on the interest rates, a rising rate of inflation, and also creating a glut of credit in the process. Increased and ready availability of relatively cheap credit provides an impulse to borrow and spend on the part of the American consumer. The banks would naturally encourage the consumer to borrow as the banks stand to gain from the transaction, (and given the record of government-bank relations in past crises) being reasonably confident of a bailout by the government in case of difficulty. Such credit expansion would be expected to impact adversely on America's domestic savings and the external current account deficit. It follows that the United States would be continually subject to developments that impact negatively on its internal and external current account balances, building up to imbalances.

Thirdly, to maintain the status of the dollar as the world's currency requires a "strong" dollar, and the United States has often publicly proclaimed one.[46] A dollar which is "strong" vis-à-vis the world's remaining currencies does not make for a competitive United States in a globalized world economy though. This inherent lack of competitiveness factor, along with the credit creation in America referred to earlier, makes a strategy of production for exports directed at the United States market the logical choice for other countries, and more so for a developing country that has a disciplined labor force willing to work at a low wage. The system thus has a tendency to create trade deficits in United States and counterpart trade surpluses elsewhere, and, indeed such a peculiarity would extend to any arrangement in which a national currency worked as an international currency.

Thus we note that there are structural elements inherent in the architecture of the dollar based international currency system, and these structural elements may work to cause a continuity of deficits on the United States external current account.

Some East Asian proposals for reform

To be able to deal better with the issues raised, the Zhou Xiaochuan article puts forth a set of proposals on how to make the international currency system less prone to imbalances. Perhaps at the heart of Zhou Xiaochuan's arguments is the proposal to reduce the international currency role of the dollar in the short term with a view to gradually shifting over the longer term to an international currency instead. Immediate measures proposed to gradually reduce the international role of the dollar comprise extending the use of SDRs so that the SDR may substitute for the dollar in foreign exchange reserves and may also be used in the pricing of commodities. For the longer term the suggestion is to create global currency to replace the dollar, which currently improvises as one. The creation of a multilateral agency to manage such a global currency is also proposed. It is then suggested that the SDR may be developed into this proposed global currency. The specifics of Zhou Xiaochuan's proposals are set out below.

Thus for the short-term, the article proposes that "special consideration should be given to giving the SDR a greater role" and thus to potentially "lay a foundation for increasing SDR allocation to gradually replace existing reserve currencies with the SDR."[47] Such a move would diversify the range of instruments available for international transactions and reserves, and hence moderate the existing role of the dollar, *qua* an international currency.

For the long-term, Zhou Xiaochuan's article proposes a super sovereign reserve currency, "a bold initiative that requires extraordinary political vision and courage," with a stable anchor on the lines of Keynes's bancor.[48] The article works out a three-fold criterion to be met by such an international reserve currency. Firstly, this international reserve currency should be anchored to a stable benchmark and issued according to a clear set of rules in order to ensure orderly supply. Secondly, its supply should be flexible enough to allow timely adjustment according to the changing demand. Third, such adjustments should be disconnected from economic conditions and sovereign interests of any single country. Such an international reserve currency "not only eliminates the inherent risks of credit-based sovereign currency, but also makes it possible to manage global liquidity." A world monetary authority is also proposed, to manage the international reserve currency, and this "global institution could be used to both create and control the global liquidity" keeping in view the global economic conditions, as distinct from conditions in a particular national economy. Such a proposal seeks to divorce the decision making in the international monetary system from purely national concerns of any one economy. In particular when a country's currency is no longer used as the yardstick for global trade and as the benchmark for other currencies, the exchange rate policy of the country would arguably be more effective in adjusting economic imbalances. Such a development could be expected to "significantly reduce the risks of a future crisis and enhance crisis management capability."[49]

A separate suggestion that reflects a more widely held view in East Asia as well as elsewhere regarding what might be termed the dysfunctional nature of the multilateral institutions is to seek an early warning mechanism, a concept that the East Asians have been working with at CMI. It is proposed that the IMF take cognizance of the risks arising from the dollar based international currency system, and to this end develop a mechanism to monitor, assess and warn in context of likely problematic economies and distress situations. "In the short run, the international community, particularly the IMF, should at least recognize and face up to the risks resulting from the existing system, conduct regular monitoring and assessment and issue timely early warnings."[50] In the present circumstances, one could surmise that it is the dollar based international currency system and the United States economy that the IMF was being asked to monitor and issue early warnings about, and that the suggestion is that IMF should proceed to do so immediately.[51] The fact that such a mechanism is proposed implies that the existing Article IV consultations, often mentioned by the IMF as the bedrock of its monitoring and surveillance activity, are insufficient.[52]

The American response to Zhou Xiaochuan's proposals only seemed to validate the concerns raised in the article. The initial United States response was to say that the proposals would be considered, thus indicating the seriousness that it attached to the matter. But no sooner had the Treasury Secretary Timothy Geithner uttered these words that the markets saw the dollar plummet very fast, causing Geithner to "correct" the "misunderstanding" created by his remarks.[53] Governor Bernanke followed up to further set the record straight, and then President Obama himself spoke to remove any remaining doubts about the dollar's future as he saw the matter. The Chinese officials too confirmed that the intent was not to undermine the dollar. And, finally, Richard Cooper, the Keynesian éminence grise of international monetary affairs, wrote up a brief to say that dollar would continue in its present role for years.[54] The episode served to expose the brittle nature of the system. It became clear that the international currency system is fragile and remains seriously vulnerable.

More generally, Zhou Xiaochuan's proposals have been seen as "more than maneuvering" and indicative of a "medium to long-term strategy" on the part of China's policymakers "to gradually move towards systematically reforming the international currency system"; and, as Li Rogou's remarks cited above suggest, this strategy would seem to predate the global financial crisis.[55] The assessment in this regard that acquired a certain definitiveness on account of the 2008 global financial crisis is that the sources of crises are systemic risks, the countries with the non-reserve currencies are at a disadvantage in the international monetary system, the IMF should enhance surveillance over the major economies and over capital flows, and it should also increase the representation of developing countries as well as accelerate quota reform.[56]

But any substantive reform of the international currency system, which would involve a large number of countries, can at best be a long-term project. The United States, the only country with veto power on the IMF board, would very likely resist reforms that could in any manner weaken its power-broking influence in the current system.[57] For the United States it would mean conceding its considerable and unique advantage of seigniorage in a global context, the facility of having the dollar as a universal unit of account, the ability to borrow interest free, and the freedom to run deficits and postpone macroeconomic adjustment. One cannot therefore realistically contemplate the United States accepting reform voluntarily in the foreseeable future. In the absence of systemic reforms, China's rapidly growing trade, its rapidly growing foreign exchange reserves, its imperative to invest overseas, and its extensive assistance to the developing countries, create a need to develop the renminbi as an international currency and as a key reserve currency.[58]

The Chinese policymakers on balance feel that a multicurrency system is coming, and that such a change is in their interest and ought to be promoted.[59] Chapter 4 noted the increasing regional and international role of the renminbi. This process of internationalization of renminbi, given the nature of the objective combined with the fact that China is a developing country and is making the attempt in an era of fiat currencies, that is to say in the absence of any link between the renminbi and another asset such as gold, can perhaps only be gradual, and remains modest for now notwithstanding its rapid advancement. Increasing use of renminbi in the region and beyond may eventually make its inclusion in the basket of currencies that make up the SDR unavoidable; with a weight that reflects China's share in world trade and world GDP as well as the fact that it is the United States's biggest creditor. Such a development would also likely give China a greater say in any IMF reform.

Though it has been argued by some that the onset of the global financial crisis in 2008 may have stalled the implementation of the strategic goal of achieving convertibility of the renminbi under capital controls,[60] the events and the discussion in chapter 4 above show that it is far more likely that the global financial crisis has speeded up the process.

IV: FINAL WORDS

The issue of what are appropriate economic policies is a singularly important one for East Asia, and its approach to economic policies has been driven by the imperative to further its economic and social development. East Asia's development goals remain distant for now. For example China, for all its economic size, has a per capita income that as a fraction is less than one-tenth of that of the United States;[61] therefore there is much ground to be covered in the East Asian view than just gaining parity in the economic size of the economies.

East Asia therefore cannot forego its approach to economic policy that has served its development effort so well. The East Asian perspective on the role of the state in economic policy that was so forcefully ignored by the multilateral financial institutions, in particular by the IMF, in course of the Asian financial crisis in 1997 was to be upheld and validated in practice some ten years later in course of the global financial crisis in

2008. The 2008 crisis saw an active involvement of the state in the efforts of the governments of the United States, Western Europe and other economies to forge a way out of the financial morass, leaving the East Asians with a sense of *deja vu*.

The forceful implementation of the Washington Consensus in East Asia in 1997 by the IMF and others was not without far reaching consequences though. We saw in chapter 2 that it set in motion efforts in East Asia to create circumstances so that the region would never again need to rely on multilateral agencies such as the IMF for financial support. We also noted in chapter 3 that these efforts, which began with cooperation in finance, built up in due course in to broader economic and financial cooperation.

The Asian financial crisis also led to a quiet questioning of the international currency system in East Asia. Even though the East Asian economies largely managed to avoid the worst impact of the global financial crisis 2008, the crisis did seem to bear out the region's worst fears about the international currency system and its dissatisfaction sharpened as a result.

Between 1997 and 2008, East Asia as an economic entity grew and integrated rapidly, with China's economy and trade exhibiting exceptional performance. With it's increasingly hub like function in the region, its rapid economic integration with the other East Asian economies, its growing enmeshment in the global trade and investment flows and its large foreign exchange reserves, China succeeded in developing a certain influence in the world economy and a new authority in the region that is unprecedented in modern times. Its determination to protect and consolidate its economic gains took on a more assertive character, and as we saw in chapter 4, China speeded up its efforts to develop an international role for its currency. China's assessment of the problems with the international currency system was also evident in the substantive proposals that its central banker published for an international currency to gradually replace the dollar.

The two financial crises, that is, the Asian financial crisis of 1997 and the global financial crisis of 2008, thus served to distinguish Asian views on economic policy from those of the multilateral financial institutions and the transatlantic economies. The economic paradigm based on organizing principles such as the markets know best and the state should be absent from the economy, that the dollar suffices as the international currency, a paradigm that had so long provided the framework for policy, was openly questioned in thought and practice.

With the crisis of 2008, the advanced economies suffered a loss of authority in their approach to economic policy, and with China's emergence the G-7/8 grouping suffered a loss of legitimacy as an institution for economic governance. The G-20, which emerged as a replacement of G-7/8, too lacked "legitimacy" as a multilateral organization for the governance of the world economy; its deliberations tended to be dominated by the G-7/8 and within that group by the United States in particular.[62] Even though in finding a way out of the global financial crisis the usual market friendly policies were set aside and the state and public funds brought into play, very much vindicating the East Asian's views in course of the Asian financial crisis, the transatlantic economies remain in denial for now.

More and more it would appear the East Asians may have developed the confidence to be assertive on economic policy, and if the point of view is not sufficiently considered in the multilateral financial institutions then the East Asians may seek to work in their usual low key, incremental fashion to further develop and shape regional institutions better suited to further their economic development.

NOTES

1. See Joseph Stiglitz, Globalization and its discontents (London: Allen Lane, 2002), p. 74.
2. See John Williamson, What Washington means by policy reform, in John Williamson, ed., Latin American adjustment: How much has happened? (Washington DC, Peterson Institute, 2002).
3. See discussion of shock therapy in Russia in for example Joseph Stiglitz, Globalization and its discontents (London: Allen Lane, 2002), pp. 142-151. A discussion that brings out the rather mixed record of the application of the Washington Consensus set of policies may be found in Dani Rodrik, Goodbye Washington Consensus, Hello Washington Confusion, mimeo, January 2006.
4. Ha-Joon Chang has convincingly shown how today's developed economies in course of their industrialization followed interventionist policies that were the very opposite of the ones implied by the rubric Washington Consensus. See Ha-Joon Chang, Kicking away the ladder, (London: Anthem Press, 2002).
5. Yong Wook Lee, The Japanese challenge to the American neoliberal order (Stanford: Stanford University Press, 2008), p. 3 and pp 169-170.
6. See Kaname Akamatsu, A historical pattern of economic growth in developing countries, Journal of Developing Economies 1962, Kiyoshi Kojima, The 'flying geese' model of Asian economic development, Journal of Asian Economies 2000, and Terutomo Ozawa, Institutions, industrial upgrading, and economic performance in Japan (Cheltenham: Edward Elgar, 2005)
7. See for example discussion in Meredith Woo-Cumings, ed., The developmental state (Ithaca: Cornell University Press, 1999).
8. See Hu: zero-sum game anachronistic for Sino-US ties, People's Daily Online, January 17, 2011.
9. See Li Hongmei, Why Premier Wen shrugs off "China Model"?, People's Daily, March 15, 2011, and China's development "not a model," Xinhua, March 14, 2011. http://news.xinhuanet.com/english2010/china/2011-03/14/c_13777218.htm
10. Joseph Stiglitz records that the World Bank nonetheless avoided studying the East Asian success cases and did so only after Japan insisted on such work and paid for the study. See Joseph Stiglitz, Globalization and its discontents (London: Penguin, 2002), p. 91.
11. See Yong Wook Lee, The Japanese challenge to the American neoliberal order, (Stanford, Stanford University Press, 2008), p. 171.
12. Joseph Stiglitz, Globalization and its discontents, (Penguin, London, 2002), p. 91.

13. See Joseph Stiglitz, Challenging the Washington Consensus, An interview with Lindsey Schoenfelder, The Brown Journal of World Affairs, Winter/Spring 2003, vol. 9, no. 2, pp. 33-40.

14. See Yong Wook Lee, The Japanese challenge to the American neoliberal order (Stanford: Stanford University Press, 2008), p. 174.

15. See Andrew Sheng, From Asian to global financial crisis (Cambridge: Cambridge University Press, 2009), p. 33.

16. See Yong Wook Lee, The Japanese challenge to the American neoliberal order, (Stanford, Stanford University Press, 2008), p. 12-15. A number of plausible reasons for Japan's AMF proposal as a means for advancing purely Japanese interests have also been advanced. Japanese banks and manufacturers may have seen possibilities in the AMF as extending a rescue to Japan's private sector. Second, the AMF provided a mechanism for Japan to apply its own crisis management mechanism. Third, a successful AMF would have provided a boost to Japan's leadership role in Asia. It is worth mentioning here that if we consider CMI as an Asian mechanism or device, then this mechanism did help the East Asian economies weather the global financial crisis of 2008 better than the advanced economies.

17. See Andrew Sheng, From Asian to global financial crisis, (Cambridge: Cambridge University Press, 2009), p. 34.

18. See Yong Wook Lee, The Japanese challenge to the American neoliberal order (Stanford: Stanford University Press, 2008), p. 13.

19. A large and growing literature documents the crisis and the policies adopted to cope. See for example George Cooper, The origin of financial crises, (New York: Vintage Books, 2008), Andrew Gamble, The spectre at the feast (Basingstoke: Palgrave, 2009), Carmen Reinhardt and Kenneth Rogoff, This time is different, (Princeton: Princeton University Press, 2009), and Andrew Sorkin, Too big to fail (New York: Viking Books, 2009), among others.

20. See Mark Weisbrot and Juan Montecino, The IMF and economic recovery: Is fund policy contributing to downside risks? Center for Economic and Policy Research, Washington DC, October 2010. http://www.cepr.net/index.php/publications/reports/the-imf-and-economic-recovery

21. See discussion regarding G-20 below.

22. See Yong Wook Lee, The Japanese challenge to the American neoliberal order (Stanford: Stanford University Press, 2008), p. 174. Also see discussion in Simon S. C. Tay, Asia alone, (Singapore: Wiley, 2010), pp. 22-29.

23. See Yong Wook Lee, The Japanese challenge to the American neoliberal order (Stanford: Stanford University Press, 2008), p. 174-175.

24. See Simon S. C. Tay, Asia alone (Singapore: Wiley, 2010), pp. 22-29; and Yong Wook Lee, The Japanese challenge to the American neoliberal order (Stanford: Stanford University Press, 2008), p. 22 and p. 173.

25. See Yong Wook Lee, The Japanese challenge to the American neoliberal order (Stanford: Stanford University Press, 2008), p. 175.

26. See Paul Bowles, Asia's post-crisis regionalism: Bringing the state back in, keeping the (United) States out, cited in Yong Wook Lee, The Japanese challenge to the American neoliberal order (Stanford: Stanford University Press, 2008), p. 176.

27. The United States had been variously running a trade deficit vis-à-vis Western Europe and Japan for the most part of the 1960s to 1980s.

28. In a previous chapter we noted the resilience of the "global imbalance" in the United States-China context in the face of appreciation of the renminbi even though the theory on the subject would have led us to expect the opposite.

29. See Peter G. Peterson, The morning after, The Atlantic Monthly, October 1987, p. 43.

30. See Peter G. Peterson, The morning after, The Atlantic Monthly, October 1987, p. 46.

31. The Economic Review and Policy Dialogue was launched at the same time as the CMI at the APT Finance Ministers Meeting of May 2000, with the stated purpose of

preventing crises. The APT Finance Ministers Meeting of May 2006 set up an expert group to improve monitoring and surveillance. See discussion in Chapter 3 above.

32. Li Ruogu, cited by Simon Rabinovitch in "China officials call for displacing dollar, in time," *Reuters*, July 6, 2009, http://www.reuters.com/article/idUSTRE 5650WO20090706. Li Ruogu was a vice governor of People's Bank of China at the time.

33. C. Fred Bergsten, Obama has to tell Beijing some hard truths, Financial Times, November 29, 2010.

34. A US Treasury official in conversation with one of the authors in March 2011 mentioned that currency manipulation was one of a set of issues with China, and if China say conceded something in one area, say the Security Council, the pressure regarding currency manipulation would recede somewhat. Also see Alan Beattie, Big guns muffled as currency wars enter a lull, Financial Times, May 12, 2011.

35. Zhou Xiaochuan, Reform the international monetary system, China Daily, March 23, 2009. Also see: http://www.pbc.gov.cn/english/detail.asp?col=6500&id=182

36. This is commonly referred to as the "Triffin Dilemma," after Robert Triffin who wrote extensively on these issues, from 1950s to 1970s, and first formulated the specific issue, just as the Bretton Woods system was coming apart because of an excess of dollars. Triffin identified the problem for the US Congress in 1960 but it took another 10 years before the system came apart.

37. Zhou Xiaochuan speech referred to may be accessed at: http://www.pbc.gov.cn/english/detail.asp?col=6500&id=178 .

38. The article by Zhou Xiaochuan brought to mind the more summary assessment by General Charles de Gaulle in his press conference of February 4, 1965. "We consider that international exchanges must be established, as was the case before the great worldwide disasters, on an unquestionable monetary basis which does not bear the mark of any individual country."

39. See Nicholas Kaldor, The dollar crisis, The Times, September 6, 7 and 8, 1971. Reprinted in Nicholas Kaldor, Further essays on applied economics (London, Duckworth, 1978), pp. 62-64. Cited in Jane D'Arista, The evolving international monetary system, Cambridge Journal of Economics 2009, 33, pp. 633-652. On August 15, 1971 the United States unilaterally terminated the convertibility of dollars into gold.

40. Jacques Rueff, cited in Fred Hirsh's interview of Jacques Rueff in The Economist, February 13, 1965.

41. One interesting if somewhat unusal point of view was that the United States ran the large persistent deficits to enable the developing countries to develop. The argument was that United States imports of developing country manufactures enabled a country to industrialize. And as a particular developing country industrialized in this process, it would yield its place to another developing country. Hence in fullness of time the whole "periphery" would industrialize through exporting manufactures to the United States. See Michael P. Dooley, David Folkerts-Landau, and Peter Garber, An essay on the revived Bretton Woods system, NBER working paper 9971, September 2003. http://www.nber.org/papers/w9971.pdf?new_window=1

42. Premier Wen Jiabao is reported to have said: "We have lent a huge amount of money to the United States and of course we're concerned about the security of our assets and, to be honest, I am a little bit worried, . . . That's why . . . I would like to urge the US to keep its commitment and promise to ensure the safety of Chinese assets." See Olivia Chung, Wen puts US honor on the debt line, March 14, 2009, Asia Times Online. Also see Michael Wines, China's leader says he is 'worried' over U.S. treasuries, New York Times, March 14, 2009.

43. See, for example, discussion in Mattias Vermeiren, The global imbalances and the contradictions of US monetary hegemony, Journal of International Relations and Development, vol. 13, no. 2., June 2010, pp. 105-135.

44. This American seignorage is often referred to as America's "exorbitant privilege."

45. For example see discussion in Andrea Boltho, The dollar era, New Left Review no. 72, November/December 2011, pp. 145-151; and in C. Fred Bergsten, The dollar and

the deficits: How Washington can prevent the next crisis, Foreign Affairs, vol. 88, no. 6, November/December 2009.

46. A relatively recent affirmation of this policy came from the United States Treasury Secretary Timothy F. Geithner and the chairman of the federal reserve, Benjamin S. Bernanke. Speaking at a Council of Foreign Relations event on April 26, 2011, Geithner said:

> Our policy has been and will always be, as long as I will be in office, that a strong dollar is in the interest of the country. . . . We will never embrace a strategy to weaken the dollar.

See A Conversation on the Economy with Timothy F. Geithner, at: http://www.cfr.org/economics/conversation-economy-timothy-f-geithner/p24825 Mr. Bernanke was quoted to have stated at a press conference on April 27, 2011:

> The Federal Reserve believes that a strong and stable dollar is both in American interests and in the interest of the global economy.

See Reuters, Bernanke says strong dollar in U.S. and global interest, April 27, 2011, at: http://www.reuters.com/article/2011/04/27/us-usa-fed-dollar-idUSTRE73Q7BH20110427

47. Zhou Xiaochuan, Reform the international monetary system, China Daily, March 23, 2009. Also see: http://www.pbc.gov.cn/english/detail.asp?col=6500&id=182

48. Back in the 1940s, Keynes had already proposed the introduction of an international currency unit named "Bancor," based on the value of 30 representative commodities. The proposal was not accepted. The collapse of the Bretton Woods system, which was based on Henry Dexter White's approach, indicates that the Keynesian approach may have been more farsighted.

49. The article also mentions using SDR in the long run, but one may infer that the character of the SDR would change significantly if it were to meet the three-fold criteria laid out above. This aspect of matter is not spelled out in any detail in the proposal. See Zhou Xiaochuan, Reform the international monetary system, China Daily, March 23, 2009. Also see: http://www.pbc.gov.cn/english/detail.asp?col=6500&id=182

50. Zhou Xiaochuan, Reform the international monetary system, China Daily, March 23, 2009. Also see: http://www.pbc.gov.cn/english/detail.asp?col=6500&id=182

51. There has been some development in context of monitoring economies by the IMF since Zhou Xiaochuan's article appeared. For example, it may be noted that at a recent G-20 meeting in Pittsburgh, "The leaders pledged to rethink their economic policies in a coordinated effort to reduce the immense imbalances between export-dominated countries like China and Japan and debt-laden countries like the United States, which has long been the world's most willing consumer. "The United States will be expected to increase its savings rate, reduce its trade deficit and address its huge budget deficit. Countries like China, Japan and Germany will be expected to reduce their dependence on exports by promoting more consumer spending and investment at home. "The ideas are not new, and there is no enforcement mechanism to penalize countries if they stick to their old habits. But for the first time ever, each country agreed to submit its policies to a "peer review" from the other governments as well as to monitoring by the International Monetary Fund. "That in itself would be a big change, given how prickly national leaders have often been toward outside criticism of their policies." See Edmund S Andrews, Group of 20 agrees on far-reaching economic plan, New York Times, September 26, 2009. The Economist noted that the "Developing countries are uneasy about formalising such a realignment. They are publicly supportive, but that may only be because they suspect it will be impossible to police." See The G20 summit, Regaining their balance, Economist.com, September 26 2009.

52. In course of a conversation with the author in March 2011, a United States Treasury official suggested that some of IMF's findings in course of its 2011 Article IV

consultations with the United States were unacceptable for the latter, and that the United States had the necessary votes in the IMF Board in support of its point of view.

53. See Anahad O'Connor, Geithner affirms dollar after remarks send it tumbling, The New York Times, March 26, 2009.

54. See Richard N. Cooper, The future of the dollar, Peterson Institute Policy Brief, September 2009.

55. Gregory Chin and Wang Yong, Debating the international currency system: What's in a speech, China Security, 2010, vol. 6, no. 1, pp. 13-14.

56. See Bo Qu, Dynamic engagement: China's preference to international monetary cooperation, mimeo, May 3, 2010.

57. Mattias Vermeiren, The global imbalances and the contradictions of US monetary policy, Journal of International Relations and Development, 2011.

58. A particular problem during the 2007-08 global financial crisis was the drying up of dollar finance for trade and hence a restrictive environment for China's economic growth. See Patrick McGuire and Goetz von Peter, The US dollar shortage in global banking, BIS Quarterly Review, March 2009.

59. Gregory Chin and Wang Yong, Debating the international currency system: what's in a speech, China Security, 2010, vol. 6, no. 1, p. 14-15. Chin and Yong cite Yu Zhonghua, "To check the hegemony of the US dollar by cultivating a multi-polar balance," Guoji jinrong bao [International Financial News], August 6, 2009, http://ifb.cass.cn/show_news.asp?id=18591. Yu Zhonghua is a professor and deputy director of the Institute of International Finance at Liaoning University.

60. See Wang Yuan Long, A geological and functional "three-step strategy" for renminbi's internationalization, in China Economist, November-December 2009.

61. Based on IMF data for 2011.

62. See proceedings of the Global Economic Governance Conference, Washington DC, October 7-8 2010. http://policydialogue.org/events/meetings/global_economic_governance_conference_washington_dc_october_7-8_2010/materials/

SIX

East Asia as a community in flux

I: INTRODUCTION

This chapter argues that the emergence of China as a major economy, globalization and the processed manufacturing it facilitated, the two financial crises—the Asian one of 1997 and the global one of 2007 that is still reverberating—and the economic and financial cooperation that have taken place in East Asia, all have worked to change the very concept of post Second World War (postwar) East Asia from a US-centric formal security structure to an informal and increasingly China-centric economic region. The end of Cold War too helped to de-emphasize the relevance of America's security relationships, bringing a sharper focus on economic development in the region. This shift in East Asia's character continues.

The idea of East Asia as a region

Rhetorical book titles such as Kishore Mahbubani's *Can Asians think?* raise the obvious question in the reader's mind: how should we understand Asia, and is there an Asian identity?[1] The question goes unanswered in Mahbubani's books but one factual answer is that Asia is a European construction, a geographical concept, which stands for a large Eurasian landmass. Once we accept Asia as such a geographical entity, we find ourselves facing the next quandary, that is, whether the inhabitants of this landmass envisage an Asian identity, which is to ask whether the idea of Asia has become an indigenous concept. There is indeed nothing in the history of this landmass to suggest such an identity, one which may socially, culturally or politically bind the populations of the diverse lands that stretch from some ill-defined point in the Urals in the west to Bering Straits in the east, and from the Siberian islands of Sevenaya Zemlya that run into the Arctic Circle in the north to the southern extremity where East Timor touches Australia. One cannot but affirm the obvious that there is simply no Asian identity that corresponds to this geography.

We are then left with the question of how to understand East Asia, a term frequently used in economic and political analysis.

As is discussed in this chapter, it was the postwar security policies of the victor, that is, the United States, vis-à-vis the countries in the geographical neighborhood, rather than the aspirations of individual countries in East Asia, that defined East Asia for the better part of the second half of the twentieth century.

We find that this postwar East Asia divided according to geopolitical considerations into two "sub-regions." One of these was Northeast Asia, comprising the geographically contiguous territories of Japan, Korea and Taiwan, being lands that share the Confucius traditions and culture. As this chapter shows, Northeast Asia's defining characteristic was the tight bilateral treaties that each of the three countries had with the United States.[2] The other sub-region was Southeast Asia comprising chiefly the present day ASEAN nations, most of which have significant minorities of overseas Chinese who are active in the region's business and commerce.[3] These Southeast Asian nations, just beginning to emerge from European colonial rule unlike Northeast Asian countries, focused on non-intervention and non-alignment in their international relations. And these new nations eventually settled on their own form of multilateralism. Thus each of the two sub-regions practiced a different approach to regional matters. This is how East Asia appeared before the American rapprochement with China that began in the 1970s and the subsequent collapse of Soviet Union, events which preceded China's emergence as an economic power.

China's economy emerged much faster than the expectations of even the most optimistic of the pundits, rising within the space of some three decades from its modest beginnings as an economic backwater until the policy shift in January 1979, when China was the world's eleventh largest economy, to become the world's second largest economy and trader by 2010; an economic powerhouse. The wind in China's sails was the globalized world economy with which the timely shift in China's policy jived well. The initial impetus came from the overseas Chinese investing on the Mainland, but foreign direct investment from other sources did not lag behind much.[4] China's growth process drew in the region, and the two financial crises, in 1997 and 2007, respectively, highlighted the robustness of the evolving regional relationships. Efforts were undertaken to formalize the mutually beneficial linkages in the region. China served as the economic hub, dwarfing Japan.

A feature common to these countries is the fact that in the postwar period they offer the only cases of making in all likelihood a successful transition from "developing countries" to "developed countries." This is most clear for Japan and Korea, as well as the city-state of Singapore and

China's Special Administrative Region of Hong Kong. China too shows strengthening technological capabilities, a record of sustained economic growth where large areas of the country can be seen as engaged in the process of credibly "catching up," giving reason to believe that the transition may be made.[5]

We argue in this chapter that the idea of East Asia began life as a postwar geopolitical concept, and the next section considers this proposition, but, as discussed later in the chapter, the basis for the perception of East Asia as a region (specifically the nature of association in this geographical space) seems to have varied with shifts in geopolitics and wealth.[6]

II: AMERICA'S POSTWAR SECURITY IMPERATIVES IN EAST ASIA

The United States "adversaries" in this postwar East Asia were Communism and the Communists. In due course this meant the Soviet Union, the Peoples Republic of China, "their" halves of Korea and Vietnam, that is, the land under the control of the Communist regimes, and as Southeast Asian colonies became independent nations, the Communist parties in these countries. The United States initially sought to contain the perceived Soviet threat, with the apparent threat from a Communist China added on shortly thereafter. To best contain these perceived threats the United States felt it needed strong anticommunist allies that would help it to pursue a collective security strategy in the area. But it was also an American concern that United States should not be drawn inadvertently into a war by the policies or other acts of one of the allies, that is get drawn into a war not of its own choosing. Hence the United States also evidenced a pragmatic need to control its allies.[7]

Northeast Asia

Given the necessity for the close control of its allies, the approach that the United States adopted in pursuing alliances in Northeast Asia was the asymmetric bilateral alliance between a strong and dominant United States and a much smaller and weaker Asian ally, in preference to a multilateral NATO style alliance, as the former method enabled a more substantial hold over the ally.[8] The bilateral framework used in dealings with Japan, Korea and Taiwan was also necessarily formal and legalistic involving binding treaties, and, in the case of Japan and Korea, it also involved stationing of American troops in Asia.

This system of alliances, termed the San Francisco system or more picturesquely the hub and spoke system, puts the United States at the center as the metaphorical hub and the various allies make up the spokes. The hub deals directly and independently with each ally or spoke, but the allies or spokes do not necessarily deal directly with each other. Substantial crossties amongst the three American allies, that is to say among the "spokes," were not encouraged. The Northeast Asian system thus consisted of three spokes linked to the United States hub. Lacking crossties amongst the spokes, Northeast Asia constituted a "region" perhaps only in American perception—as a system envisaged in the context of United States geostrategic goals during the Cold War.

United States strategic objectives necessarily included some economic development of its East Asian allies so as to help strengthen and stabilize these countries, and also to ensure that these economies stand out as examples of economic prosperity in contrast with the Communist adversary.[9]

Southeast Asia

The situation in Southeast Asia immediately after the end of the Second World War was less well defined, though a return to colonial control was in prospect and indeed came about. In due course the European colonizers withdrew, the independent postcolonial Southeast Asia panned out differently from Northeast Asia, with the specifics in each case varying according to the country and the respective colonial power. The situation of these countries was categorically dissimilar from what obtained in Northeast Asia. In general Southeast Asia's early postcolonial leaders showed an aversion to power politics, alliances and spheres of influence, which they saw as an extension of the interests of the erstwhile colonial powers and of the emerging superpower rivalry between the Soviet Union and the United States. The Southeast Asian nations developed applicable versions of non-intervention and non-alignment. Non-intervention meant that these nations would not interfere in each other's national affairs, and non-alignment meant that they would not align themselves with one superpower or the other.[10]

For there to be a consensus among a relatively large number of countries, which did not wish to impose on each other by intent or by design, the process preferably had to be non-legalistic and also informal, and indeed such a process evolved in the meetings of the Asian Relations Conference and the Bandung Conference.[11] Early initiatives toward a multilateral security alliance in Southeast Asia stumbled badly.

Nonetheless substantial and sustained efforts were made by the United States and the United Kingdom at creating multilateral defense organizations in Southeast Asia with the ostensible purpose of containing the Communist threat. These efforts did not meet with much success initially, but in due course some of the Southeast Asian nations banded together with erstwhile colonial powers and the United States under a multilateral security treaty, the SEATO pact (the acronym stood for Southeast Asia Treaty Organization). SEATO failed to establish its relevance and could not survive the end of Vietnam War. The experience with SEATO discouraged further efforts at creating multilateral security structures in Southeast Asia.[12]

But in a time of superpower rivalry, Southeast Asia could in a broad sense rely on that very rivalry for its security. Besides, these Southeast Asian countries also benefited from some American economic support. In due course the Southeast Asian nations came together in ASEAN, a non-defense multilateral organization to promote cooperation in the region. The informal non-interventionist manner that characterized the ASEAN and *the ASEAN way* is said to have been inspired by the Asian Relations Conference and the Bandung Conference procedures.[13]

Finally, as differences between the Communist regimes in Soviet Union and China grew, China came to be seen as an adversary of the Soviet Union and, in its efforts to contain the Soviet Union, the United States successfully sought to cultivate relations with China, treating China as a kind of an additional spoke. As a part of this build up of the United States-China relationship from the 1970s onwards, China's entry into the multilateral institutions and its access to the world economy were eventually facilitated, albeit with conditions which were often much harsher than those faced by any other developing country, by the United States at the expense of Taiwan.

III: EAST ASIA AND SECURITY IN THE AFTERMATH OF THE COLD WAR

East Asia and American policy after the Cold War

The collapse of Soviet Union in 1989 brought the American-led anti-Communist effort and its corollary, the Cold War era, to a close. The post Cold War security perceptions in East Asia presented a rather vague and uncertain landscape. The American bilateral treaties in Northeast Asia, respectively with Japan, Korea and Taiwan, did not end when Communism ended as a political force. The collapse of the Soviet Union meant that the Communist threat had vanished and this suddenly made these treaties look like relics of a bygone era. The United States troops, generally an unpopular feature with the host country public, remained garrisoned in Japan and South Korea. In Southeast Asia, the bilateral alliances with the Philippines and Thailand continued. Philippines and Thailand both remained in the category of a "major non-NATO ally" of United States in its "Global War on Terror" (GWOT), and both contributed small contingents to the "Coalition of the Willing" in Iraq for brief periods, as did Japan.[14] In the case of Philippines though, the American troops finally left in 1991 and United States vacated its base there; subsequently, it negotiated a right of return for these troops should circumstances so warrant in the future.

ASEAN accepted the reality of bilateral security treaties as long as it did not imply any collective action on its part.[15] The issue of a post Cold War security community in Southeast Asia was brought up frequently, and just as often it found no takers in the ASEAN moots. Indonesia rejected military pacts and Thailand pronounced military alliances to be obsolete.[16] Malaysia laid down the criterion that "one man's security should lead to another's assurance," which seemed to say that security must be achieved with the adversary, not against him.[17] Eventually in 1993-94, the ASEAN turned its Post Ministerial Conference into a security discussion, naming the dialogue as the ARF (the acronym stands for ASEAN Regional Forum). ARF maintained ASEAN's rejection of multilateral defense treaties, and also its doctrine of non-intervention. The ARF amounted to a dialogue on security, not a defense pact for armed action, and worked to narrow the scope of the common security norm by setting out three stages of security cooperation: confidence building, preventive diplomacy, and "elaboration of approaches to conflicts."[18] The point has been made that the relatively large size of the ARF membership and the ASEAN norms of non-intervention and decision through consensus often impede discussion of various insurgencies and border clashes in the ARF.[19] Such criticism seems to misunderstand the nature and purpose of the ARF. The size of membership in itself ought not to be a problem; NATO too is a large organization. And differences of opinion tend to be the norm in large multilateral organizations. But the critical point is that the ASEAN Regional Forum is not a multilateral defense pact against a perceived adversary. Its very existence downplays such a scenario and enhances the value of a dialogue.

Another important element in the changing post Cold War situation was the visible impact of rapid economic growth in East Asia. At the end of the Cold War Japan stood out as the world's second largest economy, and South Korea and Taiwan too had become self-sufficient and prosperous economies. The earlier economic reliance of the three on the United States had been substantially lessened if not largely turned into mutually advantageous relationships. China was beginning to emerge as a major processed manufacturing economy, and given the relatively open character of its economy, there was a tendency for the economies of the neighbors to be drawn in by this activity.

It was in the post Cold War shift in the American stance on economic assistance and economic policies that brought a shock to East Asia. The post Cold War America sought an end to protectionism and official development assistance. Indeed the new American mooted policy framework, often referred to as the Washington Consensus, had no place for official capital flows and official economic assistance, mercantilism, state intervention in the economy, industrial policies and picking industry champions—in fact the very policy instruments that East Asian governments had used to such good effect in their successful drive for economic growth. Instead it sought open markets and freedom for movement of goods and capital of the developing economies. But the full force of this shift in the American stance on economic policies perhaps dawned on the East Asians only in their worst days, in the course of the Asian financial crisis of 1997. It was an article of faith in East Asia that America would have swung in with maximum support to the afflicted economies in course of the Asian financial crisis, if such a crisis had occurred during the Cold War. With the Cold War over, American seemed an admonishing spectator watching East Asia descend in to the economic abyss. In Ha Joon Chang's perception the proverbial ladder that the Western countries had used and relied upon to climb up to industrialization and riches had now been kicked away to prevent others from climbing up.[20] The "ladder" had only been lowered for a period because the exigencies of the Cold War had so dictated.

Reflecting on the outcome

Thus the postwar East Asian community's defining institutions were the bilateral and treaties and other security pacts with the United States. This postwar East Asia, the outcome of a "top down" approach conceived and enforced by the United States with the authority of the undisputed and unchallenged victor of Second World War, was essentially an Asian extension of American geopolitical interests. Its objectives were to contain Communism and, in order to better achieve that goal, also to develop the economies and societies of the allied Asian countries; both to strengthen and stabilize these allies and also to present an attractive and shining alternative to the relative lack of economic progress under the Communist system. As an adversary, the Peoples Republic of China naturally stood excluded from these arrangements.

The United States alliance with Japan sat well with Japan's historical tendency to align itself with the dominant power, even as Japan rose to be the world's second largest economy, and in contradistinction to what international relations theory would lead one to expect.[21] It was indeed the intention of Mr. Yoshida Shigeru, the Japanese prime minister at the time, that the alliance would take care of Japan's security, and Japan could then devote itself fully to economic growth, a view that dovetailed with the American aims in the region. The alliance has also been reassuring for the neighbors about Japan's future intentions.[22]

End of the Cold War notwithstanding, the United States has decided to continue to keep American troops in place in East Asia, and thus perhaps to create an effective leverage for the United States in its dealing with its East Asian allies and beyond, pointing perhaps to an ill-defined purpose and task in applying the treaties.

In this manner United States strategy that reflected its worldwide postwar security interests defined its relationships in this part of the world, and hence also defined East Asia as a region. And even though America's bilateral relationships in the region were principally about security, the relationships provided for an economic component. In a post Cold War world the United States policymakers did not appear to see East Asia with the earlier priority though. The United States visualized itself as supreme in what it now saw as its moment in a post Cold War unipolar world.

Besides the usual longstanding contentions about borders, there is one piece of unfinished business that continues to cloud the security situation in East Asia, and it dates back to the end of American occupation of Japan. In relinquishing control to Japan, the United States handed over islands that were also claimed by other countries in that geographical vicinity and could therefore be considered as disputed territory. Such territories included Dokdo islands (also known as Liancourt Rocks) claimed by Korea, and Daioyu islands claimed by China. The islands of Okinawa, also known as Ryukyu Islands, allegedly a sovereign entity historically, are also disputed territory.[23] Whilst Japan thus obtained control via the United States, the Second World War victor, seeds were sown for mistrust, disputes and tense political relations, and this history continues to cast its long shadow. The Kuril Islands, though disputed by Japan, had been handed over to the Soviet Union in recognition of the latter's claim by the Allied command in course of the postwar occupation of Japan.[24]

Second, a number of "security" issues continued to emerge in East Asia. Seemingly new, these issues were related to the division of Korea, the control over disputed islands, and the nature of the United States's role in East Asia, and the recent manifestations included the sinking of a South Korean ship, the arrest of a Chinese seaman by Japan in the vicinity of the disputed Diaoyu Islands, a fresh airing in the transatlantic press of old border disputes in South China Sea, and the exchange of artillery shelling between the two Koreas after South Korea held military exercises in the disputed Yeonpyeong Island area. A large segment of the South Korean public though believed the sinking of the South Korean ship to be a covert American act in order to create an anti-North Korea security threat narrative.[25] But even as the United States sought Chinese involvement in its efforts to resolve the various Korean "crises,"[26] thus indicating its limits in being able to achieve a settlement on its own, the Chinese press saw the Diaoyu Islands incident to have been instigated by the United States, and the differences over South China Sea given undue prominence by the United States administration.[27] The Chinese press also judged that the United States was trying to create an anti-China alliance in the region, besides "saber rattling."[28] The United States actively encouraged Japan to take up a larger security role in East Asia and to build up credible defense capabilities to enable it to do so.[29] On the other hand, the United States chose to practically ignore the Russian president Medvedev's visit to the disputed Kuril Islands, even though Japan strongly protested the visit.[30]

The economic processes integrating the region around the dynamic Chinese hub implied growing Chinese authority in East Asia. Unless China tied itself up in regional disputes, it was difficult to see how China's dominant economic position in the region could be escaped from. At the same time, United States preoccupation with the GWOT and an absence from Asian moots may have reduced its profile in East Asia.[31]

IV: THE ECONOMIC COORDINATE: A COMMUNITY OF EAST ASIAN ECONOMIC INTERESTS

The beginnings of the present day economic "catch up" in East Asia go at least as far back as America's desire after the Second World War to showcase its allies in Northeast Asia as examples of prosperity, so as to counter the lure of communist and socialist societies. Clearly, there were reasons grounded in geopolitics that caused the United States to actively support a course of strengthening East Asian economies.

Japan, NIEs and Southeast Asia

With the "threat" of communism looming large after the Second World War in China and Korea, the United States responded with a vision of a regional economy in East Asia driven by the revived Japanese industry, with access to raw materials that it would need, and also with access to overseas markets for its exports. This postwar American blue print for Japan's economic and social development importantly included some economic assistance to Japan to rebuild itself from the wartime destruction that it had endured, and, to facilitate this process, Japan's economic reach had to be extended over its erstwhile colonies.[32] President Truman's words at the time convey the urgency of the matter:[33]

> Make every effort to see to it that political and economic progress in Japan is such as to demonstrate the advantages of close association with the United States and our ability as a democracy to deal with the [development and security] problems of Asia.

Japan's economic recovery began shortly after the Second World War. Japan would have good access to its erstwhile imperial hinterland and itself become self-supporting in the process.[34] In this Cold War phase Japan was the development model in a milieu of protection and controls, with economic policy devised and closely implemented by the state, and with some American economic support. South Korea's development was to closely follow Japan's example, and both South Korea and Taiwan were greatly influenced by postwar Japan's path to prosperity. The latter two economies, assisted by American and Japanese capital and technologies, successfully followed state directed export-oriented policies, mercantilist in their essence, much as Japan had demonstrated. This was quite in keeping with the tradition of Friedrich List's and Alexander Hamilton's thinking, and would be readily recognized as such by students of European and American industrialization.[35] Southeast Asia in turn was influenced by the pattern of development in Northeast Asia.

In Japanese perception, Japan's development was the first step in the development of other East Asian economies: this was the flying geese model of economic development, with Japan leading the formation and the other proverbial geese trailing behind, with state policy having a substantial and fundamental role in the economy.[36] In this scheme Korea and Taiwan, in the second tier of the formation, were quick to follow Japan's example, and this was followed in due course in a relatively more moderate way by the third tier in the formation, the Southeast Asian economies.

Some American economic assistance was forthcoming in all cases, with large Chinese business communities amongst the minority communities of Southeast Asian countries greatly augmenting the entrepreneurial resources in those economies. These developments occurred in a global situation of protection and economic controls, as well as substantial state direction of economic policy, and served to provide a boost to intra-regional economic activity.

The shift in the American economic policy framework

Japan had become the world's second largest economy by the 1980s and was increasingly assertive by the end of that decade, about the time that Soviet Union appeared to be on the verge of collapse. Japanese assertiveness was also evident in its projection of its export-oriented and state directed development model as the approach best suited to lifting developing countries out of poverty. Both South Korea and Taiwan had industrialized following Japan, and Southeast Asia appeared to be undergoing a similar transformation. Japanese firms and banking houses were perhaps the most active among the foreign business presence in a China that seemed to be gearing up for development.

As was noted earlier, the United States had been supportive of the development efforts of Japan, South Korea and Taiwan, and more generally in East Asia, but chiefly as a part of a grand strategy to contain Communism. With the collapse of Soviet Union, the Communist threat had evaporated. The end of Cold War therefore brought a sea change in the American view on development policies it had promoted and the economic assistance it had extended for that purpose. The United States now set aside its previous support for a Japanese style model of state directed policy planning and economic controls. America now stood for a laissez faire approach in which state intervention had to be eliminated, economic controls and regulations whittled down to the bare minimum, entrepreneurs and private initiative were to be encouraged, and the outcome was to be decided by free markets, which were seen as autonomous and unquestioned arbiters of "efficiency" and "welfare." Freedom of movement of goods and capital had to be ensured. Developing countries in need of development funds were expected to seek the money from private banks, a country's creditworthiness permitting, and not look to official bilateral or other assistance. In case a country was in trouble with the private banks, it could seek International Monetary Fund's (IMF's) assistance, and in extending assistance the IMF would ensure the implementation of the new policy framework. This set of policies has often been referred to as the "Washington Consensus," a term variously attributed to Sanjaya Lall and John Williamson. The Japanese approach to economic development was under threat.

It was against this backdrop that Japan encouraged and financed a study of the East Asian development experience at the World Bank. The study took several years to complete. Though the research showed that the developmental state had been critical in the emergence of Japan, South Korea, Taiwan and others, pressure from the World Bank's senior management caused this finding to be played down; instead, the World Bank's "East Asian miracle" publication attributed the region's rapid economic development to the observance of World Bank and IMF policy advice, with the World Bank arguing that the Southeast Asian economies had relied even less on the state and more on the market than the latter in its development process.[37] The East Asians though generally saw their economic progress as an outcome of a determined developmental state and thought the World Bank study to be in denial in this respect.[38] None of the East Asian states was prepared to accept that it was "the miracle of the market" that had been the cause of their development. Notwithstanding all this discussion, the practical implications of the very determined and as it turned out non-negotiable shift in economic policy on the part of the United States were felt as the Asian financial crisis set in and the United States refused to extend official assistance to East Asia or to support any state-led effort to help the afflicted. In particular the United States was quick to counter and shoot down the Japanese effort to launch the Asian Monetary Fund that would adhere more to the Japanese perceptions about economic policies, and which would not have the United States as a member.[39]

In this manner the onset of an American promoted globalized world economy that was increasingly devoid of controls and protection, with relatively free flows of goods, services and capital combined with China's shift to a market economy.

China's approach to development and its impact on the region

This globalized world economy which China faced as it contemplated rapid development constituted a critical difference with the earlier milieu of protection and controls, with state interventions in the economy being the norm, in which Japan, Korea, Taiwan and the Southeast Asian states had so successfully developed. China therefore could not quite adopt and replicate the policies that had served the earlier developers in East Asia so well. The new American economic policies and the ensuing globalization had closed that particular route.

But the advent of globalization greatly facilitated the "processed manufacturing" approach to industrialization and development. China therefore liberalized its economy to an unprecedented degree as a part of its WTO accession process. Though the industry that was being created in China remained export-oriented, the approach to manufacture and trade reflected the "processed manufacturing" concept, with each of the participating economies in the region producing some goods or services respectively for the metaphorical final assembly shop—a role that was increasingly being assumed by China. Intra-regional trade shot up at a remarkable pace. China's adherence to an exceptionally liberal trade regime for a developing country greatly facilitated the organization of the region into what has often been referred to as "Factory Asia."

For countries in the region, China's processed manufacturing based approach to its development, with China serving as the nexus in the intra-regional economic transactions, compared very favorably with the earlier one pursued by Japan. Japan, in keeping with its times, had remained protectionist both regarding inward foreign direct investment and imports, whereas China's development was characterized by significantly greater openness, and that was more helpful to the regional economies. Also the impact of "processed manufacturing" activity was more immediate in participating countries and more of a simultaneous enmeshment, as distinct from Japan's model of a lead goose showing the upward flight to others' economies in second and third formations, as appropriate and in fullness of time. China was thus able to integrate better with the regional economies than was Japan during its years of high growth. As Japan's share of East Asian trade fell, China's increased.[40] Efforts were undertaken to consolidate the emerging trade relationships in the region through formal agreements.

China's economic ascendancy therefore brought about economic integration in East Asia, marked by rising quantum and value of intra-regional trade.

More generally, in time and with the rise of China, the attractiveness of the Japanese economic development experience lessened as a model for other economies in the region. The basic factor that perhaps worked against the Japanese style developmental state was the change in the organization of the world economy from one where national economies were "closed," and access was provided on a selective and preferential basis, to a more open system that simply did not permit protection and controls of an earlier era. China's processed manufacturing approach seemed much more in tune with the new times.

Critics also see other reasons behind the fall of the Japanese development model, and relate it to developments in Japan.[41] These reasons prominently include, first, the Japanese corporations had pulled back from the regional economies in the aftermath of the Asian financial crisis, thus increasing the latter's difficulties. Second, Japan devalued the yen in course of the Asian crisis, thereby again increasing the difficulties of the afflicted regional economies in their efforts to improve the trade balance. Third, the Japanese corporations were generally reluctant to transfer technology to firms in the regional economies. Fourth, the bursting of the Japanese financial bubble and the continuing inability of the Japanese economy to regain the earlier growth trajectory implied that Japan had not got everything right. However, on reflection some of these reasons may only have created an adverse feeling in the region towards Japan, but they do not seem particularly germane to the fall of the Japanese model.

To sum up, economic integration in East Asia, signified by increasing intra-regional trade and investment, began with the growth of the Japanese economy, as was indeed the United States intention.[42] Such regional integration picked up speed with Korea's growth, and has snowballed with the emergence of China. The ASEAN FTA and the three ASEAN+1 agreements are an attempt to consolidate the fast sprouting trade and investment related developments, as is the work towards an ASEAN+3 agreement. China's own preference for non-intervention and informal structures strengthens the ASEAN way and the ASEAN institutional hub serves as the forum for locking in a number of economic developments.

China's rapid growth and the centripetal forces generated by this growth in the region continue to further the integration of the East Asian economies. In a short space of time China has become the world's largest exporter and its second largest trader. It has also become the main trading partner for the countries in the region, displacing chiefly the United States and the European Union. In some of the East Asian economies, China is now the largest source of final demand, thereby tying up the economic performance in those economies closely to developments in the Chinese economy.[43] The rapid build up of intra-regional trade is supported by intra-regional investment. China's official assistance to some of the neighboring countries complements these developments. Large business communities of overseas Chinese are present in countries throughout the region. These overseas Chinese business communities facilitate intra-regional economic activity.

Thus with the expansion of the Chinese economy, East Asian economic development acquired a momentum of its own, reducing the material significance of United States economic involvement in the region. An event of some significance in further determining the nature of the postwar East Asia as an economic entity was the Asian financial crisis, and the global financial crisis which followed some ten years after the Asian one too was formative for East Asia.

The two financial crises and an East Asian identity

The two financial crises shifted attitudes in the region towards mutually beneficial economic and financial cooperation amongst the regional economies; such coming together much guided by needs of the moment. The two crises also enhanced China's authority in the region. The first of the two crises, the Asian financial crisis of 1997, occurred a few years after East Asia had been proclaimed as a miracle of economic development by the World Bank, and the second one, the global financial crisis of 2008, came after China had established itself both as a regional hub for trade and investment, and also as a significant player in the larger world economy. The two financial crises inadvertently helped the region to discover an "identity," albeit one grounded in economic transactions, and also helped the region to better understand the working of international financial institutions as well as the working of the world economy.

The first of the two financial crises, the Asian one, coming on the heels of the shift in American stance on economic policy, caught the region by surprise. Though the hot money flows and the problem of economic management these flows were causing to some of the economies that had freshly liberalized the financial sector under IMF advice was comprehended, the financial crisis and its debilitating impact on the economic and social fabric of a country had not been experienced earlier in East Asia in the postwar period. Faced with the problems caused by the crisis, the East Asians felt a sense of bewilderment when it became evident that United States would not be extending to them the kind of financial help it had invariably extended to the Latin American economies when those economies had faced financial and economic crises, with Mexico being the most recent example at that point. The afflicted economies thus sensed indifference in the attitude of United States as it seemed to stand aloof from East Asian plight. Indeed, in the perception of the afflicted economies the United States made matters worse for them in two ways. It stymied the creation of the Asian Monetary Fund proposed by the resource rich Japan, thereby denying them the potential assistance from such a source. And it supported what East Asians saw as harsh and unhelpful IMF policy advice and conditionality that could and did only worsen the plight of the afflicted economies even as the IMF policy prescriptions helped to bail out the American banks. Of course both developments, the imposition of the Washington Consensus policy framework by the IMF and the rejection of the Japanese effort to devise an alternative policy framework through the proposed institution of the AMF, publicly affirmed the strength of American commitment to its new stance on economic policy.[44]

Thus the first crisis forced the region to consider how best it might be able to protect itself against vagaries and vicissitudes of international finance, in face of what it perceived as an unhelpful attitude on the part of the United States, an attitude which seemed to be grounded in a different set of economic beliefs. The economies in the region came together on the ASEAN forum to deliberate the issues, and in the process to consider the creation of mechanisms for self-protection. The crisis also forced East Asia to focus on and to understand the working of international financial institutions, particularly the IMF, and that greatly clarified thinking of the countries on the desirability and development of regional financial institutions.

As noted in chapter 2 above, the East Asians eventually devised a two-fold response: the initiation of the ASEAN+3 mechanism, and the Chiang Mai Initiative; the latter being pursuit of policies that would help achieve some independence from the IMF and hence from a particular aspect of the multilateral system. The ASEAN+3 mechanism initially organized by Malaysia evolved a life and authority of its own in due course.[45] Apart from serving as a forum that regularly brought together the relatively larger economies of Northeast Asia with the smaller ones of Southeast Asia, the process also led to the creation of heads of government meeting between the three Northeast Asian countries, viz., China, Japan and South Korea. On the other hand the development of the Chiang Mai Initiative (CMI) did in fact considerably lessen in time the relevance of and the reliance upon the IMF. And if IMF assistance were not to be sought, there would be no obligation to follow IMF advice. In undertaking the CMI,[46] East Asia was exhibiting a capability to organize and cooperate as a multilateral economic community with interdependent interests, and its own distinct concepts of economic development and economic policy. This was the pragmatic basis of the region's emerging identity. Thus the "chance" occurrence of the Asian financial crisis was arguably a *sine qua non* for the initiation of the ASEAN+3 process and for the initiation of regional cooperation in finance that followed and continues to develop and expand in scope as well as in size. For East Asia this amounted to a parting of the ways with the American economic orthodoxy, and an assertion of its own economic beliefs. At the same time any loss of influence by the IMF meant a loss of American influence in East Asia, as America was the sole veto-wielding member on the IMF board.

The financial cooperation that developed after the Asian financial crisis in the form of the CMI arrangements, and the post crisis policies followed in East Asia, chiefly a build up of foreign exchange reserves, helped the region to cope with the second crisis, the global financial crisis, as did the rapidly growing intraregional trade linkages. Given the CMI arrangements, the substantial foreign exchange reserves, and robust economic performance, the East Asian economies showed a certain confidence in their own capabilities to manage the global financial crisis of 2008 as it unfolded; such confidence had been found wanting in course of the Asian financial crisis. The full measure of this achievement is seldom understood. For example assurance of such mutual support was seen to be lacking even in the Eurozone, where Greece, a member of EU and the Eurozone, was forced to seek IMF assistance in the continuing aftermath of the 2008 global financial crisis; assistance from France and Germany, both advanced economies as well as founding members of the EU, notwithstanding.

As performance in the advanced economies faltered with the onset of the 2008 crisis and confidence in the efficacy of self-regulating markets sank, there was a rush in United States and Europe to use state interventions as instruments of economic policy. The theoretical basis of economic policy was now recognizably in disarray.[47] America's worldwide pursuit of laissez faire polices including the implied approach to the lack of regulation of financial institutions and markets[48] and the consequent belief in self-correcting markets were widely judged to have deepened the global financial crisis, if not caused it. As the global financial crisis unfolded, such regulatory frameworks as were founded on a belief in self-correcting markets appeared deeply flawed and in need of substantial reform; they could no longer be advocated for implementation with any confidence elsewhere.[49] The East Asians weathered the 2008 global financial crisis in much better shape than the advanced economies and with a new self-confidence. There was thus a palpable shift in thinking regarding the merits of the East Asian approach as the advanced economies resorted to interventionist measures ordinarily identified with "state capitalism" or "socialism." The global financial crisis led to a shift in the perception regarding the soundness of economic policies based on self-correcting markets vis-à-vis those of the kind pursued in East Asia.

The 2008 global financial crisis also called into question the efficacy, viability, and continuation of the international economic, financial and monetary systems based on a national currency, namely the dollar, in its present form. The dollar had come under pressure as the crisis developed, giving cause for concern to holders of dollar assets and exposing the fragility of international monetary arrangements based on a national currency. Thus the second of the two crises also exposed the limits and the vulnerability of the dollar based international monetary system, and thus prodded China to speed up its policy regarding the use of renminbi in regional trade and finance as well as in international transactions.

Objective conditions drove the East Asian economies to cluster together in the two crises, with China as perhaps the *primus inter pares*, the latter effect being more explicit and in evidence on the second occasion. China's economic strength and prospects of continuing growth gave it the confidence to act decisively in both the crises. United States did not feel the need to directly assist in the first crisis other than support the IMF's stance, and it was not in a position to help in the second crisis, rather itself looking to China's help to bail out the world economy, whilst it sought to avoid the kind of "Washington Consensus" style adjustment policies that the IMF continued to advocate for the developing countries. East Asia had "delinked" from the United States and the multilateral system on this occasion in that it did not stand in need of any assistance.

The result of the two financial crises could be summed up as follows. Firstly, the response of the region to the two crises helps to highlight the effectiveness of East Asia as an economic community, albeit an informal one, but one displaying a capability to respond to and resolve the specific economic problems being encountered. The East Asia that came into sharp relief after the Asian financial crisis and dealt with the global financial crisis with visible authority had started to take shape in the early 1990s following the earlier development of Japan and the NIEs on the back of American assistance, and is increasingly more of an indigenous effort. It is also chiefly a community of interdependent economic interests, which is developing in an environment of a non-protectionist and globalized world economy, and is protective of such an environment because it continues to benefit from it. Its economic policies are determined in the region. Its trade and investment links with China continue to deepen and grow as China develops.

V: WHITHER EAST ASIA: THE SECURITY-ECONOMIC INTERACTION IN THE REGION

We have noted that economic support from United States was helpful to Japan, Korea and Taiwan, and then Southeast Asia, in their efforts to achieve high economic growth. China's entry in to the world economy too was facilitated by the United States. In acting thus, the United States had strategic motives, chiefly to contain the Soviet Union and negate the ideology that Soviet Union so powerfully symbolized. Thus whilst the American assistance had a role initially, the East Asian economic development has now taken off with its own independent dynamics, increasingly with a mind of its own. East Asia region continues to present a complex geopolitical prospect, where security and economic interests are deeply intertwined between the different regional players and a large presence of foreign, that is, American, troops. In this context, we deal with the different perspectives of the United States, China, Japan, South Korea and Southeast Asia.

United States objectives

The United States economy has benefited substantially from East Asia's growth and prosperity. East Asia's unlimited supplies of manufactures to the United States at increasingly affordable prices, along with the equally unlimited supply of dollars to buy these goods with, has been beneficial for America in more ways than one. It has been beneficial for the financial interests in the United States which have used the Asian dollars to generate unprecedented profits. It has been beneficial for the American corporate interests in affording them space for factories and unlimited supplies of low wage labor, to their profit. And it has been beneficial for the proverbial person on the American street in providing her/him with affordable manufactures, and also with the credit to buy these goods. There is little desire to disturb this arrangement on the part of the United States, but the fact that it means increasing American indebtedness to East Asia. Within East Asia, if the American public pronouncements of American authority are any guide, it is just the money owed to China that seems to be an immediate source of concern. Indebtedness to Japan, Korea and Taiwan seems to matter much less, perhaps because, with American forces on the ground in Japan and Korea, and Taiwan perceiving itself as dependent on American security guarantees, United States can "get tough" with them. As for China, Secretary of State Hillary Clinton ponders the question: how do you get tough with your banker.[50] And the Australian foreign minister finds Secretary Clinton's approach to economic management quite normal and "rational" and speculates how to deal with the "subrational and deeply emotional" Chinese: his "rational" answer to the quandary is to wage war! These are the very depths of the moral abyss that a great power now plumbs in its economic adversity.

This relationship between East Asia and the United States, qualitatively different from the one experienced for a good part of the earlier postwar period, is widely perceived as "symbiotic," and defined as "living together of unlike organisms."

The recent American policy on China, say over the past ten years or so, exhibits a certain "eccentricity," if it is not to be seen in some disarray. From the tense days of the accidental bombing of the Chinese embassy in Belgrade by the CIA,[51] and the Hainan incident, which saw an American "surveillance" aircraft brought in to land by China for violation of its airspace followed by an American apology,[52] subsequent identification of China as a "strategic competitor,"[53] and then the pledge to defend Taiwan by "whatever it took,"[54] we saw a further ratcheting up of the Sino-US tensions in the inclusion of North Korea in the "Axis of Evil."[55] Post 9/11 we see some moderation in the American stance, a more friendly attitude towards China and the participation in the six party talks to negotiate peacefully with North Korea. As the global financial crisis shakes up the very foundations of the American economy, another shift occurs. Secretary Clinton visits China and recalls the Chinese proverb that people in the same boat fight the storm together, as a preface to seeking Chinese financial assistance,[56] and the American government's financial and economic leadership seeks Beijing's indulgence. A China visit by a modest appearing American president, behaving out of character for holders of that high office, follows. Then we see yet another shift in the American stance. Beijing is widely portrayed as a potential if not actual currency manipulator, the Dalai Lama is recalled from his meditation and slumber to meet the American president in the White House, America decides to sell arms to Taiwan,[57] and the American president dashes through "Asian democracies" of India, Indonesia, Japan and Korea, also including Vietnam in his travels, but avoiding China, even though China is the very visible subtext of these travels and travails.[58] The beginning of an American effort to construct a new great wall of China, this time only to hem in that country, is evident. China must do more is the new mantra from Washington. Roller coasters are largely an American pop culture phenomenon and this roller coaster of US-East Asia ties is as "thrilling" as it gets.

The United States seeks to be an active participant in East Asia, a geographic space that in its definition encompasses the Pacific; it seeks to be one that decides "the agenda," even as it sees its ability to get "action" according to "the agenda" receding with time.[59] For the moment the United States serves as a large export market, able to pay for those goods because of its power of seigniorage. The issue is whether this seigniorage can continue. And even if it were to continue, the question of a sustained and viable financial relationship with East Asia remains. The answer to that question lies chiefly in the economic strength of the United States. The United States needs visible leverage to deal with its creditors, and maintaining military power in the region provides a form of leverage and influence: a reported 40,000 American troops are in Japan (two-thirds of the number are said to be stationed in Okinawa), and another 28,500 American troops remain in South Korea. The "threat" from North Korea has replaced the Soviet "threat." Military power and its deployment in East Asia also enable the United States to project itself as a provider of security in the region.

Not unreasonably and like other countries, the United States is also making efforts to hitch a ride on Asia's continuing economic success. But unlike other countries it also wishes to run the show. It has launched a Trans-Pacific Partnership, known by the acronym TPP, in an effort to create a free trade area that encompasses economies on both sides of the Pacific under its "leadership." The project reflects American concern about being sidelined in the growing Asian trade networks.[60] For the moment there seem to be eight countries viz., Australia, Brunei Darussalam, Chile, Malaysia, New Zealand, Peru, Singapore, and the United

States, with a ninth, namely Vietnam, tidying up its domestic economy to meet the membership requirements.[61] For the proposed arrangement to be beneficial there ought to be substantial trade between the members or the prospective of this arrangement. The major East Asian economies, viz., China, Japan, and Korea are yet not there, thus significantly reducing the gains from the arrangement. For any meaningful enlargement of the TPP membership to the latter three nations, the efforts may come up against a number of hurdles, including but not restricted to Japan and Korea's reservations on trade liberalization. As and when a TPP materializes, it is not clear who might be its beneficiaries. In the longer term the United States may be seeking a Free Trade Area of the Asia Pacific (FTAAP) with APEC as the focal point.

China's concerns

A rapidly growing Chinese economy serves as the economic motor in what is now a fast integrating economic region. Thus we have regional economic interdependence in East Asia that strengthens the economic links between Northeast Asia and Southeast Asia through the Chinese economic hub, and also creates the space for crossties amongst the different countries. China emergence has gradually moderated the impact of the earlier American and European economic linkages, and the region as we have noted is now in search of organizational forms to lock in the bottom up intra-regional economic interaction and developments. The process is aided considerably by the business community including the Chinese ethnic minorities in a number of Southeast Asian countries that are active and major players in the respective economies. The economic freedoms that define the globalized world economy facilitate this process.

The two financial crises have separately enhanced China's authority in the region. The first of the two crises helped to better understand the nature of American, Chinese and Japanese interests in the region. In the first crisis, the United States stood behind the IMF, displaying what the East Asians perceived as an indifference to their plight. Japan devalued the yen, thereby making an export led recovery for others that much more challenging, and Japan also failed to make much headway with its Asian Monetary Fund proposal. It could not stand up to the American opposition in the latter instance. China did not devalue, thereby sharing the burden of adjustment with its neighbors. For China the first of the two crises directly led to cooperation on financial aspects. The second crisis showed the fragility of the dollar based world financial system, and it also laid bare the limits of the laissez faire economic model pursued by the advanced economies.

China identifies its priority to continue with its rapid development, and therefore China obviously stands to gain from peace and stability in a globalized world economy and more so in the region; the production and trade structures of the Chinese economy are well geared to taking advantage of such an environment. The policy pronouncements from Beijing with an emphasis on a peaceful and stable neighborhood that should also stand to gain from China's economic growth reflect this. The neighbors are thirteen in number, and East Asia is not mentioned in this context.[62] Chinese leaders use the guidelines of "do good to our neighbors, treat our neighbors as partners" (*yulin weishan, yilin weiban*) and "maintain friendly relations with our neighbors, make them feel secure, and help to make them rich" (*mulin, anlin, fulin*).[63] The omission of East Asia in such statements also highlights the difficulty of formulating policy when dealing with an ill-defined concept in geographical and political terms.

In the process of development China's policies towards its neighbors have helped to successfully integrate the economies in the region, to the benefit of all participants. Some of these relationships have been formalized through bilateral and multilateral economic agreements, including trade agreements, whilst negotiations continue to formalize the more complex aspects. China stands to gain from a general opening up of intraregional trade because it liberalized its trade regime to a greater degree than the other economies in the region. And it has pursued this aim of liberalization through the trade agreements it has concluded in the region, generally going the extra mile to the benefit of the other party.

Taiwan's case, potentially perhaps the most difficult one in terms of relations with China, offers a reasonably good example of how China and economies in the region are adjusting advantageously to China's rise even as they get closer in terms of economic linkages, and notwithstanding substantial political differences. Business links with Taiwan have deepened, as bilateral trade and investment flows have multiplied manifold. Taiwan's considerable initial reluctance towards such linkages gave way as the substantial economic advantages of doing business with China became evident and the business view won over the policymakers.[64] The growing economic ties have been consolidated through a recent bilateral economic agreement that on balance serves Taiwan's economic interests more than China's. An increasingly vocal and influential business lobby in Taiwan argues for better political relations with China. China as well as the majority of Taiwan population subscribes to the "One China" principle.[65]

But China's perceived security concerns are also growing in keeping with the country's increasing economic size and its growing worldwide trade and investment linkages. The latter require secure arrangements that sustain a globalized world economy, and that make for stability in economic partner countries and efficient logistics for transfer of goods and materials.[66]

Japan's concerns

The United States is arguably keen that Japan, where it has troops, serve as a linchpin for a larger American presence in East Asia, something that, given the region's unpleasant history under Japanese occupation during the Second World War, may not be welcome in the region.[67] The issue of Japan's identity remains unresolved even these many years after the Second World War ended; the alliance with the United States did not help clarify this aspect, and Japan's past continues to cast a shadow over its relations with China, Korea, Taiwan, Southeast Asia, and Russia.[68] It has still to conclude and sign a peace treaty with Russia to formally end the Second World War hostilities. The hub and spoke model with no crossties nature of the alliance with the United States froze mistrust between Japan and the countries in the region rather than encouraging reconciliation between them. For example, in the specific case of Japan-China relations, Victor Cha has noted:[69]

> The United States also sought to control Japan's relationship with China, fearing that a recovering Japan would see China as its natural economic partner. Some US officials, including Dulles, were concerned that this economic logic could cause Japan to gravitate toward the communist bloc. Dulles flew to Tokyo in December 1951 to obtain a commitment that Japan would not conclude a bilateral treaty with communist China. The resulting "Yoshida letter" was an extraordinarily powerful example of the exertion of US control over an ally, the scale of which did not become fully known until it was later revealed that Dulles actually drafted the letter.

Japan has an unfortunate history in the twentieth century, and that continues to affect its relationships. Japan colonized Korea and Taiwan and occupied parts of China. Japan's colonization and occupation were invariably seen as harsh. But there are different versions of Japan's history, and the variations reflect both mistrust and substance. Better political relations may have helped reduce the significance of this matter, and the alliance with the United States may not have been helpful in improvement of Japan's relations with its neighbors. It is a puzzling fact that Japan has failed to craft enduring political ties of trust with its neighbors in spite of substantial economic links. For now Japan remains diplomatically marginalized in its own region, even as it is America's most prominent ally in East Asia.

The Shigeru doctrine and the 1955 system, said to underpin Japan's policies, seem not to resonate with their old authority any longer.[70] "Japan as number one," and "Japan that can say no," words so often heard in the 1980s, appear to be slogans from another, bygone age.[71] The economic problems that began to surface in the 1990s, the declining population numbers, a rapidly growing China, and questioning of the US-Japan alliance has caused some soul searching in Japan. Japanese efforts at assuming a "leadership" position in Asia faltered in the instance of the Asian Monetary Fund, when its interests seemed to conflict with those of the United States. Earlier Japan had stayed away from the East Asian Economic Caucus proposed by Malaysia, because the United States was not included in that group. Japan's position in Asia is thus an awkward one, and clearly something of a contradiction: the United States would like Japan to lead Asia, but only if it happens in consultation with and as guided by the United States. This is not a tenable position because the very alliance with the United States determines how Japan is viewed in East Asia and compromises its capacity to be an independent player.

At one point Japan raised the possibility of China and Japan working for an Asian NATO, a proposal made presumably with the United States consent if not at its prodding. Separately Japan under Prime Minister Hatoyama also took the initiative to seek a regional accord in an East Asian community, without quite explicitly clarifying whether United States would be welcome as a member in such an organization. The proposal did not carry.

Koizumi's advisor on foreign affairs summed up the outlook and said that Japan's two goals were to maintain the US-Japan alliance and be a responsible and reliable actor in Asia; as a middle power Japan could not be expected to compete with United States or China.[72] But Japan also harbors a fear of being abandoned by the United States and needs to consider that the United States may have lost influence in East Asia over the years, having got itself involved in wars in Southwest and West Asia that do not reflect Japanese aims or priorities, much less those of larger East Asia.

The present Japan-China relationship is summed up as "cold politics-hot economics." Japanese firms are increasingly sourcing production in China, and Japan-China trade is growing rapidly, eclipsing the Japan-US trade. Good economic and trade relationships have led to institutionalizing of official links and contacts, including those amongst the heads of government.[73] In a recent dispute involving the internment of a Chinese seaman in the Diaoyu/Senkaku Islands vicinity, it was reported to be the affected Japanese business community that encouraged the government to release the seaman, as China had sought, and thus to settle the matter, even though the United States publicly asserted that the disputed islands were covered by the terms of US-Japan bilateral security treaty.[74]

The large majority of Japanese does not harbor any ill will toward China and feels that economic growth in China would be good for Japan.[75]

A question mark hangs over Japan's future political role in Asia as the sluggish American economy loses some of its weight whilst China's economic surge continues. It is a fact that in modern times Japan has historically aligned itself with the world's dominant power, be it China, Britain or the United States. And such conduct on Japan's part has defied the prognosis advanced by international relations theory that an emerging power makes an effort at balancing the dominant power.[76]

Korea's concerns

South Korea has drawn closer to China over the last fifteen years chiefly as a result of growing trade and investment links. It has a history of stable relations with China, which had been masked by the Cold War. China's border dispute with Korea was settled with North Korea, with China reported to have ceded some 60 per cent of the Korean claim. A growing Chinese economy offers Korea exceptional opportunities, and Korea accepts the greater economic integration and open borders that China finds helpful. China has been Korea's largest market since 2003. Already by 2004, over 25,000 South Korean firms that reportedly had production facilities in China.[77]

Reunification of Korea is an overriding policy goal. Both North and South Korea regard the current division of the peninsula as temporary, but differ on the form and strategy for unification. The basis for the unification goal is claimed to be some 5000 years of common history, common language and culture, and the claim of a single bloodline, thus possibly mixing myth with reality. China's handling of the North Korean nuclear issue has contributed to the development of Korea-China relationship. Both countries also found United States too confrontational in the six party talks. Chinese view is that engagement with North Korea helps improve North Korea's economy, and if that happens then the Korean problem may be solved in an acceptable manner. Engagement with North Korea that leads to economic interdependence and political reconciliation, and is therefore consistently helpful to reunification, seems to be the pragmatic course to take. Engagement began in 1993 and has continued since with the object of fostering reform and openness in North Korea. There has been a rapid expansion of trade with North Korea, and investment in the special economic zone of Kaesong Park has grown. Economic cooperation with North Korea has popular support. China's trade and investment with North Korea outstrips that of South Korea though.

A particular South Korean concern is the humanitarian disaster that would likely occur if North Korea were to just collapse. One rather more nuanced view holds that after four generations, the young Koreans have no first hand knowledge of the threat from North Korea and the war that took place and poverty that followed, and in practice the goal of reunification might not be such a priority.[78]

Korea's relations with the United States are complex, as the Koreans see an American role in creating their present situation. The United States accepted Japan's supremacy over the Korean peninsula in the 1905 peace treaty, which Theodore Roosevelt negotiated between Russia and Japan.

Arguably the United States through this move ensured Japanese supremacy in Northeast Asia, hence also sowing discord and making reconciliation between Japan and other countries in the region unlikely at least for some time. The 1943 assurance given by Franklin Roosevelt that in due course Korea would be free and independent once it had been liberated from Japan was also not honored by the United States. South Korea fears that the United States might initiate a conflict on the peninsula that might devastate the country, and therefore finds the American doctrine of preemptive war as an instrument of state policy very worrying. The vast majority of Korean public opposes the GWOT and associated actions.[79]

The South Korean-United States alliance appears less important to both parties than it did during the Cold War. United States raises concerns about North Korea's missiles and nuclear weaponry, and perceives a military threat. South Korea on the other hand views North Korea principally as an issue of national unification and sees it more in economic and cultural terms, the attitude of the government varying with the party or person in power though. Even as North Korea went nuclear in October 2006, South Korea remained suspicious of United States motives in its response, and was more supportive of engagement. South Korea is reported to have pointed out that North Korea had not succumbed to pressure for some past fifty years and was unlikely to do so now. In South Korean perception, managing the nuclear issue is a necessary step to reunification. South Korea sees North Korea as a distant relative rather than an enemy, and has downgraded North Korea as a security threat.[80] China shares South Korea's goal of a peaceful transition in North Korea. South Korean opinion surveys show that South Koreans find the United States more of a threat than China. There is a belief in South Korea that the United States is exacerbating the division and increasing the possibility of war. In relation to China the concern voiced is about an economic slowdown there.[81]

Reunified or otherwise Korea faces the problem of coexisting in a region with two large countries, that is, China and Japan, and a superpower with substantial interests in the region, that is, the United States. China's rise is forcing South Korea to confront a region radically different from the one that has existed for the first fifty years of the postwar period. Most international relations experts and American policy makers see the United States as South Korea's obvious and benign ally. But China's proximity and size means that it cannot be ignored. South Korea has a similar short-run policy orientation as China, and does not feel threatened by China. Korea provides the best example that the world does not fear China the way the transatlantic media feels it should. Over the past fifteen years the US role in the region and in Korea has been scaled back and that of China has increased.

One particular aspect is that China alone amongst the major players seems to have a regional policy or a "game plan." In course of its own development its policy of "do good to your neighbors" offers an opportunity for the South Korean economy to benefit from China's economic growth. China also seems to be keen on extending its open economy approach to its neighbors via the proposed trade agreements, of which a bilateral China-Korea FTA and the ASEAN+3 FTA would apply to Korea. The United States offers only the pursuit of a nuclear free North Korea but wishes to seek that goal very much in its own way. Japan offers little to Korea in terms of a regional policy. South Korea seems more worried by Japan's militarization than it is by China's. The dispute with Japan about Dokdo Islands remains unresolved. Korean public perception of China is more positive than that of other major powers, as opinion polls and surveys show.[82]

Southeast Asia's concerns

The nations of Southeast Asia are very much involved in economic development, and keen to keep clear of power politics for this reason. China's emergence has been directly beneficial both in trade relations and in the area of general economic assistance and therefore in the nation building projects.

In Southeast Asian countries, economic success seems to have helped to further a process of coalescing around ASEAN, imbibing the organization with confidence, with doubts about *the ASEAN way* approach surfacing only if the economies seemed to falter, or security seemed to be threatened. ASEAN's norm of non-intervention has been central to the evolution of its place in East Asian diplomacy. Thus the approach of avoidance of such traditional multilateral security treaties that require collective intervention, and the approach of exerting the non-intervention norm in regional affairs, of exclusion of non-Asians from the decision making processes in the Asian organizations whilst continuing to consult with them on issues of mutual interest, and avoidance of formal structures, legalities and procedures, possibly reached its highest form in Southeast Asia in the ASEAN and *the ASEAN way*. The ASEAN process further enhanced its relevance and applicability with the addition of the dialogue partners dimension that enabled interaction with other major players.

China's involvement with ASEAN has built up rapidly since it became an ASEAN dialogue partner in 1996. China participation in ASEAN moots helped to increase ASEAN's influence and give it new directions. China's own preference for non-intervention and non-legalistic processes, and for nation-building objectives jives well with ASEAN's. Even though China is the economic hub of the region, it is ASEAN that has served as the de jure focal point for the substantive multilateral economic and political dialogue that takes place in East Asia, in formats of AS-

EAN+1, ASEAN+3, ASEAN Regional Forum (ARF), and the East Asian Summit (EAS).

The Asian financial crisis tested the ASEAN approach and the organization's resilience. ASEAN's answer to economic uncertainties was the CMI, ASEAN FTA and the ASEAN plus initiatives with its neighbors to the north in trade and economic cooperation. The eventual answer to the security conundrum in this context was the ARF, which sought "common security" but at the same time firmly rejected "collective intervention."[83]

Individual countries in Southeast Asia differ on the perceptions regarding regional security. Singapore has voiced its particular concerns, the city-state perched at the extremity of the Malayan peninsula dressing up its views as those of East Asia, that Asia could not function properly and may be at risk from China without a large American footprint in Asian matters, thus raising the question as to what are the Asian values that Singapore often espouses.[84] Mr. Lee Kwan Yew visited Washington to seek American involvement in Asian affairs, and in doing so he echoed a point of view quite popular among some in the United States. New York Times reported some of Mr. Lee Kwan Yew's concerns in the following words:

> One of his concerns now, Mr Lee said, is that the United States has become so preoccupied with the Middle East that it is failing to look ahead and plan in this part of the world.
> "I think it is a real drag slowing down adjustment to the new situation", he said, describing what he called a lapse that worries Southeast Asian countries that count on Washington to balance the rising economic and diplomatic power of China.[85]

Mr. Lee Kwan Yew also expressed his concern over China's military build up. In his judgment in two or three decades into the future a modern high-tech People's Liberation Army was very likely, and he thought that a "blue water fleet with aircraft carriers cannot just be to deter foreign intervention in a conflict between Taiwan and Mainland."[86] He has nevertheless remained reticent, if not altogether silent, about the specific threat that was causing him alarm. The Chinese responses to such rhetoric tend to be reassuring. Public personalities in Singapore appear to have a commonality of views with Mr Lee Kwan Yew, and a subsequent book by Singapore's Mr. Simon S. C. Tay perhaps helps in understanding the problem. Mr. Tay feels that the global financial crisis has led to a parting of the ways for Asia and the United States. Policies must be devised to bring them together as such togetherness would be advantageous for both.[87] A *People's Daily* columnist though assured the ASEAN countries of China's peaceful and cooperative attitude towards its neighbors, where the ASEAN countries outnumber the larger three, and regretted the invitation by Mr. Lee Kwan Yew to "Uncle Sam" to be the arbiter in East Asia.[88]

VI: SUMMING UP

In the postwar world, the nebulous shape of the region described broadly as East Asia, with the Pacific often added on particularly by the United States, has reflected an interaction between the continuing efforts at projection of power by the United States, the increasing economic empowerment of the region, and the effective assertion of postcolonial norms by some of the countries in the region to guide inter-state relations. The concept of the region has thus varied as this interaction has evolved. Right after the Second World War, United States sought to "contain" the erstwhile USSR and "Red China" chiefly through bilateral military alliances supplemented with some economic support, initially defining East Asia as Japan, Korea and Taiwan; China was included only as the adversary.

The region is conceived differently by China, Japan and the United States. In Chinese understanding there is a concept of neighboring countries, but not Asia and this may be indicative of China's priorities to assist in and facilitate the development in the region. A peaceful and prosperous neighborhood is arguably the indigenous concept of what region and "regionalism" might mean for China, and it is a concept with a long history. References to Asia are more frequent in Japanese pronouncements, suggesting ambitions of a leadership role. United States refers often to Asia-Pacific, possibly revealing its desire for an overarching global reach.

In the post Cold War world as the region's economic success and prosperity became evident we had the economies that had achieved the East Asian miracle constituting a World Bank defined regional economic space, but China was again not among these economies. As economic prosperity spread across the region, it helped introduce concepts of a Pacific Rim and a Pacific Century.[89] Subsequently with a rapidly emerging China and a fast integrating region we have a new China-centric East Asia.[90]

The security arrangements in East Asia are chiefly a legacy of the Cold War days and remain US-centric, though US authority has perhaps been much diluted as the East Asian economies developed. The agreements underlying the security structure remain in place, even though the supporting arguments have lost their logic. The politics of these arrangements involved the definition of the region in a manner so as to exclude China in terms of regional economics and politics and to see it as an unambiguous adversary at least until the Nixon visit in February 1972 and the ensuing US-China rapprochement. After the end of the Cold War phase, the treaties remained in place holding out the prospect of America's continuing leverage over its treaty allies in the post Cold War issues. In this new scenario, with North Korea providing the new "threat,"

America and some other nations in the region, contrary to what international relations theory might suggest, have sought to "balance" the new emerging China, whilst not foregoing the economic gains that deepening interaction with China holds out.[91]

Intra-regional linkages are an important aspect of the increasing economic prosperity that East Asia is experiencing. China's emergence is central to this phenomenon. China is invariably willing to go the extra mile in order to meet the development aspirations of its neighbors, and its economic policies toward its neighbors, are clear both in concept and in implementation. Countries in the region are working through ASEAN as well as bilaterally to formalize the intra-regional processes of economic cooperation. The region very much wishes to see a continuation of this economic prosperity. In the economic sphere the East Asian countries have clarity on the desired ends and the benefits. The countries are also very clear on the means to be deployed in achieving economic growth.

It is a remarkable fact that in the postwar period, countries of East Asia are the only ones amongst the developing economies to have either made the shift to the developed group of economies, or are visibly in the process of doing so and on track to do so. The region is no longer dependent financially on multilateral institutions. The intra-regional trade continues to grow. Central to the continuation of this story is China's economy. This China-centric economic region now stands in stark contrast to the East Asia of postwar security arrangements. The East Asia that China faced in its earlier interaction in the region was one that built up around a US-centric security structure.

In comparison with the economic developments, the security situation in the region is vague, ill-defined, with little clarity about the means and ends. Security issues include firstly, contentions about interstate boundaries and disputed islands territories. Secondly, there is the nuclear status of North Korea and the issue of reunification on the Korean peninsula. Third is the issue of Taiwan and the one China policy. Some in the region also see the increasing militarization of Japan as a major problem. Japan has an unusual twentieth-century history in the Asian context, and there is a lack of trust in the region vis-à-vis Japan. This lack of trust is explained by the colonization of parts of Asia by Japan, and by Japan's close alignment with American policy. These are not novel issues but they have acquired a new significance with the emergence of China and a lack of any definitive policy on the part of the United States, other than perhaps a desire to remain the dominant power in Asia Pacific. When tensions build up in a particular security context in the region, we invariably see moves motivated by economic and financial interests to arrive at some solution so that the economic development process can move on. For example trade interests were important for Japan and may have caused it to backtrack on the arrest of the Chinese seaman in the waters of

Diaoyu / Senkaku Islands. Economic interests seem to trump "security" considerations.[92]

The United States appears not to have a long-term agenda that would be attractive for the region as a whole, and seems to vacillate amongst different geostrategic priorities, and possibly also remains uncertain about the means at its disposal to achieve such long-term ends as it may conceive, notwithstanding its exceptional military hardware and technology. American perception of China shifts between a strategic partner to a competitor, at times seen as a G-2 candidate and on other occasions advising China's neighbors to be wary of China.[93] East Asians are somewhat reluctant to a future of China versus the rest, and appear unwilling to be drawn into such a course no matter how hard they are prodded, though at times the smaller Asian economies are not averse to using such leverage as one of the bigger countries might offer vis-à-vis another.

In East Asian perception, their aspirations were resisted by the United States on a number of fronts. APEC *sans* the United States was not acceptable to America, neither were the East Asian Economic Caucus and the Asian Monetary Fund, even though the latter may arguably have lessened the pain of the region's economies afflicted by the Asian financial crisis in 1997.[94] The conjecture that in the Asian financial crisis, the US would have responded differently if the Cold War was on and USSR had been standing is not lost on East Asians who suffered through that crisis. The United States has variously both ignored and courted ASEAN and ASEAN related moots in recent years. With China's rapid rise, United States authority in the region appears to have been further diluted. The American initiatives for East Asia invariably seek to create regional organizations that include "non-Asians," for example Australia and New Zealand, who, in Dr. Mahatir's words, consider themselves to be "Europeans."

Looking to the future, one is encouraged to speculate that for the region much would depend on sustained growth in China, which could be expected to help buttress the region's economic performance given the trade and investment linkages. With time China's currency would necessarily take on a regional and an international role, though the precise path taken in the process remains foggy. Any reduction in the role of the state in the economy and a larger role for market forces, a likely development, implies growing income and wealth inequalities. Social pressures are likely to grow as a result. The manner in which East Asia interacts with economies on the farther shores of Pacific would depend much on how the American economy performs, and how Japan's economy performs and its policy towards United States plays out. Efforts at economic cooperation accords between the three northeast economies of China, Japan and South Korea, if sustained, may help to moderate differences on territorial issues and would have a salutary impact on the geopolitical tensions in the region.

NOTES

1. Mahbubani seems to consider a region from Israel to Japan as the extremities of the "New Asian Hemisphere." See Kishore Mahbubani, The new Asian hemisphere, Public Affairs (New York, 2008).

2. See Amitav Acharya, Whose ideas matter, Agency and power in Asian regionalism (Singapore, ISEAS, 2010), pp. 42-43.

3. The Council for Foreign Relations definition of Northeast Asia does not include Taiwan, even though China as well as Taiwan subscribe to the one China policy, and Taiwan is geographically adjacent to China and Japan. See http://www.cfr.org/region/478/northeast_asia.html. The concept of Southeast Asia as a political entity was reportedly used first in August 1943 at the Quebec Conference when the Allied powers established a separate Southeast Asia Command (SEAC) covering Burma, Malaya, Sumatra and Thailand. The Potsdam Conference in July 1945 extended SEAC's responsibilities to cover rest of the Netherlands East Indies and Indochina south of sixteenth parallel. Only North Vietnam, Philippines and Laos were excluded. See CM Turnbull, Regionalism and nationalism, in Nicholas Tarling, ed., The Cambridge history of Southeast Asia, volume 4 (Cambridge: Cambridge University Press, 1999), p. 258.

4. Li Lanqing, the former Vice Premier of China recalls:

> [China] having no model upon which to pattern its opening up policy, had to grope its way through trial and error. It all began in January 1979, when a Hong Kong businessman's letter asking for permission to open a factory in Guangdong Province was sent to Deng, who by then was the de facto top leader in China. Upon reading the letter, Deng wrote down the instruction, "As I see it, Guangdong should be given a free hand to give this sort of thing a try."

See Li Lanqing, Breaking through, The birth of China's opening-up policy (Oxford: Oxford University Press, 2009), p. 73. More generally, Taiwan, along with Hong Kong, is credited with playing a central role in the initial years of China's economic development under Deng Xiaoping. See discussion in Randall Jones, Robert King, and Michael Klein, The Chinese economic area: Economic integration without a free trade agreement, OECD Economics Department working paper no. 124, Paris 1992.

5. India is often suggested as a potential economic challenger of China, often judged as having the potential to overtake China. The discussion is generally hypothetical and often draws on the assumption that India is politically a more stable entity. There is now a growing literature on such comparisons. All season pundits readily offer guidance how this could be brought about soon. See for example Martin Wolf, What India must do to catch up with and possibly outpace China, Financial Times, February 15, 2006.

6. Brian Cumings, Parallax visions, Making sense of American-East Asian relations at the end of the century (Durham: Duke University Press, 1999), pp. 177-179.

7. See Victor D. Cha, Powerplay: Origins of the US alliance system in Asia, International Security, vol. 34, no. 3, Winter 2009/10, pp. 158-196.

8. See Victor D. Cha, Powerplay: Origins of the US alliance system in Asia, International Security, vol. 34, no. 3, Winter 2009/10, pp. 158-196.

9. See Victor D. Cha, Powerplay: Origins of the US alliance system in Asia, International Security, vol. 34, no. 3, Winter 2009/10, p. 184.

10. See Amitav Acharya, Whose ideas matter, Agency and power in Asian regionalism (Singapore: ISEAS, 2010), pp. 3-28. Acharya though highlights the role of Nehru in formulating ideas and concepts. But the successful Indonesian nationalist struggle led by Soekarno against the Dutch may have been the more relevant and powerful influence.

11. The Asian Relations Conference, technically a non-official gathering, was organized by the non-governmental Indian Council on World Affairs, and it was convened

by Jawaharlal Nehru in 1947 and again in 1949. The Bandung Conference was an Afro-Asian meeting and the key issue was "non-intervention." See Amitav Acharya, Whose ideas matter, Agency and power in Asian regionalism, (Singapore, ISEAS, 2010), pp. 34-36 and 54-60, respectively.

12. SEATO included only the Philippines and Thailand from Southeast Asia. Unlike NATO, an attack on one member was not to be considered an attack on all the alliance members. Also referred to as the Manila Pact, after the city where the agreement was signed in 1954, SEATO had become non-functional by 1973. Collective intervention by SEATO powers in Vietnam War was sought twice by the United States, France and the Philippines withholding support in the first instance, and France and Pakistan in the second. South Vietnam could not be a SEATO member because of the 1954 Geneva accords ending the French Indo-China war.

13. See Amitav Acharya, Whose ideas matter, Agency and power in Asian regionalism (Singapore: ISEAS, 2010), pp. 69-81.

14. The categorization of "Major Non-NATO Ally" does not amount to a mutual defense pact. In the matter of the Japanese troops in Iraq, the New York Times reported as follows:

> In all, 38 nations sent soldiers over the past six years, typically in groups numbering in the low hundreds, in rotations that were usually brief and sometimes even furtive. Japan sent a force but announced that it would not fight. Dutch troops had to be deployed just to guard it.

See Rod Norland and Timothy Williams, Iraq force soon to be a coalition of one, New York Times, July 29, 2009.

15. See Amitav Acharya, Whose ideas matter, Agency and power in Asian regionalism (Singapore, ISEAS, 2010).

16. Singapore and Malaysia are party to the *Five power defence agreement* that includes the United Kingdom, Australia, and New Zealand as well, and provides for consultations in case of an aggression against Malaysian peninsula. Drawn up in 1971, in the wake of Britain's exit from "east of Suez," the perceived threat at the time was conceived to be from Indonesia. See Dr Khoo How San, The five power defence arrangements: If it ain't broke, in Pointer: Journal of the Singapore armed forces, Oct-Dec 2000.

17. See Amitav Acharya, Whose ideas matter, Agency and power in Asian regionalism (Singapore, ISEAS, 2010), pp. 113-119.

18. See Amitav Acharya, Whose ideas matter, Agency and power in Asian regionalism (Singapore, ISEAS, 2010), pp. 120-121.

19. Ellen L Frost, Asia's new regionalism (Boulder, Lynne Rienner, 2009), pp. 136-138.

20. Ha Joon Chang, Kicking away the ladder, Development strategy in historical perspective (London, Anthem Press, 2002).

21. Japan's history of aligning itself with the dominant power has been widely noted. See for example discussion in Andrew Gordon, A modern history of Japan, From Tokugawa times to the present (Oxford, Oxford University Press, 2003), p. 4 and p. 115; and David Kang, China Rising (New York, Columbia University Press, 2010), p. 155. Also see Brian Cumings, From Japanese imperium to American hegemony, in Charles Armstrong, ed., Korea at the center (Armonk, ME Sharpe, 2006) and R. Taggart Murphy, Japan's policy trap (Washington DC, Brookings, 2004). International relations writers such as Evelyn Goh though are silent on this departure from the expectations of international relations theory by the Japanese.

22. See David Kang, China Rising (New York, Columbia University Press, 2010), p. 156.

23. Andrew Gordon writes: ". . . in 1879 Japan forced the Ryukyu king to abdicate and incorporated the Ryukyu Islands as the prefecture of Okinawa," noting that the Chinese government also claimed control of Ryukyu Islands. See Andrew Gordon, A modern history of Japan, From Tokugawa times to the present (Oxford, Oxford Uni-

versity Press, 2003), pp. 74-75. Interestingly, Benedict Anderson, citing Tessa Morris-Suzuki, recalls as follows in context of Ryukyu Islands:

> She illustrates in wonderful detail the abrupt transformation that came with the Meiji Restoration in the way that the Ainu and the Ryukyu islanders were regarded and handled. It had long been the policy of Tokugawa shogunate to forbid Ainu to dress as Tokugawa-Japanese or adopt Tokugawa-Japanese customs and traditions; similarly envoys from Ryukyus bringing tribute to Edo were instructed to dress as exotically Chinese as possible. In both instances the idea was to separate these (barbarian) peripheral peoples as far as possible from the imperial centre. But with the rise of Meiji official nationalism, there was a complete reversal of policy: Ainu and Ryukyu were now regarded as primitive and ancient types of the same Japanese race as the Meiji oligarchs themselves. Every effort, persuasive and often more coercive, was made to Japanify them (with variable success).

See Benedict Anderson, Western nationalism and Eastern nationalism, Is there a difference that matters, New Left Review, May-June 2001, pp. 31-42, specially p. 36.

24. More recently, North Korea is seen as a cause for concern. The importance of American security relationships declined as the "threat" of the erstwhile USSR evaporated, and the DPRK "threat," highlighted by President Bush in his "Axis of Evil" speech, receded for a while as it was to a large degree subsumed in the six party talks. The priority of action on the North Korean front further suffered with the advent of a new administration in Washington, until a change of government in Korea combined with a number of incidents to again bring it to the top of the security agenda.

25. Financial Times reported as follows on the sinking of the Cheonan corvette: "Many ordinary South Koreans say that their government is merely seeking a convenient scapegoat for what was a mistake on the part of the South's navy, or what was a "friendly fire" incident involving the US military." See Christian Oliver, Daniel Dombey and Song Jung-a, S Korea blames Pyongyang for sunk warship, Financial Times, May 19, 2010.

26. See Zbigniew Brzezinski, America and China's first big test, Financial Times, November 23, 2010, and Helene Cooper and Martin Fackler, White House seeks China's help, New York Times, November 24, 2010.

27. See for example discussion in Li Hongmei, Is China befriending the distant while alienating neighbors? People's Daily online, November 12, 2010.

28. See Li Hongmei, USS Washington comes upsetting Northeast Asia, People's Daily online, November 29, 2010. Also see discussion in Li Hongmei, Is China befriending the distant while alienating neighbors? People's Daily online, November 12, 2010.

29. See, for example, the discussion in New York Times editorial, A rising China, May 6, 2005.

30. For a discussion of aspects of territorial issues, see Jean-Marc F. Blanchard, "Economics and Asia-Pacific Region Territorial and Maritime Disputes: Understanding the Political Limits to Economic Solutions," Asian Politics & Policy, Vol. 1, No. 4 (October/December 2009), pp. 682-708.

31. See, for example, the discussion in Bernard K Gordon, US perspectives on East Asian economic integration, Journal of Economic Development, vol. 31, no. 2, December 2006, pp. 149-169.

32. See Bruce Cumings, From Japanese imperium to American hegemony, in Charles Armstrong, ed., Korea at the center (Armonk, ME Sharpe, 2006), p. 82.

33. President Truman, cited in Victor D. Cha, Powerplay: Origins of the US alliance system in Asia, International Security, vol. 34, no. 3, Winter 2009/10, p. 184.

34. See Bruce Cumings, From Japanese imperium to American hegemony, in Charles Armstrong, ed., Korea at the center (Armonk, ME Sharpe, 2006), pp. 80-86.

35. See Friedrich List's The national system of political economy, 1885 translation by Sampson S Lloyd (Roseville: Dry Bones Press, 1999-2000). Bruce Cumings discusses James Fallows discovery after five years in search of an English translation of List's work in a Tokyo bookshop. See Bruce Cumings, The Korean crisis and the end of "Late" development, New Left Review, Sept-Oct. 1998.

36. See Kaname Akamatsu, A historical pattern of economic growth in developing countries, Journal of Developing Economies, 1962, March-August, pp. 3-25.

37. See The East Asian Miracle: Economic growth and public policy (World Bank Policy Research Reports), (Washington DC, World Bank, 1994). Joseph Stiglitz, who directed the World Bank's East Asian Miracle project, says that the study found that the East Asian economies had been so successful "not only in spite of the fact that they had not followed most of the dictates of the Washington Consensus, but *because* they had not." These findings, according to Stiglitz, had been toned down in the published report; nonetheless, the "study laid out the important roles that the government had played." See Joseph Stiglitz, Globalization and its discontents (London: Penguin Allen Lane, 2002), p. 91.

38. See, for example, the discussion in Meredith Woo-Cumings, ed., The developmental state (Ithaca, Cornell University Press, 1999); and Alice Amsden, The rise of the rest, (Oxford, Oxford University Press, 2001).

39. See Yong Wook Lee, The Japanese challenge to the American neoliberal world order (Stanford: Stanford University Press, 2008).

40. David Kang, China Rising (New York, Columbia University Press, 2010).

41. David Kang, China Rising (New York, Columbia University Press, 2010).

42. See Bruce Cumings, From Japanese imperium to American hegemony, in Charles Armstrong, ed., Korea at the center (Armonk, ME Sharpe, 2006).

43. The Economist's EIU Viewswire reported as follows:

> Although the US is still the most important source of final demand for Asia as a whole, recent research from the European Central Bank suggests that China is now a greater source of final demand than the US for the Philippines, South Korea and Taiwan.

See Asia economy: Regional economic growth is set to slow, EIU ViewsWire, November 8, 2010, http://viewswire.eiu.com/index.asp?layout=VWArticleVW3&article_id=527579037&region_id=420000442&country_id=&channel_id=190004019&category_id=&refm=vwCh&page_title=Article

44. China is often mentioned as a country that also opposed the creation of the Asian Monetary Fund. Andrew Sheng, a witness to the diplomacy during the crisis, though records that United States and European Union were categorically opposed to the idea, ASEAN countries, South Korea and Taiwan were supportive, whereas China in his view was silent. See Andrew Sheng, From Asian to global financial crisis (Cambridge: Cambridge University Press, 2010), pp. 38-39.

45. Simon Tay records in detail that after the failure of APEC and the United States to assist in the managing the fallout from the Asian financial crisis, Prime Minister Mahatir convened the first ASEAN + 3 meeting in December 1998. See Simon S. C. Tay, Asia alone (Singapore, Wiley, 2010), pp. 24-26. Kent Calder and Min Ye however suggest that it was perhaps South Korea which took the initiative, but do not cite the specifics. See Kent Calder and Min Ye, The making of Northeast Asia (Stanford: Stanford University Press, 2010).

46. The CMI comprised currency swap arrangements. The total quantum of these arrangements expanded substantially with time, as did ease of access. The increased levels of foreign exchange reserves lent credibility to the currency swap arrangements.

47. See for example discussion in Robert Skidelsky and Christian Westerlind Wigström, eds., The state of economic crisis and the state of economics (Basingstoke, Palgrave, 2010).

48. See, for example, the discussion in Henry Kaufman, The road to financial reformation, Warning, consequences, reforms (Hoboken, Wiley, 2009).

49. New York Times quoted Alan Greenspan as follows:

> Facing a firing line of questions from Washington lawmakers, Alan Greenspan—the former Federal Reserve chairman once considered the infallible "maestro" of the U.S. economy—admitted Thursday that he was wrong to trust free markets to regulate the financial system without stronger government oversight.

See Brian Knowlton and Michael M. Grynbaum, Greenspan "shocked" that free markets are flawed, New York Times, Thursday, October 23, 2008.

50. The Guardian newspaper reported a conversation between Hillary Clinton, the American secretary of state, and Kevin Rudd, the Australian foreign minister, as follows:

> According to the note of Clinton's lunch with Rudd in Washington: "The secretary affirmed the US desire for a successful China, with a rising standard of living and improving democracy at a pace Chinese leaders could tolerate. . . . The secretary also noted the challenges posed by China's economic rise, asking: 'How do you deal toughly with your banker?'"
> Rudd responded by calling himself "a brutal realist on China," arguing for a policy of "integrating China effectively into the international community and allowing it to demonstrate greater responsibility, all while also preparing to deploy force if everything goes wrong." He described Chinese leaders as "subrational and deeply emotional" on Taiwan, a frequent source of tension with the US.

See Ewen MacAskill, WikiLeaks: Hillary Clinton's question: how can we stand up to Beijing? Australia's ex-PM Kevin Rudd advised US secretary of state to welcome Beijing onto world stage but keep force as a last resort, Guardian, December 4, 2010.

51. See Eric Schmitt, In a fatal error, CIA picked a bombing target only once: The Chinese embassy, New York Times, October 22, 1999.

52. See David E Sanger and Jane Perlez, US sends Beijing formal statement expressing regret, New York Times, April 11, 2001.

53. In a news story "Bush reassures China," BBC reported as follows: "Mr Bush has indicated a shift in American position when he described China as a "strategic competitor" rather than a potential "strategic partner." "On Monday, the State Department confirmed that the new administration was dropping former President Clinton's so-called "three No's" policy:

- No support for Taiwan independence
- No recognition of a separate Taiwanese Government
- No backing for Taiwanese membership of international organizations

"The move reflects strong support in Congress for Taiwan, especially among President Bush's Republican Party." See BBC, "Bush reassures China," March 23, 2001.

54. See David E Sanger, US would defend Taiwan, Bush says, New York Times April 26, 2001.

55. President Bush's State of the Union address, January 29, 2002.

56. New York Times reported as follows on Secretary Clinton's China visit:

> She thanked Yang for China's 'continuing confidence' in the United States, as the largest foreign buyer of Treasury securities. He offered a noncommittal statement that China would decide where to invest its foreign exchange reserves on the basis of safety, value and liquidity.
> In an interview Sunday that was broadcast on Dragon Television, Clinton pressed her case for why China should continue to buy U.S. Treasury bonds.
> "It's a good investment; it's a safe investment," she told Yang Lan, the host of the show.

> The Chinese government, Clinton said, had an even more compelling incentive to keep buying: It needs the United States to recover as a market for Chinese goods. To jolt the economy back to life, she said, the United States needs to be able to take on more debt.
> "We are truly going to rise or fall together," she said. "We are in the same boat, and, thankfully, we are rowing in the same direction."

See Mark Landler, Clinton urges China to fight climate change, New York Times, February 22, 2009.

57. See US and China: tetchy twins, editorial in the Guardian, February 8, 2010.

58. See, for example, the discussion in Robert D Kaplan, Obama takes Asia by sea, New York Times, November 11, 2010, and in Pankaj Mishra, Obama, the street kid from Jakarta knows that US dominance of Asia is over, Guardian, November 8, 2010.

59. See for example Sewell Chan, Summit shows U.S. can still set agenda, if not get action, New York Times, November 12, 2010. Also see Philip Stephens, A history of the world in 250,000 cables, Financial Times, November 29, 2010.

60. See for example Fred Bergsten's interview in Asahi Shimbun, November 6, 2010.

61. See White House press release, *Trans-Pacific Partnership: Progress Towards a Regional Agreement,* November 13, 2010. http://www.whitehouse.gov/the-press-office/2010/11/13/trans-pacific-partnership-progress-towards-a-regional-agreement.

62. Though East Asia as defined here overlaps with most of the neighboring countries.

63. See Wei Liang, China: Globalization and the Emergence of a New Status Quo Power?

64. Initially there was considerable resistance on the part of the Taiwan authorities against economic linkages with China. This official resistance did not stop illicit investment and trade transactions, which grew manifold. Taiwan, along with Hong Kong, is credited with playing a central role in the initial years of China's economic development under Deng Xiao Ping. See discussion in Randall Jones, Robert King, and Michael Klein, The Chinese economic area: Economic integration without a free trade agreement, OECD Economics Department working paper no: 124, Paris, 1992.

65. The "One China" principle is softened by the Chinese concept of sovereignty, which is distinctly different from the Westphalian one; a point which Hong Kong's situation so forcefully articulates: the Chinese concept of sovereignty is more flexible and accommodating of differences between a nation's constituting units. See David Kang, China rising (New York, Columbia University Press, 2010).

66. For a discussion of aspects of China's foreign policy imperatives, see Sujian Guo and Jean-Marc F. Blanchard (co-editors), "Harmonious World" and China's New Foreign Policy (Lanham: Lexington Books, 2008).

67. There is a point of view among some in the Asian press that the United States is actively encouraging disputes between China and Japan so as to facilitate a larger security role for Japan in East Asia. See, for example, discussion in Feng Zhaokui, Diaoyu dispute sowed by US, in China Daily, September 15, 2010, and Peter Lee, Japan poured oil on troubled waters, Asia Times, October 2, 2010.

68. In discussing nationalism Benedict Anderson makes a curious observation: "One could add that in Japan itself, there are some people who regard themselves as a kind of White." See Benedict Anderson, Western nationalism and Eastern nationalism, Is there a difference that matters, New Left Review, May-June 2001, pp. 31-42, especially p. 32. It is also worth noting that in Apartheid South Africa Japanese were classified and treated as "white."

69. See Victor D Cha, Powerplay: Origins of the US alliance system in Asia, International Security, vol. 34, no. 3, Winter 2009/10, p. 186.

70. David Kang, China rising (New York, Columbia University Press, 2010).

71. "The Japan that can say no, why Japan will be first among equals," was the title of a book by Shintaro Ishihara and Akio Morita published in 1989. The more recent version carries the same title. See Shintaro Ishihara, The Japan that can say no (Touch-

stone Books, 1992). "Japan as number one," was the title of another book, very popular in its time. See Ezra F Vogel, Japan as number one, (New York: Harper Collins, 1980).

72. David Kang, China rising (New York, Columbia University Press, 2010). Also, this proposition is a far cry from the days of "Japan that can say no," and "Japan as number one."

73. David Kang, China rising (New York, Columbia University Press, 2010).

74. The New York Times reported as follows:

> While Washington remained officially neutral on China's and Japan's conflicting claims of sovereignty over the islands, Secretary of State Hillary Rodham Clinton said the islands came under America's treaty obligations to defend Japan in case of attack. The statement angered China, which believes the United States' cold-war-era security alliances in Asia are being used to contain it.
> Mrs. Clinton's comment was welcomed in Japan, where concerns about China's rise have forced the year-old Democratic Party government to seek stronger ties with the United States and reverse its previous calls to remove an American air base from Okinawa.
> "For peace and stability in this region, the presence of the United States and its military is important," Mr. Kan told reporters after meeting Mr. Obama, "and this recognition has been shared by me and many people in the country, as well as our neighboring countries."

See Martin Feckler, Leaders of China and Japan meet on summit's sidelines, New York Times, November 13, 2010. Earlier, the New York Times reported that the shortfall in rare earths supplied by China to the Japanese firms was an important consideration in the release of the Japanese seaman: "According to a survey of Japanese companies conducted last week by the ministry and released Tuesday, all 31 companies involved in such trade that responded to the survey said disruptions of the shipments increased since Sept. 21. They said exports were effectively blocked at numerous Chinese ports because of abnormal amounts of paperwork and increased inspections." The Japanese Economic Minister Akihiro Ohata was reported to have commented: "The government strongly wants this to be corrected."
See Chinese and Japanese leaders meet in Europe, New York Times, October 5, 2010. More generally, Kent Calder and Min Ye have argued in their recent book that the occurrence of security disputes leads to urgent efforts to resolve the matter because of the significant economic stakes that might be adversely affected. See Kent Calder and Min Ye, The making of Northeast Asia (Stanford, Stanford University Press, 2010).

75. See David Kang, China rising (New York, Columbia University Press, 2010).

76. See James C Hsuing, China's second ascent and international relations theory, APSA 2009 Toronto Meeting paper.

77. See David Kang, China rising (New York, Columbia University Press, 2010).

78. Charles Armstrong reports that economic and security considerations argue against a push for unification. Armstrong writes:

> Most South Koreans today neither fear a North Korean invasion nor desire a North Korean collapse. . . . the general attitude might be described as a desire for 'containment': keeping the North alive but at bay, if necessary through economic assistance, so long as it is not too costly to the South. This is a far cry from the fervent hope for unification that motivated South Koreans for decades after the initial division, but it follows logically from the economically pragmatic world-view that dominates contemporary South Korea.

See Charles Armstrong, Contesting the peninsula, New Left Review, May-June 2008, p. 130.

79. David Kang, China rising (New York, Columbia University Press, 2010).

80. David Kang, China rising (New York, Columbia University Press, 2010).

81. David Kang, China rising (New York, Columbia University Press, 2010), p. 117.
82. David Kang, China rising (New York, Columbia University Press, 2010).
83. Acharya records that both points of view, non-interventionist and interventionist, were argued out in ASEAN meetings over 1997-98. "NGOs . . . backed by Western donor agencies . . . [wanted an] . . . interventionist posture towards Burma." The non-interventionist elements in ASEAN wanted "constructive engagement," but Anwar Ibrahim of Malaysia wanted "constructive intervention," whilst Surin of Thai foreign minister sought "flexible engagement." Both Anwar Ibrahim and Surin were seen by their ASEAN peers as influenced by the "West"; Surin was labeled a "Western stooge" by the media, and Anwar Ibrahim left office shortly thereafter. See Amitav Acharya, Whose ideas matter, Agency and power in Asian regionalism (Singapore, ISEAS, 2010), pp. 123-133.
84. Benedict Anderson offers a rather skeptical view of "Asian values" in an otherwise scholarly discourse. Anderson writes: "These 'values' were too brazely rhetorical, as euphemisms of certain state leaders to justify authoritarian rule, nepotism and corruption." See Benedict Anderson, Western nationalism and Eastern nationalism, Is there a difference that matters, New Left Review, May-June 2001, pp. 31-42, especially p. 31.
85. See Seth Mydans and Wayne Arnold, Modern Singapore's creator is alert to perils, New York Times, September 2, 2007. More recently, Simon S. C. Tay of Singapore has written a book explaining the importance of United States involvement in Asia. See Simon S. C. Tay, Asia alone, The dangerous post-crisis divide from America (Singapore, Wiley, 2010)
86. See US risks losing global clout – Lee Kuan Yew, at manilatimes.net, October 29, 2009.
87. See Simon S. C. Tay, Asia alone, The dangerous post-crisis divide from America (Singapore, Wiley, 2010)
88. See Li Hongmei, Nothing to be fretted about, People's Daily online, November 6, 2009.
89. Bruce Cumings, Parallax visions (Durham, NC, Duke University Press, 1999).
90. With the advent of rapid economic growth in India, the economic statistics for a number of successful Asian economies, such as China and India, unlike in many ways, were aggregated to advance the concept of an Asian Century.
91. With the world experiencing rapid change in the economic balance with consequent implications for politics, the international theorists appear to be rethinking concepts. One line of thought explores non-Western or non-Eurocentric approaches to inter-state relations. See for example Amitavv Acharya and Barry Buzan, eds., Non-Western international relations theory (London, Routledge, 2010), and James C. Hsuing, China's second ascent and international relations theory, APSA 2009 Toronto Meeting paper.
92. Also see the discussion in Kent Calder and Min Ye, The making of Northeast Asia (Stanford, Stanford University Press, 2010).
93. The Financial Times published the following report on Mrs Clinton's advice to the Cambodian government.

> Mrs. Clinton is on a nearly two-week trip to Asia designed to reinforce US diplomatic influence in the region. On a visit to Cambodia on Monday, she said the Obama administration would resume talks about cancelling $450m in debts from the 1970s that the government owed the US and she cautioned Cambodia's leaders against becoming too dependent on China. In recent years, Cambodia has forged a particularly strong relationship with Beijing.
> "I think it is smart for Cambodia to be friends with many countries," she said. "It's like our relationship with other countries. You look for balance. You don't want to get too dependent on any one country."

See Geoff Dyer, China rebuffs US offer on disputed islands, Financial Times, November 2, 2010. Having heard out Clinton's advice with patience, Cambodia proceeded to sign more agreements on economic cooperation with China. See Jamil Anderlini, China lifts profile in Cambodia, Financial Times, November 4, 2010.

94. See Amitav Acharya, Whose ideas matter, Agency and power in Asian regionalism (Singapore, ISEAS, 2010), p. 154 and p. 157.

Bibliography

Acharya, Amitav, *Whose ideas matter, Agency and power in Asian regionalism*, (Singapore, ISEAS, 2010).

Acharya Amitav and Barry Buzan, eds., *Non-Western international relations theory*, (Routledge, London, 2010).

Akamatsu, Kaname, "A historical pattern of economic growth in developing countries," *Journal of Developing Economies*, 1962, March-August, pp. 3-25.

Amsden, Alice, *Escape from Empire* (Cambridge, MIT Press, 2009).

———, *The rise of the rest* (Oxford, Oxford University Press, 2001).

Anderlini, Jamil, "Wall St banks to launch renminbi funds," *Financial Times*, May 12, 2011.

———, "China lifts profile in Cambodia," *Financial Times*, November 4, 2010.

———, "Beijing looks to broaden renminbi use," *Financial Times*, August 17, 2010.

———, "China to deploy foreign reserves," *Financial Times*, July 21, 2009.

Anderlini, Jamil, Song Jung-a, and Lindsay Whipp, "S Korean treasuries sought by China," *Financial Times*, August 18, 2010.

Anderson, Benedict, "Western nationalism and Eastern nationalism, Is there a difference that matters," *New Left Review*, May-June 2001, pp. 31-42.

Andrews, Edmund S., "Group of 20 Agrees on Far-Reaching Economic Plan," *New York Times*, September 26, 2009.

Antkiewicz, Agata, and John Whalley, China's new regional trade agreements, NBER working paper 10992, December 2004.

D'Arista, Jane, "The evolving international monetary system," *Cambridge Journal of Economics* 2009, 33, pp. 633-652.

Armstrong, Charles, "Contesting the peninsula," *New Left Review*, May-June 2008.

ASEAN Secretariat, Joint Media Statement of the 14th AEM+3 Consultations, Manado, Indonesia, August 12, 2011.

———, The Joint Ministerial Statement of the 14th ASEAN+3 Finance Ministers' Meeting, held in Ha Noi, 4 May 2011.

———, The Joint Ministerial Statement of the 13th ASEAN+3 Finance Ministers' Meeting, held in Tashkent, May 4, 2010.

———, The Joint Media Statement of the 12th ASEAN+3 Finance Ministers' Meeting, held in Bali, May 3, 2009.

———, The Joint Ministerial Statement of the 9th ASEAN+3 Finance Ministers' Meeting, May 4, 2006, Hyderabad, India.

———, The Joint Ministerial Statement of the 8th ASEAN+3 Finance Ministers' Meeting ,May 4, 2005, Istanbul, Turkey.

———, The Joint Ministerial Statement of the ASEAN+3 Finance Ministers Meeting, May 6, 2000, Chiang Mai, Thailand.

Asia Regional Integration database at: http://www.aric.adb.org/fta.php?id=1&ssid=3&title=ASEAN%20Free%20Trade%20Area

Austria, S., "East Asian Regional Cooperation: Approaches and Process," Philippine Institute for Development Studies Discussion paper Series No. 2003-02, 2003.

Bangkok Post, "ASEAN and Korea a perfect fit," June 27, 2009.

———, "Taiwan aims for Asean FTA," November 10, 2009.

Barboza, David, "As China invests US could lose," *New York Times*, May 4, 2011.

———, "Inflation in China poses big threat to global trade," *New York Times*, April 17, 2011.

———, "In China, tentative steps towards global currency," *New York Times*, February 11, 2011.
———, "China Passes Japan as Second-Largest Economy," *New York Times*, August 15, 2010.
———, "As China's Wages Rise, Export Prices Could Follow," *New York Times*, June 7, 2010.
———, "Foxconn Increases Size of Raise in Chinese Factories," *New York Times*, June 6, 2010.
Bayly, Christopher, and Tim Harper, *Forgotten wars, Freedom and revolution in Southeast Asia* (Cambridge, Harvard University Press, 2007).
BBC, "Bush reassures China ," March 23, 2001.
Beattie, Alan, "Round two in currency war: A phoney US victory," *Financial Times*, October 7, 2011.
———, "Big guns muffled as currency wars enter a lull," *Financial Times*, May 12, 2011.
———, "Watchdog says IMF missed crisis risks," *Financial Times*, February 9, 2011.
———, "International economy: a display of disunity," *Financial Times*, October 22, 2010.
———, "Joshua Chaffin and Kevin Brown, Wen warns against renminbi pressure," *Financial Times*, October 6, 2010.
Bergsten, Fred C. "Obama has to tell Beijing some hard truths," *Financial Times*, November 29, 2010.
———, "Fred Bergsten's interview in Asahi Shimbum ," November 6, 2010.
———, "The dollar and the deficits: How Washington can prevent the next crisis," *Foreign Affairs*, volume 88, no. 6, November/December 2009.
———, Pacific Asia and the Asia Pacific: The Choices for APEC, PIIE Policy Brief, July 2009
———, ed., *International adjustment and financing 1985-91* (Washington DC, IIE, 1991).
Bergsten, Fred C., Charles Freeman, Nicholas R. Lardy, and Derek J. Mitchell, "China's Challenge to the Global Economic Order," in *China's Rise: Challenges and Opportunities*, (Washington DC, PIIE, 2009).
Blanchard, Olivier, and Francesco Giavazzi, "Rebalancing growth in China: A three-handed approach," MIT Dept of Economics working paper 05-32, November 25, 2005.
Bland, Ben, "Vietnam: A question of balance," *Financial Times*, November 24, 2011.
Blitz, James, "Britain and China strengthen relations," *Financial Times*, September 8, 2011.
Boltho, Andrea, "The dollar era," *New Left Review* no. 72, November/December 2011, pp. 145-151.
Bowles, Paul, "Asia's post-crisis regionalism: Bringing the state back in, keeping the (United) States out," *Review of International Political Economy*, vol. 9, no. 2 (May, 2002), pp. 230-256.
Brender, Anton, and Florence Pisani, *La crise de la finance globalisee*, Editions La Decouverte, Paris 2009 (translation by Francis Wells distributed as Anton Brender and Florence Pisani, *Globalised finance and its collapse*, Brussels, Dexia, 2009).
Brown, Kevin, and Robert Cookson, "Singapore aims to be renminbi hub," *Financial Times*, April 19, 2011.
Brown, Kevin, Robert Cookson, and Geoff Dyer, "Malaysian bond boost for renminbi," *Financial Times*, September 19, 2010.
Brown, Kevin, and Geoff Dyer, "Hu defends China's role in global recovery," *Financial Times*, November 13, 2009.
Bryant, Ralph C., et al., eds., *External deficits and the dollar* (Washington DC, The Brookings Institution, 1988).
Buzan, Barry, "A World Without Superpowers: de-centered globalism," LSE IDEAS and International Relations Department public lecture, May 10, 2011.
Brzezinski, Zbigniew, "America and China's first big test," *Financial Times*, November 23, 2010.

Calder, Kent, and Min Ye, *The making of Northeast Asia* (Stanford University Press, Stanford, 2010).
Chang, Ha-Joon, *Institutional Change and Economic Development* (Anthem Press, London, 2007)
———, *The East Asian development experience, The miracle, the crisis and the future* (Zed Books, London, 2007),
———, *Kicking away the ladder, Development strategy in historical perspective* (Anthem Press, London, 2002).
Cha, Victor D., "Powerplay: Origins of the US alliance system in Asia," *International Security*, vol. 34, no. 3, Winter 2009/10, pp. 158-196.
Chan, Sewell, "Summit shows U.S. can still set agenda, if not get action," *New York Times*, November 12, 2010.
Chen, Lurong, Production sharing and East Asian regional trade liberalization, mimeo, June 2009.
Cheng, Leonard K., and Zihui Ma, China's Outward Foreign Direct Investment, mimeo, December 2008.
Chiang, Johnny C., talk at Carnegie Council in New York, July 13, 2010.
Chiang, Min-Hua, and Bernard Gerbier, Taiwan and the Transformation of Asia-USA Economic Relationship: From the Triangular Trading Bloc to the Four-Corner Structure, La Chronique des Amériques, Novembre 2008 N°19.
Chin, Gregory, and Wang Yong, "Debating the international currency system: What's in a speech," *China Security*, 2010, vol. 6, no. 1.
China Economic Review, "The rise of renminbi," March 2012, vol. 23, no. 3.
Chung, Olivia, "Wen puts US honor on the debt line, March 14, 2009," *Asia Times* online.
Chwieroth, Jeffrey M., *Capital ideas, The IMF and the rise of financial liberalization*, (Princeton, Princeton University Press, 2010).
Cookson, Robert, "China revs up renminbi expansion," *Financial Times*, July 28, 2010.
———, "Banks back switch to renminbi trade," *Financial Times*, August 26, 2010.
Cooper, George, *The origin of financial crises*, (New York, Vintage Books, 2008).
Cooper, Helene, and Martin Fackler, "White House seeks China's help," *New York Times*, November 24, 2010.
Cooper, Richard N., "The future of the dollar," Peterson Institute Policy Brief, September 2009.
Cowling, Keith, and Philip R. Tomlinson, "Post the 'Washington Consensus': economic governance and industrial strategies for the twenty-first century," *Cambridge Journal of Economics*, September 2011, vol. 35, no. 5, pp. 831-852.
Cumings, Bruce, *Dominion from Sea to Sea: Pacific Ascendancy and American Power*, (New Haven, Yale University Press, 2009).
———, "From Japanese imperium to American hegemony," in Charles Armstrong, ed., *Korea at the center* (Armonk, ME Sharpe, 2006).
———, Parallax visions, *Making sense of American-East Asian relations at the end of the century* (Durham, Duke University Press, 1999).
———, "The Korean crisis and the end of 'Late' development," *New Left Review*, Sept-Oct., 1998.
Davies, Ken, "On China's rapid growth in FDI," *China Daily*, March 8, 2009.
Dent, Christopher, "Free trade agreements in the Asia-Pacific a decade on: evaluating the past, looking to the future," *International Relations of the Asia-Pacific*, vol. 10, no. 2.
Dooley, Michael P., David Folkerts-Landau, and Peter Garber, "An essay on the revived Bretton Woods system," NBER working paper 9971, September 2003. http://www.nber.org/papers/w9971.pdf?new_window=1
Duhigg, Charles, and Steven Greenhouse, "Electronic Giant Vowing Reforms in China Plants," *New York Times*, March 30, 2012.
Dyer, Geoff, "China rebuffs US offer on disputed islands," *Financial Times*, November 2, 2010.

———, "End looms for era of cheap Chinese labour," *Financial Times*, June 3, 2010.
———, "Brazil and India add to pressure on China," *Financial Times*, April 21, 2010.
———, "China: No one home," *Financial Times*, February 21, 2010.
Dyer, Geoff, Jamil Anderlini, and Henny Sender, "China's lending hits new heights," *Financial Times*, January 17, 2011.
Dyer, Geoff, and Edward Luce, "Renminbi dispute looks set to haunt Sino-US economic talks," *Financial Times*, September 3, 2010.
Dyer, Geoff, David Pilling, and Henny Sender, "A strategy to straddle the planet," *Financial Times*, January 17, 2011.
The Economist, "What's Schadenfreude in Chinese?" August 20, 2011.
———, "Taiwan-China trade talks, Chinas in a bull session," April 19, 2010.
EIU Viewswire, "China economy: Reform push," April 18, 2012.
———, "Asia economy: Regional economic growth is set to slow," November 8, 2010.
———, "Asia's economy: ASEAN's China gamble," August 10, 2010.
Economic Times, "Scindia, China-Asean FTA may hit trade balance," in April 23, 2010.
Erixon, Fredrik, and Razeen Sally, "Trade, globalisation and emerging protectionism since the crisis," ECIPE working paper no: 02/2010.
Fairbank, John K., ed., *The Chinese World Order: Traditional China's Foreign Relations* (Cambridge, Harvard University Press, 1968).
Fairbank, John K., and Merle Goldman, *China, A new history*, 2nd edition (Cambridge, Harvard University Press, 2006).
Farchy, Jack, "LME eyes renminbi move for metals," *Financial Times*, April 16, 2012,
Feckler, Martin, "Leaders of China and Japan meet on summit's sidelines," *New York Times*, November 13, 2010.
Feldstein, Martin, ed., *International economic cooperation* (Chicago, University of Chicago Press, 1988).
Feng, Zhaokui, "Diaoyu dispute sowed by US," *China Daily*, September 15, 2010.
Feridhanusetyawan, Tubagus, "Preferential Trade Agreements in the Asia-Pacific Region," IMF working paper, WP/05/149, July 2005.
Financial Times, "The return of Chinese inflation," editorial of March 14, 2010.
Frost, Ellen L., *Asia's new regionalism* (Boulder, Lynne Rienner, 2009).
Fukushima, Akiko, "Japan's perspective on Asian regionalism," in Michael J. Green and Bates Gill, *Asia's new multilateralism* (New York, Columbia University Press, 2009).
Funabashi, Yoichi, "China's peaceful Ascendancy," in *Yale Global*, December 19, 2003.
Fung, Hung-Gay, et. al., Market Impediments, Trade, and Foreign Direct Investment: Evidence from China's Round-Tripping working paper, November 2006.
Gamble, Andrew, *The spectre at the feast* (Basingstoke, Palgrave, 2009).
Grabel, Ilene, "Not your grandfather's IMF: global crisis, 'productive incoherence' and developmental policy space," *Cambridge Journal of Economics*, September 2011, vol. 35, no. 5, pp. 805-830.
Gopinath, Gita, Oleg Itskhoki, and Brent Neiman, "Trade prices and the global trade collapse," NBER working paper no:17594, November 2011.
Gordon, Andrew, *A modern history of Japan, From Tokugawa times to the present* (Oxford, Oxford University Press, 2003).
Gordon, Bernard K., "US perspectives on East Asian economic integration," *Journal of Economic Development*, vol. 31, no. 2, December 2006, pp. 149-169.
Gorst, Isabel, "Kazakhstan and China agree $1bn currency swap," *Financial Times*, June 13, 2011.
Grimes, William W., "The Asian Monetary Fund reborn? Implications of Chiang Mai Initiative Multilateralisation," in *Asia Policy*, no. 11, January 2011, pp. 79-104.
———, *Currency and contest in East Asia* (Ithaca, Cornell University Press, 2009).
Guardian, "US and China: tetchy twins," editorial February 8, 2010.
Hasegawa, Tsuyoshi, *Racing the enemy* (Cambridge, Harvard University Press, 2005), pp. 268-274.

He, Dong, and Robert N. McCauley, "Offshore markets for domestic currency: Monetary and financial stability issues," HKMA working paper 2010.

Hille, Kathrin, "Renminbi fund to support overseas expansion," *Financial Times,* March 14, 2011.

Hille, Kathrin, and Robin Kwong, "Foxconn wants clients to share wages burden," *Financial Times,* June 7, 2010.

Hiratsuka, Daisuke, "Production Networks in Asia: A Case Study from the Hard Disk Drive Industry," ADBI working paper 301, Tokyo July 2011.

Hirsch, Fred, Interview of Jacques Rueff in *The Economist,* February 13, 1965.

Hook, Leslie, "Rmb internationalisation: first steel then the world," *Financial Times,* July 8, 2011.

Hsuing, James C., "China's second ascent and international relations theory," paper presented at APSA Toronto Meeting 2009.

Hu Xiaolian, "A Managed Floating Exchange Rate Regime is an Established Policy," July 15, 2010.

Huang, Yukon, "Eye China's coasts, not its currency," *Financial Times,* August 10, 2010.

Hudson, Michael, "Washington cannot call all the shots," *Financial Times,* June 14, 2009.

Tin-bor Hui, Victoria, "How China was ruled," *American Interest* March-April 2008.

———, *War and State Formation in Ancient China and Early Modern Europe* (Cambridge, Cambridge University Press, 2005).

IMF, "World Economic Outlook April 2010" (Washington DC, IMF, 2010).

IMF, "Annual Report 1997" (Washington DC, IMF, 1997).

Independent Evaluation Office of the IMF, "IMF Performance in the Run-Up to the Financial and Economic Crisis: IMF Surveillance in 2004–07" (Washington DC, IEO-IMF, January 10, 2011)

Ishihara, Shintaro, *The Japan that can say no* (Touchstone Books, 1992).

Ito, Takatoshi "RMB as number one: When will the Chinese RMB become a regional currency?" mimeo, University of Tokyo, April 10, 2011.

Jacob, Rahul, "China wage rises brings shift in production," *Financial Times,* September 6, 2011.

———, "China factories eye cheaper labour overseas," *Financial Times,* November 8, 2011.

Jacob, Rahul, Patti Waldmeir, and Barney Jobson, "Walmart presents irresistible target," *Financial Times,* October 20, 2011.

Jones, Randall, Robert King, and Michael Klein, "The Chinese economic area: Economic integration without a free trade agreement," OECD Economics Department working paper no: 124, Paris 1992.

Jung-a, Song, and Robert Cookson, "South Korea seeks to shift reserves to China," *Financial Times,* May 4, 2011.

Kaldor, Nicholas, "The dollar crisis," *The Times,* September 6, 7 and 8, 1971.

———, *Further essays on applied economics* (London, Duckworth, 1978).

Kang, David, *East Asia before the West, Five centuries of trade and tribute* (New York, Columbia University Press, 2010).

———, *China Rising* (New York, Columbia University Press, 2010).

Kaplan, Robert, D., "Obama takes Asia by sea," *New York Times,* November 11, 2010.

Katada, Saori N., and Mireya Solís, eds., *Cross Regional Trade Agreements: Understanding Permeated Regionalism in East Asia* (Berlin, Springer, 2008).

Kaufman, Henry, *The road to financial reformation, Warning, consequences, reforms,* (Hoboken, Wiley, 2009).

Kawai, Masahiro, "The role of an Asian Currency Unit for Asian monetary integration," mimeo, October 2008.

Kawai, Masahiro, and Ganeshan Wignaraja, eds., *East Asia's free trade agreements, How is business responding* (Cheltenham, Edward Elgar, 2011).

Kelleher, Ellen, "Renminbi outshines dollar amid investor demand," *Financial Times*, October 9, 2011.
Kim, Won Bae, "The rise of China and the repositioning of NAEs," *Seoul Journal of Economics*, vol. 24, no 2, 2011.
Kimura, Fukunari, "East Asian production networks and the rise of China," in Takatoshi Ito and Chin Hee Hahn, eds., *The Rise of China and Structural Changes in Korea and Asia* (Seoul, Korea Development Institute, 2010).
King, Stephen, "A focus on real exchange rate suggests that it doesn't matter," *The Economist*, June 17, 2010.
Kissinger, Henry A., *On China* (London, Penguin, 2011).
Knowlton, Brian, and Michael M. Grynbaum, "Greenspan 'shocked' that free markets are flawed," *New York Times*, October 23, 2008.
Kojima, Kiyoshi, "The 'flying geese' model of Asian economic development," *Journal of Asian Economies* 2000, reprinted in *Terutomo Ozawa, Institutions, industrial upgrading, and economic performance in Japan* (Cheltenham, Edward Elgar, 2005)
Krugman, Paul, "The Return of Depression Economics Part 2: The eschatology of lost decades," Lionel Robbins Memorial Lecture, London School of Economics, June 9, 2009.
Kurlantzick, Joshua, "China's Charm: Implications of Chinese Soft Power," Carnegie Endowment Policy Brief, no 47, June 2006.
Kwong, Robin, "Apple supplier ordered to shut China plant on environmental concerns," *Financial Times*, October 17, 2011.
———, "Why can't we be an RMB hub?" *Financial Times*, August 18, 2011.
———, "China and Taiwan sign landmark deal," *Financial Times*, June 29, 2010.
———, "Second Foxconn wage hike marks wider change in strategy," in Robin Kwong's blog in *Financial Times*, June 7, 2010.
———, "China confident of electronics role," *Financial Times*, June 3, 2010.
Landler, Mark, "Clinton urges China to fight climate change," *New York Times*, February 22, 2009.
Lao Tzu, *Tao Te Ching*, translation by D. C. Lau, (London, Penguin, 1963).
Lau, Justine, and Geoff Dyer, "CNPC boosts war chest with $30bn loan," *Financial Times*, September 9, 2009.
Lawrence, Robert, "China in the multilateral trading system," KSG working paper, 2006.
Lee, Kwan Yew, "US risks losing global clout," manilatimes.net, October 29, 2009.
Lee, Peter, "Japan poured oil on troubled waters," *Asia Times*, October 2, 2010.
Lee, Yong Wook, *The Japanese challenge to the American neoliberal order* (Stanford, Stanford University Press, 2008).
Leahy, Joe, and James Lamont, "Brics to discuss common development bank," *Financial Times*, March 19, 2012.
Leunig, Tim, "'Reshoring' jobs from China won't happen," *Financial Times*, October 30, 2011.
Lex, "McDonald's renminbi bonds," *Financial Times*, August 20, 2010.
Li, Fion, and Sophie Leung, "Sanusi Says Nigeria Plans to Get Yuan to 10% of Reserves Soon as Possible," *Bloomberg*, September 7, 2011. http://www.bloomberg.com/news/2011-09-07/sanusi-says-nigeria-plans-to-get-yuan-to-10-of-reserves-soon-as-possible.html
Li, Hongmei, "Why Premier Wen shrugs off 'China Model'?," *People's Daily*, March 15, 2011.
———, "China's development 'not a model,'" *Xinhua*, March 14, 2011.
———, "USS Washington comes upsetting Northeast Asia," *People's Daily* online, November 29, 2010.
———, "Is China befriending the distant while alienating neighbors?" *People's Daily* online, November 12, 2010.
Li, Lanqing, *Breaking through: The birth of China's opening-up policy* (Oxford, Oxford University Press, 2009).

Lim, H., and F. Kimura, "The Internationalization of Small and Medium Enterprises in Regional and Global Value Chains," ADBI working paper 231, Tokyo 2010.

Lim, Linda Y.C. "Rebalancing in East Asia," pp. 31-35, in Stijn Claessens, Simon Evenett, and Bernard Hoekman, eds., *Rebalancing the global economy: A primer for policymaking*, Centre for Economic Policy Research, June 23, 2010,

Lin, Justin Yifu, "From Flying Geese to Leading Dragons, New Opportunities and Strategies for Structural Transformation in Developing Countries," World Bank Policy Research working paper 5702, Washington DC, June 2011.

———, "Global Imbalances, Reserve Currency and Global Economic Governance," mimeo, October 22, 2010.

Ling, Carmen, "Hong Kong Head of global transaction services at Citi" cited in Robert Cookson, "Banks back switch to renminbi trade," *Financial Times*, August 26, 2010.

List, Friedrich, *The national system of political economy*, 1885 translation by Sampson S Lloyd (Roseville, Dry Bones Press, 1999-2000).

Lyons, Gerard, "China is undermining the dollar by the back door," *Financial Times*, April 27, 2010.

MacAskill, Ewen, "WikiLeaks: Hillary Clinton's question: how can we stand up to Beijing? " *Guardian*, December 4, 2010.

Mahbubani, Kishore, "The new Asian hemisphere," *Public Affairs*, New York, 2008.

Makan, Ajay, and Kara Scannell, "Accounts probe dents Chinese stocks in US," *Financial Times*, September 30, 2011.

Marris, Stephen, *Deficits and the dollar* (Washington DC, IIE, 1987).

Masina, Pietro P., ed., *Rethinking development in East Asia, From illusory miracle to economic crisis*, (London, Curzon, 2002).

McGregor, Richard, "China to allow Renminbi trade payments," *Financial Times*, July 2, 2009.

———, "Chinese offshore investment set to take-off," *Financial Times*, May 4, 2011.

McGuire, Patrick, and Goetz von Peter, "The US dollar shortage in global banking," *BIS Quarterly Review*, March 2009.

Minto, Rob, "Shanghai: moving up a league?" *Financial Times*, January 30, 2012.

Mishra, Pankaj, "Obama, the street kid from Jakarta knows that US dominance of Asia is over," *Guardian*, November 8, 2010.

Mitchell, Tom, "No place like home for migrant workers," *Financial Times*, February 25, 2010.

———, "Labour shortage hits China export recovery," *Financial Times*, February 25, 2010.

Mitchell, Tom, Justine Lau, and Robin Kwong, "Unrest spreads among Chinese workers," *Financial Times*, June 9, 2010.

Murphy, R. Taggart, *Japan's policy trap* (Washington DC, Brookings, 2004).

Mydans, Seth, and Wayne Arnold, "Modern Singapore's creator is alert to perils," *New York Times*, September 2, 2007.

New York Times, editorial, "A rising China," May 6, 2005.

Noble, Josh, "Higher wages in China: good news for the economy," *Financial Times*, June 3, 2010.

Norland, Rod, and Timothy Williams, "Iraq force soon to be a coalition of one," *New York Times*, July 29, 2009.

O'Brien, Patrick, "The myth of Anglophone succession," *New Left Review* 24, November-December 2003, pp. 113-134.

O'Connor, Anahad, "Geithner Affirms Dollar After Remarks Send It Tumbling," *New York Times*, March 26, 2009.

OECD, "International investment perspectives," 2005 (Paris, OECD, 2005).

Oliver, Christian, Daniel Dombey, and Song Jung-a, "S Korea blames Pyongyang for sunk warship," *Financial Times*, May 19, 2010.

Owen, Geoff, "Family still has a role to play," *Financial Times*, August 4, 2010.

Pangestu, Mari Elka, "The Challenges for Trade Policy in a Dynamic World and Regional Setting: An Indonesian Perspective," ADB Institute, Tokyo, December 14, 2010.

Park, Yung Chul, "Prospects for rebalancing growth in East Asia," in Stijn Claessens, Simon Evenett, and Bernard Hoekman, eds., *Rebalancing the global economy: A primer for policymaking*, Centre for Economic Policy Research, June 23, 2010.

Park, Yung Chul, and Chi Young Song, "RMB Internationalization: Prospects and Implications for Economic Integration in East Asia," *Asian Economic Papers*, Fall 2011, vol. 10, no. 3, pp 42-72.

Pei, Minxin, "How China is ruled," *American Interest*, March-April 2008.

People's Daily, "China's 4 trillion yuan stimulus package at farewell platform," November 24, 2010.

Peterson, Peter G., "The morning after," *The Atlantic Monthly*, October 1987.

Pettis, Michael, "Do not overreact to China's currency delays," *Financial Times*, October 13, 2010.

Pilling, David, "China's spending spree deserves three cheers," *Financial Times*, May 11, 2011.

———, "Long march to renminbi convertibility," *Financial Times*, August 25, 2010.

———, "Asia: more self-contained," *Financial Times*, August 10, 2010.

———, "Change is finally afoot for China's workers," *Financial Times*, June 2, 2010.

———, "Unruffled Asia resumes its economic ascent," *Financial Times*, May 12, 2010.

Qu, Bo, "Dynamic engagement: China's preference to international monetary cooperation," mimeo, May 3, 2010.

Rabinovitch, Simon, "China export growth dips as EU slows," *Financial Times*, November 10, 2011.

———, "China's labour costs soar as wages rise 22%," *Financial Times*, October 25, 2011.

———, "China's Comac confronts aircraft duopoly," *Financial Times*, September 23, 2011.

Rabinovitch, Simon, and Robert Cookson, "China outlines plan to loosen capital controls," *Financial Times*, February 23, 2012.

Ravenhill, John, "Extending the TPP: The political economy of multilateralization in Asia," mimeo, paper presented at the Asia-Pacific trade economists' conference, Bangkok, November 2009.

Reid, Anothony, "Economic and social change, c. 1400-1800," in Nicholas Tarling, *The Cambridge history of Southeast Asia*, vol. 1, part 2, (Cambridge, Cambridge University Press, 1999).

Reinhardt, Carmen, and Kenneth Rogoff, *This time is different*, (Princeton, Princeton University Press), 2009.

Reuters, "Highlights - Key points from Shanghai's global yuan hub plan," January 30, 2012.

———, "Exclusive: China to step up ASEAN yuan trade settlement," October 20, 2011.

———, "Bernanke says strong dollar in U.S. and global interest," April 27, 2011.

Rodrik, Dani, "Goodbye Washington Consensus, Hello Washington Confusion," mimeo, January 2006.

Robison, Richard, Mark Beeson, Kanishka Jayasuriya, and Hyuk-Rae Kim, eds., *Politics and markets in the wake of the Asian crisis*, (London, Routledge, 2000).

Rogoff, Kenneth, "An open letter," July 2, 2002, http://www.imf.org/external/np/vc/2002/070202.htm

———, "The IMF strikes back," *Foreign Policy* January-February 2003.

Rosen, Daniel H., and Thilo Hanemann, "An American open door? Maximising the benefits of Chinese direct foreign investment," *Asia Society*, May 2011.

Sakakibara, Eisuke, "Market-driven Integration in East Asia," Tokyo 24 June 2009, Distinguished Speaker Seminar.

San, Khoo How, "The five power defence arrangements: If it ain't broke," in *Pointer: Journal of the Singapore armed forces*, Oct-Dec 2000.

Sanger, David E., "US would defend Taiwan, Bush says," *New York Times*, April 26, 2001.
Sanger, David E., and Jane Perlez, "US sends Beijing formal statement expressing regret," *New York Times*, April 11, 2001.
Schmitt, Eric, "In a fatal error, CIA picked a bombing target only once: The Chinese embassy," *New York Times*, October 22, 1999.
Searight, Amy, "Emerging economic architecture in Asia," in Michael J Green and Bates Gill, *Asia's new multilateralism* (New York, Columbia University Press, 2009).
Sender, Henny, and Joe Leahy, "China offers other Brics renminbi loans," *Financial Times*, March 7, 2012.
Sheng, Andrew, *From Asian to global financial crisis* (Cambridge, Cambridge University Press, 2010).
Skidelsky, Robert, and Christian Westerlind Wigström, eds., *The state of economic crisis and the state of economics* (Basingstoke, Palgrave, 2010).
Sorkin, Andrew, *Too big to fail* (New York, Viking Books, 2009).
South China Morning Post, "WTO rifts spurs ASEAN to tackle free trade," October 7, 2003.
Spence, Jonathon D., *The search for modern China* (New York, WW Norton, 1999).
Stephens, Philip, "A history of the world in 250,000 cables," *Financial Times*, November 29, 2010.
Stern, Nicholas, "The prize, perils and price of China's plan," *Financial Times*, April 28, 2011.
Stiglitz, Joseph, "Challenging the Washington Consensus, An interview with Lindsey Schoenfelder," *The Brown Journal of World Affairs*, Winter/Spring 2003, Volume IX, Issue 2, pp. 33-40.
———, *Globalization and its discontents* (London, Penguin Allen Lane, 2002).
———, "Some lessons from the East Asian miracle," *World Bank Research Observer*, (1996) vol. 11, no. 2, pp. 151-177.
Stockwell, A.J., "Southeast Asia in war and peace: The end of European colonial empires," in Nicholas Tarling, ed., *The Cambridge history of Southeast Asia*, vol. 4 (Cambridge, Cambridge University Press, 1999).
Subacchi, Paola, "'One currency, two systems': China's renminbi strategy," Chatham House briefing paper, October 2010, pp. 6-7.
Subramanian, Arvind, *Eclipse* (Washington DC, PIIE, 2012)
Sutherland, D., and B. Matthews, "'Round Tripping' or 'Capital Augmenting' OFDI? Chinese Outward Investment and the Caribbean Tax Havens," paper prepared for Leverhulme Centre for Research on Globalisation and Economic Policy (GEP), University of Nottingham, January, 2009.
Sutter, Robert, and Chin-hao Huang, "China-Southeast Asia Relations: Military Diplomacy and China's Soft Power," in *Comparative Connections: A Quarterly E-Journal on East Asian Bilateral Relations*, April 2005.
Tay, Simon S.C., *Asia Alone* (Singapore, Wiley, 2010).
Thorbecke, Willem, "Investigating the Effect of Exchange Rate Changes on the People's Republic of China's Processed Exports," ADBI working paper Series no. 202, March 2010.
Thorbecke, Willem, and Namish Salike, "Understanding Foreign Direct Investment in East Asia," Asian Development Bank Institute Working Paper 290, June 2011.
Turnbull, C.M. "Regionalism and nationalism," in Nicholas Tarling, ed., *The Cambridge history of Southeast Asia*, vol. 4 (Cambridge, Cambridge University Press, 1999).
UNCTAD, "Global Investment Trends Monitor No. 6," April 27, 2011.
———, "World Investment Report 2010" (Geneva, UNCTAD, 2011)
———, "World investment report 2009" (Geneva, UNCTAD, 2010).
———, "UNCTAD Investment brief," no. 2, (Geneva, UNCTAD, 2007).
U.S. Census Bureau, "Trade in goods with China."

Vermeiren, Mattias, "The global imbalances and the contradictions of US monetary hegemony," *Journal of International Relations and Development*, vol. 13, no. 2., June 2010, pp. 105-135.
Vlcek, William, "From Road Town (BVI) to Shanghai: FDI, IBCs and global capital flows," paper presented at Third Biennial Oceanic Conference on International Studies (OCIS) School of Political Science and International Studies, University of Queensland 2 - 4 July 2008.
Vogel, Ezra F., *Japan as number one*, (New York, Harper Collins, 1980).
Wagstyl, Stefan, "Brics: missed opportunity II," *Financial Times*, March 29, 2012.
———, "Europe to China: please chip in," *Financial Times*, October 28, 2011.
Wang, Yuan Long, "A geological and functional 'three-step strategy' for renminbi's internationalization," in *China Economist*, November-December 2009.
Wang, Yuanfeng, "Western countries should rethink consumerism," *Peoples Daily*, September 2, 2011.
Weisbrot, Mark, and Juan Montecino, "The IMF and Economic Recovery: Is Fund Policy Contributing to Downside Risks?" Center for Economic and Policy Research, Washington DC, October 2010. http://www.cepr.net/index.php/publications/reports/the-imf-and-economic-recovery
Wen, Jiabao, "Be Open and Inclusive and Achieve Mutual Benefit and Common Progress" Statement by Premier Wen Jiabao at the First East Asia Summit Kuala Lumpur, Malaysia, December 14, 2005.
Wheatley, Jonathan, "Brazil and China eye plan to axe dollar," *Financial Times*, May 18, 2009.
Whipp, Lindsay, and Jamil Anderlini, "Chinese economy eclipses Japan's," *Financial Times*, August 16, 2010.
White House, "Trans-Pacific Partnership: Progress Towards a Regional Agreement," press release, November 13, 2010.
Williamson, John, "What Washington means by policy reform," in John Williamson, ed., *Latin American adjustment: How much has happened?* (Washington DC, Peterson Institute, 2002).
Wines, Michael, "China's Leader Says He Is 'Worried' Over U.S. Treasuries," *New York Times*, March 14, 2009.
Wolf, Martin, "Evaluating the renminbi manipulation," *Financial Times*, April 6, 2010.
———, "China and Germany unite to impose global deflation," *Financial Times*, March 16, 2010.
———, "What India must do to catch up with and possibly outpace China," *Financial Times*, February 15, 2006.
World Bank, "The East Asian Miracle: Economic Growth and Public Policy," World Bank Policy Research Reports (Washington DC, World Bank, 1994).
Woo-Cumings, Meredith, ed., *The developmental state*, (Ithaca, Cornell University Press, 1999).
Wu, Friedrich, Poa Tiong Siaw, Yeo Han Sia, and Puah Kok Keong, "Foreign direct investments to China and Southeast Asia: has been losing out?," *Economic Survey of Singapore* 2002, third quarter.
Xiao, Geng, "People's Republic of China's Round-Tripping FDI: Scale, Causes and Implications," Inter-American Development Bank, no 9167, December 2004.
Xing, Yuqing, "Processing Trade, Exchange Rates and China's bilateral Trade Balances," mimeo, National Graduate Institute for Policy Studies, Tokyo, January 2011.
Xinhua, "Malaysian central bank unveils onshore RMB settlement service," March 21, 2012.
———, "Commerce minister urges deeper China-ASEAN co-op," August 16, 2011.
———, "Japan's warming to TPP poses political and diplomatic conundrums," November 14, 2010.
———, "Yuan Trade Settlement Benefits China-ASEAN FTA," October 23, 2010.
———, "ASEAN companies eye China for future growth," October 21, 2010.
———, "China-ASEAN FTA to enhance China-Malaysia ties," December 12, 2009.

Yellen, Janet, "The Asian financial crisis ten years later: Assessing the past and looking to the future," transcript of a speech to Asia Society of Southern California, February 6, 2007.

Yoshioka, Keiko, "Moves afoot to give renminbi greater international play," *Asahi Shimbun*, August 26, 2011.

Yu, Zhonghua, "To Check the Hegemony of the US Dollar by Cultivating a Multi-Polar Balance," *Guoji jinrong bao* [International Financial News], August 6, 2009.

Yuji, Charles, Horioka and Akiko Terada-Hagiwara, "The determinants and long-term projections of savings rates in developing Asia," NBER working paper no: 17581, November 2011.

Yuk, Pan Kwan, "Who's who in the yuan trading club," *Financial Times*, June 13, 2011.

Zhang, Feng, "Rethinking the 'Tribute System': Broadening the conceptual horizon of historical East Asian politics," *Chinese Journal of International Politics*, vol. 2, 2009, pp. 545-574.

Zhou, Xiaochuan, "Reform the International Monetary System," *China Daily*, March 23, 2009.

Zhou, Yan, "China should lead over single currency," *China Daily*, April 28, 2011.

Zhu, Jin, "China's wage proportion decreases for 22 years," *China Daily*, May 13, 2010.

Index

About the Authors

Dr. Wei Liang is associate professor of international policy studies and a research fellow in the Center for East Asian Studies. She teaches Global Politics, US-East Asia Trade and Investment Policy, Introduction to Trade Policy, The China Factor, and International Trade Negotiation Simulation. A graduate of Peking University, People's Republic of China, she received her Ph.D. in International Relations from the University of Southern California. Before joining the faculty at MIIS in 2007, she had teaching and research appointments at Florida International University, San Francisco State University, and Berkeley Roundtable on the International Economy (BRIE), UC Berkeley, where she did her postdoctoral research. Dr. Liang's research interests include international trade policy and negotiation, global economic and environmental governance, and international political economy with an area focus on East-Asia, U.S.-China economic relations. She has written and published widely on these issues.

Faizullah Khilji received his DPhil in Economics from University of Oxford. He has worked in various capacities in the area of economic management with the government of Pakistan, including development policy, macroeconomic policy, regulation of capital markets, competition policy, and trade policy and international trade deliberations. His last assignment was as Chairman of the National Tariff Commission and a Permanent Secretary to the Government. He has also worked with the UN Economic and Social Commission for Asia and the Pacific, Bangkok, Thailand, on issues of regional economic and financial cooperation, economic development of Southeast Asian economies, and on the role of transnational corporations in the Asia-Pacific region. He has served on the UN Commission on Investment and Technology, and on a number of WTO dispute settlement panels. He has written and published from time to time on the above issues, and also served as a resource person and lecturer, variously at universities, as well as for SAARC, UNCTAD, UN ESCAP, UNFPA, World Bank, and WTO.

www.ingramcontent.com/pod-product-compliance
Ingram Content Group UK Ltd.
Pitfield, Milton Keynes, MK11 3LW, UK
UKHW041628031026
15587UKWH00001B/149

9 780739 170823